THE HERB

HASHISH VERSUS MEDIEVAL MUSLIM SOCIETY

THE HERB

HASHISH VERSUS MEDIEVAL MUSLIM SOCIETY

BY

FRANZ ROSENTHAL

LEIDEN
E. J. BRILL
1971

PRINTED IN THE NETHERLANDS

TABLE OF CONTENTS

CHAPTER ONE

INTRODUCTION

Next to the control of sex as the most pressing issue confronting human society, the control of the instinct and need for play among men has been a matter of constant concern and considerable experimentation. Man is *homo ludens,* the playing animal, and the means by which he has sought to fulfill this side of his nature have not always been consistent with the best interests of the group organization necessary for human existence. Gambling is the outstanding example of a playful flight away from harsh reality which at times may lead rather too far away from it. The consumption of stimulants or depressants in solid, liquid, or gaseous form, beyond the requirements of nourishment and without any thought of normal physical need, is another. As it may affect not only man's mental state but at times also his physical functioning on a temporary or permanent basis, it is the kind of play that bears careful watching by society.

Islam is well known for the strictness of its attitude with respect to what it considers permissible means of amusement and relaxation for the individual. The Prophet's personal experience of the environment he lived in and the views he formed as a result set the course. Wine and gambling are expressly interdicted in the Qur'ān. It was easy for the guardians of the Muslim community to make the most of these prohibitions and, by and large, to enforce them. Expectedly, individual rebellions have been numerous in the course of history. It depended on circumstances of time and locale how strong such rebellions would become and what forms they would take. The problems of the consumption of alcoholic beverages, in particular, and their use and abuse have been in the center not only of social life but also of literature. As a result, an almost uncontrollably large mass of material attesting to the struggle of the individual against societal restrictions imposed upon him in this connection is available to us. A detailed and exhaustive treatment of this material would be a tremendously vast undertaking that could not be held within moderate limits. Much less formidable is the amount of information on gambling and its function in Muslim society, although it, too, is plentiful and full of unsolved and, perhaps, unsolvable questions for the historian.

The escape from the drudgery of life by means of various drugs other than alcohol expected to produce temporary physical euphoria or fleeting sensations of mental change was not barred by the authority of express statements creditable to the very highest religious sources. For this reason, attempts to counteract their consumption, even where it was suspected to be a danger to the fabric of society, were intermittent and, in the end, halfhearted. Because of its peculiar nature, the escapist use of drugs was as a rule looked upon with a certain disdain and a good deal of reticence, even where it surfaced and became so prominent as to call out for scrutiny. As will become clear in the course of this investigation, we have no way of knowing accurately how general a problem the use of drugs may have been in the past, and even for more recent times, we have, to my limited knowledge, no real hard facts to go by. It would seem very risky to generalize from the number and pitch of literary utterances or from the impressions gained by outsiders whose preparedness to receive and evaluate them it is impossible to assess. However, it is clear that Muslim authorities often considered it necessary to try to curb the use of drugs. As clearly, these attempts did not pass without arousing individual resistance. They thus produced another phase of the unceasing struggle of the individual against the society which is his creature, his savior, and his oppressor. The material presented on the following pages is meant to throw some limited light on this particular phase. If hashish has been chosen as the basis for discussion, it is because it is the most representative and, probably, the most widely used of the hallucinatory drugs employed by medieval Muslims.

Recent years have witnessed a vast outpouring of books and studies on cannabis intoxication. I have looked at some of them but have come to the conclusion that it would not be a good investment of my time to read too intensively in this literature. The knowledge of the history of hashish, especially in the Islamic period, displayed in it is pitiful and, on occasion, comical. This does not really come as a surprise, but it raises the somewhat disquieting spectre of a lack of historical understanding in the formation of views on a problem intimately concerned with man's past and future. Since so much has been written on the subject, it is possible that someone somewhere has gathered up something more than the few stock items repeated over and over again. I do not consider this likely, nor do I believe that historians and Near East experts have written on hashish and used fuller information than usual. If anything of the sort has escaped me, I have to apologize to the authors of such works and to the readers of these lines.

The modern literature on the subject stresses the need for a good deal of refinement in terminology. Thus, it is considered necessary (as was done on occasion also in the past) to make terminological distinctions between various hemp products, restricting such terms as hashish and marijuana to particular preparations made from the plant. Or terms such as addiction and habituation are broken down according to more closely defined aspects. All this, I feel, is useful to a certain degree, but it has comparatively little applicability to the medieval period and has been disregarded here. "Hashish" serves as the general term for which nowadays "cannabis" appears to enjoy preference. Terms are thus used here in the rather vague manner of common speech. To my mind, this can neither blur the picture nor make things appear more clear-cut than they are.

It has seemed to me to be the most immediate and needed task to provide information on what medieval Muslims knew about, and how they looked at, the use of drugs. To my knowledge, such information is not easily, or not at all, available elsewhere in the scholarly literature and accessible to those who are not familiar with Near Eastern languages. This has made my treatment as long as it has turned out to be, instead of the few pages I had originally meant to devote to it. While information is primary, interpretation continues to retain its proper place. In fact, interpretation of some sort or other can never be completely avoided, as it is inherent in everything we say or write. However, apart from the general theme explained above that motivates my writing on the subject and dominates it, the developing of interpretational generalities has not been my aim. In studying basic drives of human nature, presumed differences between large civilizational complexes become increasingly more elusive upon closer acquaintance with the historical situation and upon wider and deeper probing of the preserved evidence. In the case of hashish, it might be said that persistent reading of the daily newspapers and some rather superficial knowledge of Islam would suffice for anyone who might wish to do so, to guess at and describe quite accurately the general situation, the general attitudes, and the general procedures that could be assumed to have prevailed in medieval Islam with respect to the drug. This would hardly be a useful exercise. It is not the generalities but the details that count, and they have been presented here as clearly and as fully as possible. Observations encountered in the modern literature, unless they are derived from such properly scientific work as chemical analysis or controlled experimentation, can often be duplicated from Muslim sources. It might have been useful to footnote the medieval cases with parallel passages from modern writings. However, anyone interested in this aspect can do this very easily on his own. It is more important to explain and preserve the information provided by the indigenous sources on their own terms, in the hope that the mosaic thus put together will form a meaningful picture.

Much of this study had perforce to be based upon manuscript material. It should, however, be understood that numerous other works still unpublished might profitably have been consulted for basic or, mainly, illustrative material. And much further combing needs to be done of the vast literature available in print. The manuscripts used are not of the highest quality. This is to some degree due to the special character of the subject matter, but it is also possible, and very much to be hoped, that better manuscripts are hidden somewhere in Eastern and Western libraries. The manuscripts consulted here, directly or, mostly, in microfilm, are preserved in the great collections of libraries in Ankara, Berlin, Cambridge, Gotha, Istanbul, Leiden, New Haven (Connecticut), Paris, Princeton (New Jersey), and Rabat. For the courtesy and generosity with which they were made available to me, I am deeply grateful.

CHAPTER TWO

MONOGRAPHS ON HASHISH AND SOME OF THE MORE IMPORTANT SOURCES

The extent and character of the Muslim occupation with hashish problems and hashish lore are indicated by the source material at our disposal which largely determines what the present study can, and cannot, accomplish. It may thus be advisable to present here, at the outset of our discussion, instead of waiting for its end, an outline of the literature, in chronological order as far as possible. Some of the monographs listed are not preserved and known only through quotations and bibliographical reference. Much may have been written which never became known beyond the circle of the author and his friends.

We may well suspect that nearly every poet and productive amateur writer of verse, from the thirteenth to the sixteenth centuries, wrote at least some playful poems on hashish, although these poems might at times have been excluded from published collections of his work.[1] With the exception of al-Isʿirdī's representative and early specimen of the genre, no separate listing of this material has been made here. All major, and many minor, legal works can also be assumed to have rarely been entirely without some references to hashish, but even though much of a larger size and importance has surely eluded me, most of such occasional material would not justify special listing in the following list. The same applies to other lesser and incidental references. They will be restricted to mention later on in the footnotes.

The information provided by outsiders, that is, European travelers and residents in Islamic countries, is in part as old as, and on occasion older than, some of the Oriental sources used here, but it has been left aside. Whatever use of it has been made later on is so discrete as in no way being able to becloud the Muslim outlook.

1. Ibn al-Bayṭār, ʿAbdallāh b. Aḥmad al-Mālaqī (d. 646/1248),[2] *al-Jāmiʿ li-mufradāt al-adwiyah*, IV, 39 (Būlāq 1291); French trans. L. Leclerc, in *Notices et extraits des manuscrits de la Bibliothèque*

[1] On hashish poetry, see below, pp. 72, 141 f., and 163 ff.

[2] Cf. J. Vernet, in *EI*², *s.v.* Ibn al-Bayṭār.

Nationale, XXVI (1883), 118-120; German trans. J. von Sontheimer, II, 327-329 (Stuttgart 1840-1842). Much quoted in later times, for instance, by az-Zarkashī and al-Maqrīzī.

2. Al-Isʿirdī, Nūr-ad-dīn Muḥammad b. Muḥammad Ibn Rustum (619-656/1222-1258),[1] wrote a *Rangstreit* poem of hashish and wine, preserved by al-Kutubī (d. 764/1363) and translated below, pp. 163-166. It was possibly taken over by al-Kutubī from al-Isʿirdī's *Sulāfat az-zarajūn fī l-khalāʿah wa-l-mujūn*.

3. Muḥammad b. Sulaymān (b. Muḥammad b. Sulaymān) b. ʿAbd-al-Malik ash-Shāṭibī (585-672/1189-1274),[2] *Zahr al-ʿarīsh fī taḥrīm al-ḥashīsh*, is the oldest monograph on the subject of hashish of which we have knowledge, although it appears not to have been preserved. The title is mentioned by as-Sakhāwī (831-902/1427-1497) in his biography of Ibn Ḥajar.[3] Another reference is contained in a biography from a book allegedly entitled *az-Zahr al-muḍī* (?) *fī manāqib ash-Shāṭibī*, cited by ʿAbd-al-Wahhāb ʿAzzām,[4] about which nothing further is known to me. It was presumably also the source of the third reference, by Bağdatlı İsmail Pasha (d. 1339/1920).[5] In these two cases, the author is described as Ibn Abī r-Rabīʿ al-Maʿāfirī. However, aṣ-Ṣafadī distinguishes, and, it seems, correctly, between Ibn Abī r-Rabīʿ al-Hawwārī[6] and our Shāṭibī (al-Maʿāfirī) (both of whom, he says, died in 673). Since az-Zarkashī (No. 9) uses an almost identical title (although he may have had originally *aḥkām* for *taḥrīm*), it would seem a fair assumption that he had no knowledge of ash-Shāṭibī's earlier work, which he does not mention.

4. Ibn Ghānim, ʿIzz-ad-dīn ʿAbd-as-Salām b. Aḥmad al-Maqdisī

---

[1] Cf. aṣ-Ṣafadī, *Wāfī*, ed. H. Ritter, I, 188-192 (Wiesbaden, reprint, 1962, *Bibliotheca Islamica* 6a); al-Kutubī, *Fawāt*, II, 329-334 (Cairo 1951-1953); *GAL*, I, 257.

[2] Cf. al-Yūnīnī, *Dhayl Mir'āt az-zamān*, III, 72 (Hyderabad 1374-1380/1954-1961); adh-Dhahabī, *ʿIbar*, V, 300 (Kuwait 1960-1966); aṣ-Ṣafadī, *Wāfī*, ed. S. Dedering, III, 127 f. (Damascus 1953, *Bibliotheca Islamica* 6c); Ibn al-Jazarī, *Ghāyat an-nihāyah*, II, 149 (Istanbul 1932-1935, reprint).

[3] Cf. F. Rosenthal, *A History of Muslim Historiography*, 2nd ed., 609 (Leiden 1968).

[4] *Fī mazārāt al-Iskandarīyah*, in *ar-Risālah*, VII (1358/1939), No. 338, p. 2332, cited in Saʿīd al-Afghānī's edition of az-Zarkashī, *Ijābah*, 2nd ed., 12, n. 1 (Beirut 1390/1970).

[5] Cf. *Dhayl Kashf aẓ-ẓunūn*, I, 618 (Istanbul 1945-1947).

[6] Ibn Abī r-Rabīʿ al-Hawwārī's notice from aṣ-Ṣafadī appears in substantially the same form in al-Kutubī, *Fawāt*, II, 421 f., indicating al-Yūnīnī as his source, cf. al-Yūnīnī, *Dhayl*, III, 71 f., *anno* 672.

(d. 678/1279-1280),[1] *Majlis fī dhamm al-ḥashīshah*, preserved in Ms. Princeton 2136 (= 1056 H). The ms. was written by a certain Ṭalḥah b. Muḥammad b. Ibrāhīm b. Abī l-Aʿlā al-Ḥanbalī, who is presumably not the person mentioned by as-Sakhāwī, *Ḍaw'*, IV, 9 (Cairo 1353-1355). It is dated on Tuesday, 10 Rabīʿ II 802/Wednesday, 10 December 1399.[2] The *Majlis* takes up only the last three pages (not folios) of the Princeton Ms. The name of the author appears in it as ʿIzz-ad-dīn ʿAbd-al-ʿAzīz b. ʿAbd-as-Salām b. Ghānim. The last name is written somewhat indistinctly, but the reading Ghānim corresponds better to the reading of the ms. than the ʿĀmir of the Princeton Catalogue. *GAL, Suppl.*, I, 768, lists the work under ʿAbd-al-ʿAzīz b. ʿAbd-as-Salām (ca. 577-660/1181-1262). However, the name of the grandfather is almost certain evidence for the correct attribution. The confusion is easily understandable.

Another, anonymous ms. of the work is preserved in the Berlin Ms. Wetzstein II, 1774 (= Ahlwardt, No. 5488), fols. 102a-103b, with the title *Faṣl fī l-ḥashīshah wa-taḥrīmihā*. The Berlin Ms. presents a dating problem. The text immediately preceding the *Faṣl* in the ms. is stated to have been copied in 783/1381. Ahlwardt, who lists that text under No. 1675 of his Catalogue, takes this to be the actual date when the ms. was written. However, strangely enough, he also assumes that the scribe may have misspelled his own name, the name by which, he says, he was known and which in the ms. looks somewhat like Khaṭīb بالعلما. Unless this should turn out to be the correct form of his name, it may very well be that the date of 783 belongs to the ms. from which the Berlin Ms. was copied.[3]

The Princeton Ms. does not contain the verses from the Berlin Ms., referred to below, p. 156, n. 2, or the story following upon them that identifies hashish with the *zaqqūm* tree (below, p. 46).

---

1 This is the date indicated in *GAL, Suppl.*, I, 808, cf. also H. Ritter, in *Oriens*, III (1950), 58 ff.; Ibn Kathīr, XIII, 289.

2 The tenth of Rabīʿ II was a Tuesday in 805, but I do not think that the reading "five" is possible.

3 Ahlwardt lists another work from the same ms., written by the same hand, under No. 635 of his Catalogue. He dates its author, a certain ʿAbd-al-ʿAzīz b. Munajjā b. Aḥmad al-Ḥalabī, in the seventh or eighth century of the hijrah, apparently on the strength of the 783 date just mentioned. It would be helpful if it were possible to identify this author, but I have not yet succeeded in doing so. The other available references to him are all based upon Ahlwardt, cf. *GAL, Suppl.*, II, 133; K. Vollers, *Katalog ... Leipzig*, 276 f., No. 847, II (Leipzig 1906); ʿIzzat Ḥasan, *Fihris makhṭūṭāt Dār al-Kutub aẓ-Ẓāhirīyah, ʿulūm al-Qur'ān*, 20 (Damascus 1381/1962).

For the poem at the end of Ibn Ghānim's treatise, see below, pp. 167 ff. For other verses possibly attributable to Ibn Ghānim, see below, p. 150.

5. Al-ʿUkbarī, ʿImād-ad-dīn Abū l-Faḍl al-Ḥasan b. Muḥammad b. ʿAbd-ar-Raḥmān Ibn Abī l-Baqā' (seventh/thirteenth cent.), *Kitāb as-Sawāniḥ al-adabīyah fī l-madā'iḥ*[1] *al-qinnabīyah*. The work is first mentioned by Ibn al-Fuwaṭī (642-723/1244-1323),[2] who merely says that it deals with the eating of hashish. Since it is so far known only from quotations in al-Maqrīzī and al-Badrī,[3] it is hard to say whether it was in fact so uncompromisingly pro-hashish as its title and the reaction of al-Qasṭallānī (No. 6) would seem to suggest.

Al-ʿUkbarī's death is placed in the year 690/1291 in the summary entry No. 5489 of the Berlin Catalogue where Ahlwardt has brought together the titles of works on hashish known to him. No source is indicated, but the date is plausible and is not contradicted by the statement in al-Maqrīzī allegedly showing that al-ʿUkbarī was alive in and after 658/1260; al-Maqrīzī's statement does, in fact, not refer to al-ʿUkbarī himself as being involved in the interview said to have taken place in that year (below, p. 51).

Another work by al-ʿUkbarī, entitled *Ṭārid al-humūm*, is quoted by al-Badrī, fol. 14a (below, p. 146).

6. Al-Qasṭallānī, Quṭb-ad-dīn Abū Bakr Muḥammad b. Aḥmad b. ʿAlī b. Muḥammad (Shāfiʿite, 614-686/1218-1287),[4] *Takrīm al-maʿīshah fī (bi-)taḥrīm al-ḥashīshah*. This title is cited by al-Aqfahsī (No. 10) and al-Qalqashandī (756-821/1355-1418),[5] who has *fī dhamm*. Ḥājjī Khalīfah (1017-1067/1609-1657), 1009,[6] states that al-ʿUkbarī's work gives the impression of having been provoked by that of al-Qasṭallānī. Al-Qasṭallānī, in turn, upon the appearance of al-ʿUkbarī's work, wrote a point by point rejoinder which he entitled *Tatmīm at-Takrīm li-mā fī l-ḥashīsh min at-taḥrīm*. For a commentary on al-Qasṭallānī, see below, No. 14. Not unexpectedly, the biographical sources omit these titles on hashish in their entries on al-Qasṭallānī.

---

[1] Al-Maqrīzī and, in two instances, al-Badrī (fols. 3a and 50a) omit the definite article.

[2] *Talkhīṣ Majmaʿ al-ādāb*, IV, ii, 708 (Damascus 1963).

[3] Cf. below, pp. 50 ff. The quotations in al-Badrī are to be found on fols. 3a (below, pp. 50 ff.), 24b (below, p. 78), 30a (below, p. 83, n. 3), and 50b (below, p. 101).

[4] Cf. *GAL, Suppl.*, I, 809 f.

[5] *Ṣubḥ*, II, 146 (Cairo 1331/1913).

[6] Ḥājjī Khalīfah's *Kashf aẓ-ẓunūn* is cited here according to the edition by Ş. Yaltkaya (Istanbul 1941-1943), unless indicated otherwise.

7. Ibn Taymīyah, Aḥmad b. ʿAbd-al-Ḥalīm (Ḥanbalite, 661-728/1263-1328),[1] may have written a monograph on the subject. At least, the Istanbul Ms. Reis el-küttap 1154, containing a collection of treatises by Ibn Taymīyah, lists one on hashish in its table of contents. It was to be found on fols. 218-221 of the ms., but, unfortunately, there is a gap extending from fol. 210 to fol. 222. In the list of his works in al-Kutubī, *Fawāt*, I, 81, we find a legal treatise on declaring hashish forbidden and unclean and necessitating the *ḥadd* penalty *(Taḥrīm al-ḥashīshah al-mughayyibah wa-l-ḥadd ʿalayhā wa-tanjīsuhā)*. Further evidence for a separate legal decision on hashish appears in al-Badrī, fol. 53a, where Ibn Taymīyah in his "Treatise known as declaration of the illegality of hashish" *(ar-Risālah al-maʿrūfah bi-taḥrīmihā)* is quoted. It is possible, however, that these texts were nothing else but one or more of the *fatwā*s on hashish that appear in the collected *Fatāwī al-kubrā* of Ibn Taymīyah, used here in the recent (1966?) Cairo edition, IV, 301-303, 310 f., 312 f., 322-324, and 324-326. The last two *fatwā*s may also be read in the same collection, I, 128-130, and II, 252-254. The parallel texts show some slight variants. The last one, dealing with *ghubayrā'*, is somewhat expanded at the end of the text in Vol. IV.

Another work by Ibn Taymīyah dealing with hashish is *as-Siyāsah ash-sharʿīyah*, ed. M. al-Mubārak, 94-96 (Beirut, n. y. [1966?]); French trans. H. Laoust, 111 f. (Beirut 1948).

8. Adh-Dhahabī, Muḥammad b. Aḥmad (Shāfiʿite, 673-748/1274-1348),[2] has a section on hashish in the *Kitāb al-Kabā'ir*, 84 f. (Cairo 1385/1965, the fourth printing of an edition apparently first published in 1355). It turns out to be an almost literal reproduction of the passage in Ibn Taymīyah's *Siyāsah*. There are some additional verses at the end (below, p. 156). Ibn Taymīyah is not mentioned as the source. The textual history of the *Kitāb al-Kabā'ir* in general would seem to bear investigation. In the introduction of *az-Zawājir ʿan iqtirāf al-kabā'ir*, Ibn Ḥajar al-Haytamī (909-974/1504-1567) calls adh-Dhahabī's work "attributed" *(mansūb)* to him. Ibn Ḥajar al-Haytamī resumes the passage on hashish in Vol. II, 150 f. of the edition, Cairo 1370/1951, Nos. 371-382, with a few inconsequential comments of his own.

9. Az-Zarkashī, Muḥammad (b. ʿAbdallāh) b. Bahādur (Shāfiʿite,

---

[1] Cf. *GAL*, II, 100 ff., *Suppl.*, II, 119 ff.

[2] Cf. *GAL*, 2nd ed., II, 57 ff., *Suppl.*, II, 45 ff.

745-794/1344-1392),[1] *Zahr al-ʿarīsh fī aḥkām* (or *taḥrīm*) *al-ḥashīsh* There are several mss., also listed by M. Abū l-Faḍl Ibrāhīm in the introduction of his edition of az-Zarkashī's *Burhān fī ʿulūm al-Qur'ān*, 9 (Cairo 1376-77/1957-58). None of the mss. used here for the edition of the text (below, pp. 175 ff.) is particularly good, but since the work was well known and much considered, it would seem likely that older and better ms. material is still in existence somewhere. The mss. available and the sigla adopted for the apparatus criticus are these:

A Berlin Ms. Wetzstein II, 1809 (= Ahlwardt, No. 5487), fols. 108a-115a, with the title *Ẓill...aḥkām...* The text preceding az-Zarkashī in the ms. is dated in Rabīʿ I 1122/May 1710.

B Berlin Ms. Wetzstein II, 1801 (= Ahlwardt, No. 5486), fols. 37a-46b, with the title *Zahr...taḥrīm...*

C Gotha 1451 (= Pertsch, No. 2096), fols. 1a-6a. Fol. 6a is written in a hand different from the preceding pages, and the title is mentioned only at the end, written by still another hand *(Zahr... aḥkām...)*. The text of this ms. omits all verses together with the context in which they are embedded. This, it would seem, was not merely the result of the linguistic incompetence of some earlier copyist but was done intentionally by someone who considered all such material irrelevant. The omission of the passages referring to ʿAlī al-Ḥarīrī (below, pp. 99 f. and 124) would also seem to have been done on purpose. The contrary assumption, namely, that these reputed omissions were, in fact, additions to az-Zarkashī's original text can be safely ruled out. Among the omitted verses are those contained in the quotation from al-Qarāfī (below, pp. 108 ff.) which are to be found in al-Qarāfī's text. Nobody would have gone back to al-Qarāfī's text in order to supply them, if az-Zarkashī had not had them in the first place.

D Berlin Ms. Petermann II, 407 (= Ahlwardt, No. 5487), fols. 216a-221b, with the title *Zahr...aḥkām...*, corresponds to Ms. Gotha but has an extremely poor text.

The section on hashish in the *Ta'rīkh al-Khamīs* by ad-Diyārbakrī, which was apparently composed in the first half of the tenth/sixteenth century,[2] is based entirely upon az-Zarkashī, cf. also al-Fanārī (No. 20). Both *Qamʿ* (No. 16) and Ibn al-Ḥanbalī (No. 18) refer to az-Zarkashī, who was, of course, also used by al-Badrī

[1] Cf. *GAL*, 2nd ed., II, 112, *Suppl.*, II, 108.

[2] *Ta'rīkh al-Khamīs*, II, 30 f. (Cairo 1302). For ad-Diyārbakrī, cf. *EI*², *s.v.*

(No. 13), in particular for the comparatively brief discussion of the legal situation where other authorities are also cited indirectly through az-Zarkashī.

The catalogue of the Ẓāhirīyah in Damascus lists az-Zarkashī's work as contained in Ms. No. 5896.[1] The Catalogue's very brief description of the contents indicates substantial agreement with az-Zarkashī. However, the Ẓāhirīyah text is stated to be an *urjūzah* poem, and not a prose text. It may have been a versification of az-Zarkashī's work (by himself?), but this assumption remains to be verified.

10. Al-Aqfahsī, Shihāb-ad-dīn Aḥmad Ibn al-ʿImād (Shāfiʿite, d. 808/1405-6),[2] *Ikrām man yaʿīsh bi-taḥrīm al-khamr wa-l-ḥashīsh.* The Princeton Ms. of the work has *bi-jtinābih* (clearly written, however, *bi-jtinābat*), for *bi-taḥrīm.* According to the old Cairo Catalogue, VII, 157, the Cairo Ms. of the work (*majāmīʿ* 114,2, fols. 71-102) is dated on Friday, 10 Rajab 792/24 June 1390, and thus was written during the lifetime of the author. As this ms. was not available, I was able only to make use of the Princeton Ms. 1822 (=890 H), fols. 1-22b. The integrity and completeness of its text are dubious and can be ascertained only with the help of the Cairo Ms. The portion dealing specifically with hashish extends from fol. 19b to the end, fol. 22b. It is possible that it in particular was considerably abridged.

Al-Aqfahsī's work contains only very little beyond the information found in az-Zarkashī. Az-Zarkashī, however, is not mentioned by name. Ibn Taymīyah's *Siyāsah* is quoted, and so is the *Takrīm al-maʿīshah* of al-Qasṭallānī. Al-Qasṭallānī may have been a common source for az-Zarkashī and al-Aqfahsī in some instances, but it would seem rather more likely that az-Zarkashī was widely used by al-Aqfahsī without acknowledgement. Al-Aqfahsī may have looked upon the sources quoted by az-Zarkashī so to speak as common property and therefore have neglected to mention az-Zarkashī's name, but even this seems hard to prove.

Ibn Ḥajar al-Haytamī (above, p. 9), *Taḥdhīr ath-thiqāt min akl al-kaftah wa-l-qāt,* which he finished on 17 Ṣafar 960/2 February 1553, states that "all the blameworthy qualities mentioned in connection with hashish are also to be found in *qāt,*[3] with additional

---

[1] Cf. ʿAbd-al-Ghanī ad-Daqar, *Fihris makhṭūṭāt Dār al-Kutub aẓ-Ẓāhirīyah, al-fiqh ash-Shāfiʿī,* 126 (Damascus 1383/1963).

[2] Cf. *GAL, Suppl.,* II, 110 f.

[3] Cf., for instance, C. Brooke, *Khat (Catha Edulis): Its Production and*

harm" (Yale Ms. L-753 [= Catalogue Nemoy, No. 1579], fol. 5a). Thus, it is hardly surprising that from fol. 9b of the Yale Ms. to the end of the treatise, the author reproduces much of the treatise of Ibn al-ʿImād (al-Aqfahsī). He also makes twice reference to az-Zarkashī and appears to have used his work directly.

Al-Aqfahsī, fol. 21a, quotes six verses "in refutation of the wicked men who have declared it permissible to eat hashish." The first and last of these verses read:

> Do not listen to one who praises drinking hashish,
> For he is not right in what he says.
> ....
> Doing something right and good could hardly be expected
> From someone who slips from the glorious right path.
>
> *(lā tuṣghiyanna li-mādiḥin shurba l-ḥashī-*
> *shi fa-innahū fī l-qawli ghayru musaddadi*
> ....
> *hayhāta an ya'tī (sic) bi-fiʿlin ṣāliḥin*
> *man zalla ʿan sanani r-rashādī l-amjadi).*

Ibn Ḥajar al-Haytamī starts out with five other verses, beginning:

> O you whose mark has become the eating of hashish
> And whose viciousness and hangover have thus become fully obvious.
>
> *(yā man ghadā akla l-ḥashīshi shiʿāruhū*
> *wa-ʿadā [ghadā ?] fa-lāḥa ʿuwāruhū wa-khumāruhū).*

Then, the six verses of al-Aqfahsī are quoted. They are, however, followed by six more verses, of which the first and the last read:

> Those who have expressed a legal opinion stating it is permissible to drink it have erred.
> It is considered disgraceful (?) by ash-Shāfiʿī and Aḥmad
> ....
> From a ruler or a scholar or an inspector
> Or a good counselor, restrained in what he does.
>
> *(qad ḍalla man aftā bi-ḥilli sharābihā*
> *fīhā ʿ-z-y (leg. khazan ?) li-sh-Shāfiʿīyi wa-Aḥmadi*
> ....
> *min ḥākimin aw ʿālimin aw nāẓirin*
> *aw nāṣiḥin fī fiʿlihī mutazahhidi).*

It is possible that all this additional material belonged to al-Aqfahsī's original text, as someone familiar with the Cairo Ms. of it may be able to verify or disprove.

11. Al-Maqrīzī, Aḥmad b. ʿAlī (principally a Shāfiʿite, 766-845/1364-1442),[1] *Khiṭaṭ*, II, 126-129 (Būlāq 1270), has a highly informa-

Trade in the Middle East, in *Geographical Journal*, CXXVI (1960), 52-59.

[1] Cf. *GAL*, 2nd ed., II, 47 ff., *Suppl.*, II, 36 ff.

tive section on "the hashish of the poor (the Ṣūfīs)." It has long been the main text on hashish known in the West because it was edited and translated with copious notes by A. I. Silvestre de Sacy in his *Chrestomathie arabe*, I, 112-132 (text), II, 115-155 (trans.) (Paris 1806); 2nd ed., I, 74-88 (text), 210-283 (trans.) (Paris 1826). Cf. also Jawad al-Muscati, *Hasan bin Sabbah*, for an English translation by Abbas H. Hamdani, 113 ff. (Karachi 1958).

When al-Maqrīzī is cited here without any further indication, the reference is to this passage. In other cases, as, for instance, the poems on hashish in *Khiṭaṭ*, II, 25 f., volume and page are indicated.

12. Shams-ad-dīn Muḥammad b. an-Najjār (Shāfiʿite), *Kitāb Zawājir ar-Raḥmān fī taḥrīm ḥashīshat ash-Shayṭān*, is repeatedly quoted by al-Badrī.[1] Ibn an-Najjār's lifetime falls into the fifteenth century, as indicated by al-Badrī's references to him as his shaykh and his late shaykh. If al-Badrī, fol. 54b, refers to the same man as seems likely, his father's name was ʿAbd-al-Wahhāb. This would exclude any possibility of identifying him with the *muqri'*, Muḥammad b. Aḥmad b. Dāwūd (788/1386 to ca. 870/1465-66).[2] The work is mentioned by Ḥājjī Khalīfah, 1120, as one of the sources of Ibn al-Ḥanbalī (No. 18), without an indication of the name of its author.

13. Al-Badrī, Abū t-Tuqā Taqī-ad-dīn Abū Bakr b. ʿAbdallāh b. Muḥammad (847-894/1443-1489),[3] *Rāḥat al-arwāḥ fī l-ḥashīsh wa-r-rāḥ*, preserved in Paris Ms. ar. 3544. The part devoted to hashish extends from the beginning to fol. 57b; fols. 58a-142b deal with wine. A brief excerpt exists in the Berlin Ms. Wetzstein II, 422,2 (= Ahlwardt 5488), fols. 70b-71a. Reference to the work is made by Ḥājjī Khalīfah, 829. The apparently very close relationship of al-Bakrī (below, p. 34, n. 5) to al-Badrī's work remains to be investigated.

On fol. 57a, al-Badrī states that he was asked to compose his work in 867/1462-63 (when he was just twenty years old). According to the Paris Ms. (dated itself on Saturday, 22 Jumādā I 1207/5 January 1793), the original ms. *(nuskhat al-aṣl)* from which it was copied was

---

[1] Cf. fols. 8b (below, p. 58), 17a-b (below, p. 97, n. 7), and 48a (below, p. 46, n. 2).

[2] Cf. as-Sakhāwī, *Ḍaw'*, VI, 308.

[3] Cf. *GAL*, II, 132, 2nd ed., II, 164, and *Suppl.*, II, 163. For the correct form Abū t-Tuqā, cf. as-Sakhāwī, *Ḍaw'*, XI, 41 f., and the cross reference in *Ḍaw'*, XI, 101. The correct form is also indicated in the Paris Ms., for instance, fol. 17b. According to as-Sakhāwī, the author was known as Ibn al-Badrī, but in his work he refers to himself as al-Badrī, and this style of reference has been adopted here.

written in 869/1464. This is stated in the colophon. However, a story taking place in the years 869-870 is told on fols. 29a-30a (below, pp. 133 f.). On fol. 22a, Nūr-ad-dīn ʿAlī b. Sūdūn al-Bashbughawī, who died in 875/1470, is called "the late." On fol. 83b, we find a communication made to the author by Aḥmad b. Khalīl as-Sakhāwī (b. 839/1436)[1] "after my composition of this book." Thus, 869/1464 could presumably be the date of the first completion and publication of the work, but if the Paris Ms. was indeed copied from a manuscript written in that year, that ms. must have contained later additions and notes by the author which were taken over into the text. Their incorporation into the text was more likely done by an intermediate copyist, and not by the one of the Paris Ms. himself. On fol. 47a, we find a note on the root *s-ṭ-l* (below, p. 75) introduced by the words, "in his handwriting, a marginal note." It is, however, not clear whether this refers to al-Badrī since we cannot be sure that he himself was the author of the verses quoted in this connection.[2]

The work of al-Badrī, by far the most comprehensive exposition of hashish lore known at present, is surprisingly well arranged. Particular topics are treated together, although it is only natural, since there is much overlapping, that information on some topic may also be found in the treatment of another. The method is loosely associative. Talking about a given topic often leads to what we would call footnote material. The section on wine contains similar excursuses on subjects such as fruits, flowers, rivers, the influence of music on animals and human beings, musical instruments, etc. Speaking about the predilection of hashish users for sweets, al-Badrī digresses with a large collection of material on the subject of sweets (fols. 25a-28a)

---

1 Cf. as-Sakhāwī, *Ḍaw'*, I, 294 f.

2 According to C.Rieu's catalogue, Ms. Brit. Mus. 1422 of al-Badrī's *Ghurrat aṣ-ṣabāḥ* was written in 875/1471 and contains a number of favorable notices for the work dating from 871/1466-67. According to as-Sakhāwī, *Ḍaw'*, XI, 41, al-Badrī claimed later in his life that the work was already written in 865/1460-61, which would make it the work of a boy of eighteen. The Bodleian Ms. 522,8 of al-Badrī's *Maṭāliʿ al-Badrīyah* is supposedly an autograph copy written in 880/1475 (cf. A. Nicoll's Catalogue, 298-300, Oxford 1835, where al-Badrī is correctly called Abū t-Tuqā). The Paris ms. of the *Rāḥah* has quotations from both the *Ghurrah* (fol. 52b) and the *Maṭāliʿ* (fols. 70a and 88a). Altogether al-Badrī cites in it no less than nine of his own works (fols. 55b, 86b, 110b, 115b, 122a, and 133a, in addition to the references just given). This seems too much for a man just twenty years old, and the general tone of the *Rāḥah* is that of a mature and accomplished littérateur. Since there is no reason to doubt the correctness of his birth date, we must be dealing here with a later recension.

whose only tenuous relation to hashish are very occasional and incidental references to hashish users and hashish intoxication. The discussion of the relationship of hashish use and homosexuality (fols. 30a ff.) is greatly expanded by material, often obscene, which has no immediate bearing upon hashish. On fols. 51b-52b, we find a discussion of the illegality of homosexuality (below, p. 85). This is al-Badrī's way of atoning for the lack of moral scruples exhibited in his long digression into the subject. The same purpose is to be served by the strenuous denunciation of hashish at the end of the discussion, which was mostly favorable to hashish use. It would appear that thereby, the young author not only saved his soul but also forestalled any attempt by the authorities of taking a close look into his own affairs. His personal attitude remains entirely unclear as we would expect (cf. below, p. 151, n. 1).

14. ʿAbd-al-Bāsiṭ b. Khalīl al-Ḥanafī (Ḥanafite, d. 920/1514),[1] *ad-Durr al-wasīm fī tawshīḥ Tatmīm at-Takrīm fī taḥrīm al-ḥashīsh wa-waṣfih adh-dhamīm*, said to be a commentary on al-Qasṭallānī (No. 6). Ḥājjī Khalīfah, 470, specifies that it is a commentary on al-Qasṭallānī's *Takrīm*, but the title indicated by Ḥājjī Khalīfah, 737, suggests rather a commentary on the *Tatmīm at-Takrīm*.

15. Fuzūlī (Fuḍūlī) (d. 963/1556),[2] *Benk u bāde*, used in the German translation by Necati H. Lugal and O. Reşer, *Des türkischen Dichters Fuzūlī Poem "Laylā-Meğnūn" und die gereimte Erzählung "Benk u Bāde" (Haşiş und Wein) nach dem Druck Istbl.* 1326 *übersetzt* (Istanbul 1943).

16. The strange treatise entitled, *Qamʿ al-wāshīn fī dhamm al-barrāshīn*, is preserved only in the Leiden Ms. or. 814,12. The Leiden Ms. gives the name of its author as Nūr-ad-dīn ʿAlī b. al-Jazzār. The ms. has no dots for Jazzār, thus making the reading somewhat uncertain. In fact, as-Sakhāwī, *Ḍaw'*, V, 171, lists a Meccan with almost the same chain of names but not identical with the author of *Qamʿ*, who is expressly stated to have been al-Kharrāz. The author of *Qamʿ* is described as a Shāfiʿite and the chief shaykh in Egypt, Cairo, and the two Qarāfahs. His *kunyah* is said to be Abū l-Ḥasan.[3]

---

[1] Cf. *GAL*, 2nd ed., II, 66, *Suppl.*, II, 52 f. For an owner's note in the handwriting of ʿAbd-al-Bāsiṭ in the Istanbul Ms. Köprülü I, 366, cf. M. Weisweiler, *Der islamische Bucheinband des Mittelalters*, 151 (Wiesbaden 1962).

[2] Cf. A. Karahan, in *EI*², *s. v.* Fuḍūlī.

[3] Cf. *GAL*, *Suppl.*, II, 429, 5b; Ḥājjī Khalīfah, IV, 570 f., in the edition of G. Flügel (Leipzig and London 1835-1858), a passage that is not included in Yaltkaya's edition.

Qamʿ is quoted by al-Fanārī (No. 20) as the work of Ibn al-Ḥasan al-Bakrī. Ibn al-Ḥasan should possibly be corrected to Abū l-Ḥasan. It is, of course, quite possible that the author's father was also called al-Ḥasan, but Ḥājjī Khalīfah, 360, seems to indicate that his father's name was Muḥammad. According to Ḥājjī Khalīfah, 360, another work by the same author, entitled *Taḥṣīn al-manāzil min hawl az-zalāzil,* was written in 984/1576-77. In any event, the date of the Fanārī ms. places the composition of *Qamʿ* before 991/1583.

In the spirit of the times, the author of *Qamʿ* concludes his work with a couple of pages devoted to his views on coffee. He praises it and considers its use legally permissible wherever it agrees with an individual. Rather cryptically, however, he mentions additives which make the use of coffee fall into the forbidden category, citing the verse:

> I was asked about coffee whether
> It is permitted and safe.
> I replied: Yes, it is safe.
> The only difficulty are those additions to it.[1]

The allusion is no doubt to drugs put into coffee. Ḥājjī Khalīfah mentions the fondness of drug addicts for coffee.[2] In the following eighteenth century, al-Idkāwī speaks of spiking coffee with opium and other drugs.[3]

17. Ibrāhīm b. Bakhshī, known as Dede Khalīfah (d. 973/1565-66), is credited with a *Risālah* on hashish, cf. No. 18.

18. Ibn al-Ḥanbalī, Raḍī-ad-dīn Muḥammad b. Ibrāhīm al-Ḥalabī (Ḥanafite, 877-971/1472-1563),[4] *Ẓill al-ʿarīsh fī manʿ ḥill al-banj wa-l-ḥashīsh.* Ḥājjī Khalifah, 1120, is our only reference so far. He describes the work as a commentary or abridgment of the *Risālah* of Dede Khalīfah (No. 17). He also informs us that Ibn al-Ḥanbalī used among his sources the *Zahr al-ʿarīsh,* presumably the

---

[1] *la-qad qīla lī qahwatu l-bunni hal*
taḥillu wa-tu'manu āfātuhā
fa-qultu naʿam hiya ma'mūnatun
wa-mā ṣ-ṣaʿbu illā muḍāfātuhā.

[2] Cf. Ḥājjī Khalīfah (Kātib Chelebi), *The Balance of Truth,* trans. G. L. Lewis, 60 (London 1957).

[3] Cf. his *Ḥusn ad-daʿwah,* in Yale Ms. L-55 (= Catalogue Nemoy, No. 1575), fol. 2a, as mentioned by L. Nemoy, in *Papers in Honor of Andrew Keogh,* 46 f. (New Haven 1938).

[4] Cf. *GAL,* 2nd ed., II, 483 f., *Suppl.,* II, 495 f.

work of az-Zarkashī (No. 9), and the *Zawājir ar-Raḥmān fī taḥrīm ḥashīsh ash-Shayṭān* (No. 12).

19. The Berlin Ms. or. 4°, 49 (= Ahlwardt, No. 5488), fols. 8a-9a, has a subscription naming a certain Maḥmūd al-Muḥammadī al-Ḥanafī as the man who has collected there the legal arguments for the forbidden character of the use of hashish. This subscription refers no doubt to the author of what is written on fol. 8a. This ends with the words, "thus, I say with the help of God," and the text on fols. 8b-9a appears to constitute the main body of Maḥmūd's treatise but is written in a clearly different hand. According to the text on fol. 8a, the author, being in Egypt and not liking it there, attended the classes of al-Barhamatūshī[1] and heard it said that his late teacher, Shihāb-ad-dīn *(sic)*[2] Aḥmad b. Kamālbāshāh considered *ghubayrā'* (below, pp. 24 f.) legal and permitted it for consumption. The author contends that he himself had never heard Ibn Kamāl Pāshā (see No. 21) say such a thing and that it was falsely and maliciously ascribed to him. From these statements it results that this Maḥmūd lived in the sixteenth century and, apparently, well into the second half of it.

20. Al-Fanārī, Maḥmūd b. Pīr Muḥammad, *Risālah fī bayān ḥurmat al-ḥashīsh wa-l-afyūn*, is preserved in the Istanbul Ms. Laleli 3675, fols. 38b-39a. The ms. is dated in Shaʿbān 991/August-September 1583. The name of the author appears on top of the page, clearly written in the same hand as the rest. It would be possible for this Maḥmūd to have been a son of Pīr Muḥammad al-Fanārī who died in 954/1547 or the following year.[3] This, however, is an entirely unsubstantiated guess.

The short treatise is a pastiche of numerous quotations, many of them written in the margins. In the text, we find two excerpts from *Qamʿ* (No. 16), of which only one is marked as such. Some passages agree with az-Zarkashī whose name is not mentioned, and al-Fanārī does indeed not quote him directly. In one case, what seems to be a literal quotation from az-Zarkashī is introduced by a reference to *al-Mawāhib al-ladunīyah* and *al-Khamīs*, biographies of the Prophet

---

[1] Shams-ad-dīn al-Barhamatūshī is mentioned three times in al-Ghazzī, *al-Kawākib as-sā'irah*, but I know of no obituary notice devoted to him. Barhamatūsh is the vocalization indicated by A. S. Atiya in his edition of Ibn Mammātī, *Qawānīn*, 110 (Cairo 1943).

[2] Ibn Kamāl Pāshā (Kemālpashazādeh) was Shams-ad-dīn.

[3] Cf. Ṭāshköprüzādeh, *ash-Shaqā'iq an-nuʿmānīyah*, II, 15 (Cairo 1310, in the margin of Ibn Khallikān, *Wafayāt*).

by, respectively, al-Qasṭallānī (d. 923/1517) and ad-Diyārbakrī (above, No. 9).

The marginal notes appear to be in the same hand. Since it is hardly likely that we have here the original ms. of al-Fanārī—his notes, so to speak, jotted down for later elaboration—, the material in the margins may have been taken over from the original work. There is, however, a reference, to a work entitled *Tanwīr al-abṣār*. If this means the work by at-Timirtāshī,[1] we would have a serious problem, not because at-Timirtāshī died in 1004/1595, only a short while after the date of the ms., but because Ḥājjī Khalīfah, 501, states that at-Timirtāshī's *Tanwīr al-abṣār* was composed in al-Muḥarram 995/December 1586, that is, *after* the date of the Fanārī ms. Thus, either the marginal notes are later additions, or, possibly, the *Tanwīr* cited is another work, and not that of at-Timirtāshī.

21. An anonymous brief treatise entitled *Risālah fī ḥurmat al-banj* is preserved in Ankara, General Library, Eski Eserler 678, fol. 147a. In the ms., the treatise follows upon another anonymous treatise *Fī bayān ṭabīʿat al-afyūn*, which is no doubt the widely distributed work by Ibn Kamāl Pāshā (873-940/1468-1534).[2] I did, however, not make sure of this while I was Ankara, and, much to my regret, I have been unable later on to consult Ibn Kamāl Pāshā's essay. It may contain points of interest in connection with hashish.

22. The Gotha Ms. of az-Zarkashī (No. 9) further contains, on fol. 6a-b, a survey of the history of hashish in Islam and some poems on the drug. Since a commentary by at-Timirtāshī appears to be indicated as the direct source of the former, we would have to date these notes in the tenth/sixteenth century, but the material quoted can safely be assumed to go back to the much earlier indirect authorities mentioned.[3]

---

[1] Cf. *GAL*, *Suppl.*, II, 427.

[2] Cf. *GAL*, *Suppl.*, II, 668 ff., and *Şarkiyat Mecmuası*, VI (1966), 71-112, where mss. of the brief treatise on opium are listed on p. 108.

[3] Cf. below, pp. 48 f., p. 78, n. 1, and p. 150, n. 4.

CHAPTER THREE

THE USE OF HASHISH

1. The Names of the Drug

Hashish has been singled out for discussion because of its prominence among the drugs used in medieval Islam. However, it must be realized that as a rule no distinction was made between the numerous different narcotics known, and it is often not easy for us to be sure whether cannabis or some other drug is intended in a given report. Some jurists seem to have been dimly aware of the problems concealed in the differences of properties and effects of different drugs, but many of those who tell stories about the use of drugs were unable to distinguish between them, nor were they particularly interested in doing so. Moreover, whenever we hear about hashish, some caution is indicated in view of the ever present possibility that the preparations used were mixtures of a number of different substances of which hashish may have been merely one and, perhaps, not the most potent one in its effect.

Ḥashīsh, *banj*, and *afyūn* (opium)[1] are the terms most frequently used, and they are also most commonly lumped together without, it seems, any clear idea of the distinctions that might exist, or should be made, between them. *Banj* in particular is a term with a long history, which, in the Muslim world, tended to be dishonorable. *Al-mubannijah* "substances having the effect of *banj*" was used as a comprehensive term for narcotic drugs.[2] The *mubannij*, who practices *tabnīj*, was a sinister figure who made use of his dark art to seduce innocent people or, even more nefariously, to have it serve as a prelude to murder and robbery.[3] As is well known, *banj*, in its pre-

[1] In his edition and translation of Maimonides, *Sharḥ asmāʾ al-ʿuqqār*, 19 f. (Cairo 1940, *Mém. de l'Institut d'Égypte* 41), M. Meyerhof states that Maimonides vocalizes *ufiyūn* and that the usual vocalization is *afiyūn*. The reprint of the work, dating from ca. 1966, omits Meyerhof's translation and notes, the most valuable part of the publication.

[2] Cf., for instance, Jābir b. Ḥayyān, *Kitāb as-Sumūm*, in the edition and translation of A. Siggel, *Das Buch der Gifte des Ǧābir Ibn Ḥayyān*, fol. 131b, p. 139 (Wiesbaden 1958), cf. also p. 154, n. 2. Siggel wrongly read "die Erlaubten."

[3] Cf., for example, the dramatic story told in Ibn ad-Dāyah, *Mukāfaʾah*, 158-160 (Cairo 1941), 88 f. (Cairo 1332/1914).

Islamic history, represented, in fact, "hemp." But in the usage of Muslim times, it was commonly the scientific word for "henbane,"[1] although we are admittedly at a great disadvantage in any attempts we might make to clarify the exact meaning of the scholarly references. Physicians and scientists appear to have been by and large consistent in their use of *banj* for henbane. ʿAlī b. Rabban aṭ-Ṭabarī, in the middle of the ninth century, speaks of three kinds of *banj*, of which the white one was in use, apparently referring to henbane.[2] The three kinds seem to be characteristic of *banj* in the meaning of henbane. It should be noted, however, that one also distinguished, as did, for instance, Ibn al-Bayṭār, three kinds of hemp; on the other hand, Ibn Jazlah and Maimonides (1135-1204) list only two kinds of *banj*.[3] When the great Rāzī (251-313/865-925) discusses deadly poisons in his *Ḥāwī*, he properly includes *banj* "henbane" but makes no mention of hemp.[4] Ar-Rāzī's authorities for the effects of and remedies for *banj* are Greek works such as Rufus' *Ilā l-ʿAwwām*,[5] and comparison of ar-Rāzī with Paul of Aegina whom he quotes shows that *banj* is indeed to be understood as henbane *(hyoskyamos)*.[6] But it is characteristic of the general confusion that the author of the *Book of Poisons* ascribed to Jābir b. Ḥayyān can speak of opium as the juice of black *banj* before he mentions the connection of opium with poppy, and it always remains quite unclear what substance he has in mind when speaking about *banj*.[7] In sum, as the author of the *Risālah fī ḥurmat al-banj*[8] put it, "*banj* is a general term, and *ḥashīsh* a specific term." Any mention of *banj* in the general literature may actually refer to hashish. On the other hand, there is no guarantee that a mention of hashish does not involve something else besides hemp and hemp preparations. Considering the original meaning of *ḥashīsh* to be mentioned immediately, it would certainly not be improper to employ it for any drug derived from plants, as all these narcotics were.

When the use of hashish became established, and the drug took

---

[1] Cf. M. Meyerhof, in *EI*², *s. v.* bandj.

[2] Cf. aṭ-Ṭabarī, *Firdaws al-ḥikmah*, ed. M. Z. Siddiqi, 402 (Berlin 1928).

[3] Cf. al-Maqrīzī and Meyerhof's ed. and trans., 10 (text), 32 f. (trans.).

[4] Cf. ar-Rāzī, *Ḥāwī*, XIX, 355 f. (Hyderabad 1374—/1955—).

[5] Cf. *Ḥāwī*, XIX, 376.

[6] Cf. *Ḥāwī*, XIX, 361, 366, and Paul of Aegina, ed. I. L. Heiberg, II, 31 (Leipzig and Berlin 1921-1924).

[7] *Op. cit.* (p. 19, n. 2), fol. 47a, p. 57.

[8] See above, p. 18.

on, and in a way retained, the role of plaything for a "select" and quasi-secret fraternity, it acquired very many names and nicknames. Hashish could very well have told the camel and the lion (or whatever else enjoyed the reputation of being distinguished by an enormous Arabic nomenclature) to hang their heads in shame, so rich was the choice of words to designate it. The hashish nomenclature was also of a similar character, consisting largely of descriptive adjectives, metaphoric usages, kennings, and the like. It did not, of course, find the loving attention of philologians, and it possessed extremely little staying power, changing rapidly over the years and differing from locality to locality. It also included the trade names for certain confections, and it rarely allows for clear distinctions to be drawn. But its size itself is significant, and it is impressive for the psychological dimensions it conceals rather than reveals.

In the first place, we must realize that *ḥashīsh* or *ḥashīshah*[1] is itself a nickname. The word as such has no specific connection whatever with the hemp plant. It may mean grass used as fodder,[2] herbs used for medicinal or other purposes, weeds that infest, for instance, a flower garden and must be weeded out with dispatch by the careful gardener,[3] and the like. We cannot be absolutely sure which of the meanings of *ḥashīsh* led to its use for the cannabis drug. It would be possible to see in it a sort of abbreviation of the expression *al-ḥashīsh al-muskir* "the intoxicating *ḥashīsh*." Most likely, it may be simply "*the* herb" as distinguished from all other (medicinal) herbs.[4] Again, we cannot be sure but it seems most likely that the nickname was intended to be of the endearing, rather than the vituperative,

---

[1] *Ḥashīshah* is the *nomen unitatis* of the collective noun *ḥashīsh*, but no distinction in the use of the two forms can be discerned. Grammatically the word may be used as a masculine if the masculine form of the noun is used, but preferably the feminine is used, regardless of the grammatical form of the word employed.

[2] All these meanings are extremely common, and no occurrences need be cited, but for the meaning of fodder, one may, for instance, refer to Ibn al-Mufarrigh al-Ḥimyarī, a poet of the seventh century, in the edition of his collected poems by Dāwūd Sallūm, 159 (Baghdād 1968).

Ḥashīsh may be legally classified together with firewood as "indifferent things" in enemy territory, as in the work by Ibn Jamāʿah (639-733/1241-1333) translated into German by H. Kofler, *Handbuch des islamischen Staats- und Verwaltungsrechtes*, 95 (*Abh. f. d. Kunde d. Morgenlandes*, XXIII, 6, 1938). Kofler, strangely enough, translates "Haschisch."

[3] Cf., for instance, the story in al-Ghazzālī, *at-Tibr al-masbūk*, 75 f. (Cairo 1378/1968).

[4] Cf. already P. Alpin, *Medicina Aegyptiorum*, 258 (Leiden 1745): "...quasi cannabem hinc herbam per excellentiam vocant."

kind.[1] At any rate, its use clearly implies that the drug had become popular and was widely used by the time of the adoption of this nickname. Conversely, if we were able to determine when it came into use, we would learn something about the obscure early history of hashish in the Muslim world.[2] Furthermore, since hashish was a nickname popularized no doubt at a particular time under particular circumstances, it is obvious that we cannot expect it to have been employed before that time, and if cannabis was known and used for hallucinogenic purposes, it must have been designated differently.

The scientific names for the plant and its products were *qinnab (qunnab)* "cannabis" and *(waraq,* sg. *waraqat) ash-shahdānaj* "(leaves of) hemp (seed)." They occur frequently in connection with qualifying adjectives such as *hindī* "Indian" and *bustānī* "garden...," or "cultivated," as against *barrī* "wild."

A form with retention of the final *s* of the original Greek, *qunbus* (this being the most likely vocalization), is disregarded by the dictionaries but amply attested.[3] Thus, the poem of Ibn ar-Rassām uses *ḥashīsha l-qunbusi.*[4] The same combination occurs in the first line of a long poem attached to Ibn Ghānim's treatise on hashish,[5] while Ibn al-Wardī (d. 749/1349) uses *al-qunbus* by itself.[6] In the West, hashish was supposedly nicknamed "daughter of *al-qunbus.*"[7] Dāwūd al-Anṭākī (d. 1008/1599) defines *qunbus* as the shrub and the seeds of *qinnab,* whereas *ḥashīshah* designated the leaves.[8] The Arabic translation of Dioscurides transliterates *qn'bs.*[9]

The foreign word *shahdānaj* had a number of slightly different forms. It presumably meant in Persian something like "royal grain," but detractors would say that it meant "queen of insanity" *(sulṭānat*

---

[1] In American usage, "weed" may be a vituperative term for tobacco. "Grass" is presently a term of endearment for marijuana. "Weed" as used for marijuana may be, I suppose, either.

[2] Cf. below, pp. 41 ff.

[3] For Syriac forms, cf. R. Payne Smith, *Thesaurus Syriacus,* 3459, 3671 (Oxford 1879-1901). Jewish Hebrew or Aramaic forms also retain the final *s.* I. Löw, *Die Flora der Juden,* I, 256 (Vienna and Leipzig 1924-1934, reprint Hildesheim 1967), cites *ḳinnab, ḳumbus* as the modern Syrian-Palestinian forms, also (I, 262) *ḳunbuz.*

[4] Cf. below, p. 157.

[5] Cf. below, p. 168. The Princeton Ms. vocalizes *al-qanbas.*

[6] Cf. below, p. 75.

[7] Cf. below, p. 36, and also p. 166, n. 4.

[8] Cf. Dāwūd al-Anṭākī, *Tadhkirah,* I, 200 (Cairo 1324).

[9] Cf. the edition of C. E. Dubler and E. Terés, II, 304 (Barcelona and Tetuán 1952-1959).

al-junūn),[1] apparently connecting *dānaj* with *dēwaneh* "crazy." The divergent forms do not merely reflect clerical uncertainty but they attest to the fact that the word was quite generally known and used. We find *shāhdānaj* with a long vowel in the first syllable.[2] Final *q* for *j* is not uncommon. The form *shādānaq* is fancifully credited to an alleged *Kitāb Sūq al-ʿarḍ fī nabāt al-arḍ* of the philosopher Muḥammad b. Zakarīyā' ar-Rāzī,[3] no doubt one of the apocryphal works ascribed to the famous Rāzī. Dāwūd al-Anṭākī says that the Egyptians call it *sharānaq*,[4] a corruption adopted into the spoken language rather than a clerical mistake.[5]

The scientific names have had an uninterrupted history from the earliest times of Muslim scholarship and literature on to the present. The time of origin of a nickname cannot be accurately determined, and literary preservation effectively masks the true time of its falling out of use. In some cases, we may guess at the particular region where a given nickname was in use, but we cannot be certain whether it did not in fact spread from there to other places. The two substantial lists of nicknames which have come down to us (see below, pp. 34 ff.) contain interesting specifications in these respects but again how true they are to reality is anybody's guess. The urge to invent picturesque terms can be assumed to have been well nigh irrestible to addicts and littérateurs alike. It added some minor intellectual fillip to a game fondly believed to engage the mind.

One of the most common designations of hashish was *al-khaḍrā'* (or, much less frequently, the masculine *al-akhḍar*) "the green one," alluding to its derivation from a highly ornamental green plant.

[1] Cf. al-Badrī, fol. 57a.

[2] Cf. E. W. Lane, *An Arabic-English Dictionary*, I, iv, 1611c-1612a, who also lists slightly different vocalizations.

[3] Cf. al-Badrī, fol. 5b. Cf. also *shādānak* in F. Steingass, *Persian-English Dictionary*, 721b.

[4] *Loc. cit.* (above, p. 22, n. 8).

[5] Speaking of conditions in Persia, E. Kaempfer, *Amoenitatum exoticarum politico-physico-medicarum fasciculi* V, 645-647 (Lemgo 1712), refers to "semen quod Sjadonéh, Pollen flosculorum quod TSjers, & Folia quae Baeng vocant," a passage already cited by Silvestre de Sacy, *Mémoire sur la dynastie des Assassins*, in *Mémoires de l'Institut Royal de France, Classe d'histoire et de littérature ancienne*, IV (1818), 49. *TSjers* corresponds to Persian *chars*, listed by Steingass, *Persian-English Dictionary*, 391a, as meaning "condensed Indian hemp-juice." Charas as well as bangh are well-known terms in India for hemp products. A picture of "charas, also known as hashish" and the chief profiteer from the drug trade, dubbed, inevitably, "the Charas King," appeared under the by-line of S. H. Schanberg in the *New York Times* of 6 October 1969, p. 14.

It has nothing to do with a possible green sheen of the finished product which may be no more than a figment of the imagination but which is not infrequently alluded to, as in a poem (by ʿAlī b. Sūdūn al-Bashbughawī?) referring to "a pill greenish in color."[1] Poets were particularly taken by the expression "green one," which they might naturally also use for other narcotic plants such as the poppy.[2] The color imagery to which it lent itself was endlessly exploited by them with long practiced skill. It may often have been considered just a poetic metaphor, but it quite clearly was current as a proper nickname.[3]

Another term connected with the vegetable origin of hashish, and, possibly, also felt to imply a color scheme, was *ghubayrā'*, in its etymological meaning, probably, "the little dust-colored one." It is claimed as the slang term for hashish used in Diyār Bakr.[4] Az-Zarkashī mentions it expressly as a nickname for hashish,[5] although he also cites ʿAlā'-ad-dīn Ibn al-ʿAṭṭār (d. 724/1324)[6] as speaking of "the *ḥashīshah* called *ghubayrā'*," which may, or may not, suggest that he thought of *ghubayrā'* as something different from cannabis. When a compound whose admixture to food would infallibly put to sleep anyone eating it is described as consisting in equal parts of blue *banj*, opium, *ghubayrā'*, and castoreum, the meaning of *ghubayrā'*, as well as *banj*, here is uncertain, but the entire concoction is anyhow fictitious.[7] *Ghubayrā'* occurs in Prophetical traditions[8] and supposedly refers to an alcoholic beverage, but nobody seems to have known anything concrete about it. Botanists claim it for the service tree or sorb.[9] Ibn Taymīyah refers to it as a *ḥashīshah*,[10] but for him,

[1] Cf. al-Badrī, fol. 22b: *bunduqah fī lawnihā khuḍrah*. Cf. also pp. 77, 83, and 137.

[2] Cf. an-Nuwayrī, *Nihāyah*, XI, 25 (Cairo 1342—, reprint ca. 1965).

[3] Cf. also below, pp. 35 and 40.

[4] Cf. below, p. 35.

[5] Cf. below, p. 176.

[6] Cf. below, p. 119, n. 3, and p. 187.

[7] Cf. al-Jawbarī, *Kashf al-asrār*, 60 (Cairo 1316).

[8] Cf. A. J. Wensinck and others, *Concordance et indices de la tradition musulmane*, IV, 458 (Leiden 1936-1969).

[9] Cf. M. Meyerhof's ed. and trans. of Maimonides, No. 405, and, for a reference from al-Kindī, M. Levey, *The Medical Formulary*, 86, 310 (Madison, Wisc., and London 1966). Al-Aqfahsī, *Ikrām man yaʿīsh*, Princeton Ms. 1822 (= 890 H), fols. 2b-3a, quotes authorities such as Abū ʿUbayd al-Qāsim b. Sallām and Mālik for the identification of *ghubayrā'* with *sukurkah* (see below, p. 109, n. 1) and for claiming Abyssinian origin for it. Ash-Shāfiʿī, *Umm*, VI, 175 (also 228 margin) (Cairo 1321-1325), cited the identification from Mālik on the authority of Zayd b. Aslam (d. 136/754).

[10] *Fatāwī*, II, 252 f., IV, 324 f.

as well as for his older contemporary Ibn al-ʿAṭṭār, it might have been something different from plain hashish. Perhaps, it was a confection made with hashish as its main ingredient. Or rather, it was transferred from some proper use to serve at times as a nickname for hashish.

Its vegetable origin was indicated by *ibnat al-qunbus (al-qinnab)* "daughter of cannabis,"[1] which also rarely appears in the masculine form of *ibn al-qinnab* "son of cannabis."[2] The way in which hashish was prepared gave it the nickname of *muḥammaṣ(ah)* "the toasted one," of not infrequent occurrence. *Muʿanbar(ah)* "amber-scented" was, on the other hand, descriptive rather than a full-fledged nickname and as such probably quite restricted.[3] *Kāfūrī*, however, does not refer to an admixture of camphor,[4] but we may trust the authorities who bring it into connection with the Park of Kāfūr in Cairo.[5] Various words for pill or pellet, such as *bunduqah*, were also familiarly used for hashish, as it was taken in pill form.[6] Its often lauded easy storage and transportability gave rise to the nickname *bint al-jirāb* "daughter of the bag," believed to have been at home in Baghdād.[7] The alleged historical origins of hashish use were honored by the terms Ḥaydarīyah and Qalandarīyah.[8] *Al-mufarriḥ* ("that which gladdens") *al-Ḥaydarī* was a suitable description of hashish.[9]

The supposed effects of hashish furnished kennings such as *hāḍim al-aqwāt* "digester of food" and *bāʿithat al-fikr* "rouser of thought,"[10] the latter being echoed also in a nickname such as *luqaymat al-fikr* "morsel of thought."[11] As much was made by addicts of the ability of hashish to show them "secret meanings," or, as we might say, to open up for them new levels of mental perception, it is not surprising

---

[1] Cf. al-Badrī, fol. 45a, and below, pp. 26 and 36. Wine is "the daughter of the vines" *(bint al-kurūm)*, cf. al-Badrī, fol. 64b, and the verses cited later on.

[2] Cf. al-Badrī, fol. 6a, below, p. 59.

[3] Cf. al-Badrī, fol. 56a (below, p. 137), and below, p. 154.

[4] As suggested in *Wörterbuch der klassischen arabischen Sprache* (letter *K*), 527b (Wiesbaden 1970), with reference to an-Nuwayrī (see below, p. 106, n. 3).

[5] See below, pp. 63 and 135.

[6] Cf. below, pp. 61 f.

[7] Cf. below, pp. 26 and 35. The prototype is "daughter of the cask" (*bint ad-dann* or *ad-dinān*) for wine, cf. al-Badrī, fols. 65a, 66a.

[8] Cf. az-Zarkashī, below, pp. 50 and 176. Forms such as *Qalandarāwī* (below, p. 40) or *Qarandalīyah* (cf. al-Bakrī [below, p. 34, n. 5]) also occur.

[9] As in the superscription of verses on hashish in the *Dīwān* of Ṣafī-ad-dīn al-Ḥillī, see below, p. 171, n. 6.

[10] Cf. Ṣafī-ad-dīn al-Ḥillī, below, p. 172.

[11] Cf. below, pp. 37 and 92.

to find "secrets" *(esrār)* as a commonly employed nickname for hashish among the Turks.[1] Medical euphemisms such as *maʿjūn* "paste, electuary" or *tiryāq* "theriac"[2] were suitable cover names for all kinds of hallucinogenic drugs, including hashish. Although *maʿjūn* at least was widely used this way at a comparatively early date,[3] the use of both terms appears to have been expanded in Ottoman times.

Particular popularity was enjoyed by *kaff*, *maʿlūm*, *zīh*, and *ṣaḥīḥ*. *Kaff* had the advantage of permitting easy and varied punning. The word ordinarily meant "palm (of the hand)," and its verbal homophone meant "to stay." Thus a poet, Taqī-ad-dīn al-Mawṣilī, would rhyme:

> Stay the hand *(kuffa kaffa)* of worries with *kaff*, for *kaff*
> Is a cure for the worried lover—
> With the noble daughter of hemp, not with the daughter
> Of a vine. Away with the daughter of the vines![4]

Kaff could also refer to the constellation of Cassiopeia, inspiring these verses:

> When the satan of worries flies away with my thoughts,
> Intent upon stealing gaiety away from me, being himself full of emotion,
> I promptly proceed to the daughter of the bag,
> As from the stars of *al-kaff* a star has come to it.[5]

The verbal root *kafā* in the meaning of being satisfied or enough could be pressed into service:

---

[1] So already in the list, below, p. 35. Modern Turkish dictionaries separate the drug *esrar* from *esrār* "secrets."

[2] Also *diryāq*, see below, p. 38. The *tiryaki* of the Karagöz theatre may be an opium smoker. For the common equation *diryāq* = wine, see, for instance, al-Badrī, fol. 61a.

[3] When Ibn Taymīyah, *Fatāwī*, IV, 315, reports on a *maʿjūn* taken customarily by some people every afternoon before the afternoon prayer, he adds that its effect is to change the mind (remove the intellect). It could very well have involved hashish. Al-Badrī has repeated references to *maʿjūn*.

[4] Cf. al-Maqrīzī, who also cites other verses containing the same play on words, cf. below, p. 155. I have no further information on Taqī-ad-dīn al-Mawṣilī.

[5] Cf. al-Badrī, fols. 10a-b and 12a:

> *idhā ṭāra shayṭānu l-humūmi bi-fikratī*
> *yarūmu stirāqa l-lahwi minnī wa-yaṭrabu*
> *ʿadaltu ilā binti l-jirābi mubādiran*
> *fa-qad jā'ahū min anjumi l-kaffi kawkabu.*

The concluding "it" refers to the bag (for "daughter of the bag," see above, p. 25); since *jā'ahū* is attested twice, a correction to *jā'anī* "come to me" would be hard to defend. For the context of these verses, cf. below, p. 146.

Give up wine, and you will be safe
From legal punishment and crime.
Be satisfied with *kaff* instead of wine.
Indeed, *kaff* is enough.[1]

When Silvestre de Sacy first encountered the term *kaff* in the verses cited by al-Maqrīzī, he suggested that *kaff* was another form of *kayf (kēf)*, well known in Persian and Arabic as a word for narcotic. This is unlikely, although the existence of the term *kayf* might possibly have helped *kaff* on its way to becoming rather widely used as a nickname for hashish. In the realm of botany, *kaff* is usually defined as purslane, and, qualified by a depending genitive, it was used to designate quite a variety of plants, all on the basis of a presumed similarity with the human or animal palm or hand. The hemp plant is described by az-Zarkashī[2] as having the size of the fingers of the hand, and Dāwūd al-Anṭākī[3] expressly employs the word *kaff* and fingers of the hand to describe the size as well as the shape of hemp leaves. A poet could very well speak of the palms *(akuff)* of hashish.[4] There can be little doubt that *kaff* as a nickname for hashish represents "palm (of the hand)," as suggested by the leaves of the hemp plant.

Maʿlūm appears to have been rather widely used.[5] Its original meaning is not quite clear. It appears qualified by "the poor (the Ṣūfīs)," yet it is possible that it is just an euphemism hinting at hashish as "the known (thing)." Perhaps, however, it should be understood as "payment, salary," hashish constituting the "pay-off" for the rigors of Ṣūfī life and the only real compensation for all of life's miseries.

Zīh is no doubt correctly identified as a nickname at home in Egypt,[6] and it is of frequent occurrence as such in the work of al-Badrī.[7] Its correct vocalization is indicated by the fact that it

---

1 Cf. al-Badrī, fol. 46b:

utruk-i-l-khamrata taslam
min ḥudūdin wa-l-jināyah
wa-ktafī bi-l-kaffi ʿanhā
inna fī l-kaffi kifāyah.

The meter *(ramal)* requires a long *ī* in *wa-ktafī*, for *wa-ktafi*.

2 Cf. below, p. 176. "Shape" may be meant as well as "size."

3 *Tadhkirah*, I, 200.

4 Cf. below, p. 60.

5 Cf. al-Badrī, fols. 45a-b (below, p. 166, n. 4), 47a-b, 56a-b (below, p. 99), and below, p. 36.

6 Cf. below, p. 36.

7 It was known already to Silvestre de Sacy from al-Bakrī's *Kawākib*.

rhymes with *tanzīh* (al-Badrī, fol. 10a). It may be more than a phonetic coincidence that the Coptic dictionary lists *sihe (nhīt)* with the meaning of "derangement (of mind)."[1] We may have here a plausible etymology of *zīh*. In analogy to *ḥashshāsh*, its user could be called *zayyāh*; this form appears once in a verse of a long poem by the littérateur, Abū l-Khayr al-ʿAqqād:

> You can observe the *zayyāh* using everything sweet,
> While the slave of beer is humble and despised.[2]

In his *Tadhkirah*, Dāwūd al-Anṭākī mentions an Anatolian *(rūmī)* kind of hemp, called *az-zkzh*, which recalls *zīh* but is hardly to be connected with it.

Ṣaḥīḥ is claimed as the Syrian nickname for hashish.[3] It probably goes back to the meaning of "sound" or "healthy." Like *kaff*, it was eminently suitable for punning by the initiated. The use of the word in the sciene of *ḥadīth* and as the title of al-Bukhārī's famous collection brought out the punster in *ḥadīth* and legal scholars, as illustrated by the story of Jamāl-ad-dīn al-Malaṭī mentioned below,[4] or by these verses:

> The jurist says to me, when he was noting in my eyes
> Allusions more obvious than the clearest evidence:
> To what special cases do you apply the most remarkable of
> The principles of relaxation? I replied: To the *ṣaḥīḥ*.[5]

"Relaxation" *(basṭ)* in these verses may also serve the purpose of a

---

Cf. Biberstein Kazimirski, *Dictionnaire arabe-français*, II, 470 (Cairo 1875): "Espèce de plante connue en Égypte, dont on préparait une boisson enivrante." In a story told by al-Badrī, fol. 17b (cf. below, p. 98), *zīh* seems to alternate with *ṭībaḥ* which would thus qualify as a further nickname (?).

[1] Cf. W. E. Crum, *A Coptic Dictionary*, 379b (Oxford 1939).

[2] Cf. al-Badrī, fol. 17a:
tarā z-zayyāha yahwā kulla ḥulwin
wa-ʿabdu l-mizri fī dhullin wa-shayni.
I have no further information on the poet.

[3] Cf. below, p. 36.

[4] Below, p. 104. Al-Badrī, fol. 4b, mystifyingly mentions "al-Bunduqī in his *Ṣaḥīḥ*, entitled *Ṣaḥīḥ al-ḥuffāẓ*," which may possibly be intended as a purely fictitious work. On fol. 13b, we hear about a lecturer under the influence of hashish who is said "to have given us a lecture on hashish from the evidence in his *Ṣaḥīḥ*."

[5] Cf. al-Badrī, fol. 12b:
yaqūlu liya l-faqīhu wa-fī ʿuyūnī
kināyātun adallu min-a-ṣ-ṣarīḥi
uṣūlu l-basṭi awjahahā ʿalā mā
tufarriʿuhū fa-qultu ʿalā ṣ-ṣaḥīḥi.
For the "allusions in the eyes," see below, p. 77.

cover name for hashish. We thus hear about someone receiving a gift to be used for "all his *basṭ*,"[1] and a destitute addict, scrounging for some little money, "revived his *basṭ (aḥyā basṭah)*."[2] Whether or not *basṭ* in these cases directly signifies hashish, it was so used, according to E. W. Lane,[3] in nineteenth-century Egypt.

Ṣaḥīḥ made for easy punning also as a medical term:

> I said to one dying of hashish
> And going from it to the grave:
> Did you really die of hectic fever?
> He replied: I died of *ṣaḥīḥ* (= being healthy).[4]

And again:

> They said: We observe the green one, weak as it is,
> Try to overcome us temperamentally, but natural temper is the stronger.[5]
> In breaking it, there is relaxation for the intelligent.
> I said to them: This is *ṣaḥīḥ* well tested.[6]

All the preceding terms may be assumed to have served principally as nicknames for hashish pure and simple. There are other terms where this is by no means that clear, as well as some which were certainly compound confections. The role of hashish in them, in preference to other narcotics, is difficult to determine, and, in general, we have presently not enough material for proper identification. We thus find *kabsh (kabshah, kibāsh)*,[7] which is no doubt

[1] Cf. al-Badrī, fol. 13b (see below, p. 80, for the context).

[2] Cf. al-Badrī, fol. 22b (see below, p. 159, for the context).

[3] *An Account of the Manners and Customs of the Modern Egyptians*, 3rd ed., II, 40 (London 1842), mentions *sheera (sheereh)* and *basṭ* as used for different hemp preparations. On *shīreh* (of Persian origin) and *basṭ*, cf. K. Vollers, in *ZDMG*, L (1896), 623, 644, and E. Graefe, *Einiges über das Ḥašīš-Rauchen*, in *Der Islam*, V (1914), 234 f.

[4] Cf. al-Badrī, fol. 12b:
qultu li-man māta min ḥashīshin
wa-rāḥa minhu ilā ḍ-ḍarīḥi
bi-ʿillati d-diqqi mitta ḥaqqan
fa-qāla lī mittu min ṣaḥīḥi.

[5] This is an imitation of the beginning of a poem by al-Mutanabbī (*Dīwān*, ed. ʿAbd-al-Wahhāb ʿAzzām, 464, Cairo 1363/1944): "I try to overcome desire with respect to you, but desire is the stronger."

[6] Cf. al-Badrī, fol. 12b:
wa-qālū narā l-khaḍrāʾa maʿ ḍaʿfi shaʾnihā
tughālibunā bi-ṭ-ṭabʿi wa-ṭ-ṭabʿu aghlabu
wa-fī kasrihā basṭun yaladhdhu li-dhī n-nuhā
fa-qultu lahum hādhā ṣaḥīḥun mujarrabu.

[7] All these forms occur in al-Badrī, fol. 23a, although *l* is written instead of *k* in *kibāsh*.

related to *shaqfah kabshīyah* in a poem by Ṣafī-ad-dīn al-Ḥillī[1] and in the verse referring to "the daughter of *al-kabsh* having made wine superfluous."[2] It would be futile to speculate whether this term had anything to do with the common meaning of the word ("ram"), some botanical application,[3] a locality in Cairo,[3a] or whatnot.

Even more doubt and uncertainty attach to *kirshah, kurūsh.* It may rather refer to some kind of cheap food, such as tripe, in which case al-Badrī's quotations of verses were merely an aside:

> I saw a person eat *kirshah,*
> A man of taste and intelligence.
> He said: I always love it.
> I said: Love of one's country is part of the faith.[4]

These verses are attributed to an-Naṣīr al-Ḥammāmī, while Shihāb-ad-dīn Aḥmad b. Ghānim rhymed:

> You who censure me for eating *kurūsh*
> Prepared with the greatest of care,
> Do not censure me because of the *kurūsh,* for my loving
> My country belongs to the signs of faith.

The intended relationship of the famous *ḥadīth* on patriotism might help to clarify the meaning of the word, but it is not clear to me.[5] Al-Badrī cites theses verses à propos a story about a certain ʿAlī al-Qayrawānī who used hashish constantly and was satisfied with making a meager living as a watchman of sugar cane (fields or

[1] Cf. below, p. 151, n. 1.

[2] Cf. al-Badrī, fol. 46b: *wa-bintu l-kabshi aghnat ʿan khumūri.* The ms. has *s,* and not *sh,* in *kabshi.*

[3] Cf., for instance, *Wörterbuch der klassischen arabischen Sprache* (letter *K*), 541a. [3a] Or in Baghdād.

[4] For these and the following verses, cf. al-Kutubī, *Fawāt,* I, 117, and al-Badrī, fol. 24a. Regrettably, neither furnishes any clear information on *kirshah, kurūsh.* For Ibn Ghānim, cf. Ibn Ḥajar, *Durar,* I, 265-267. He was born in 651 or, more likely, 650/1252, and he died in 737/1336-37. Al-Ḥammāmī died in 712/1312-13, cf. al-Kutubī, *Fawāt,* II, 604-607. Ibn Ḥajar, *Durar,* IV, 393-395, gives 669/1270-71 as his date of birth but seems to have a somewhat earlier year for his death.

[5] Whether it might be love of one's stomach? But *kirsh* may also mean associates, family, and so on, which could be the meaning applicable in this connection. It is interesting to note that the *Lisān al-ʿArab,* VIII, 232, l. 3, refers to alternate forms *(thawb) akrāsh* or *akbāsh* meaning the same thing (a kind of Yemeni garment). In a poem by Ṣarīʿ ad-dilāʾ (d. 412/1021-22), a verse clearly referring to "ram" *(kabsh)* is followed by one saying that "one who eats *al-kirsh* unwashed will have that medicine (? *ad-dawā*) drip on his moustache" (al-Kutubī, *Fawāt,* II, 469). In this scurrilous poem, which also speaks of eating coal, possibly *kirs* "dung" is meant (?). For the medical view on the value of *kirsh* as food, cf. ar-Rāzī, *Ḥāwī,* XXI, i, 363.

factories) *(ḥarāsat al-qaṣab)*. From his earnings he bought his daily ration of hashish and the rest he spent on *kirshah* together with bread. This would indeed seem to indicate that *kirshah* is some kind of food unrelated to hashish, but this is not absolutely necessary, and the problem, if it is one, must remain unsolved for the time being.

Another word of uncertain significance is *lubābah (li/abābah?)*. A *lubābah* was given to the unsuspecting bridegroom and caused him to fall asleep.[1] Hashish users are so stingy that they would not even give a *lubābah* to their friends.[2] Here, it could be some kind of food, but in the first case, it must be a narcotic (which, it is added, the person in question then continued to use but in the proper doses). A correction to *kabābah* "cubeb" seems out of the question. We might think of connecting *lubābah* with the kind of honey cake, described by E. W. Lane[3] as follows: libábeh is composed of broken or crumbled bread, honey, clarified butter, and a little rosewater: the butter is first put into a saucepan over the fire, then, the broken bread; and next, the honey." Perhaps, *lubābah* was a sweetmeat to which some narcotic, perhaps hashish, was added.

Again, we hear about a narcotic called *k-n/tbābatī*, once spelled *k-bābatī*. Metrical use shows that there was a long syllable in the beginning, and it supports the reading *-bābatī*, although the letters are vouched for only by the authority of the ms. One of the stories connected with the word speaks of the experience of ʿAlī b. Sūdūn al-Bashbughawī, who met an amīr just returned from the Ḥijāz with a number of glass jars *(marṭabān*, pl. *marāṭabīn)* displayed in front of him. The amīr asked al-Bashbughawī to taste their contents, und he unthinkingly did so. The result was that he got high, his eyes reddened, and he became very hungry.[4] Again, a combination of *k-n/tbābatī* with *kabābah* "cubeb" would be completely gratuitous, and its supposed composition remains uncertain.

There can be no doubt that *barsh* was a compound drug. It is stated, in the monograph devoted to it,[5] to be "an evil paste" *(al-maʿjūn al-khabīth)*. Its user was called *barrāsh*. Its locale is indicated to be Egypt, and it could be assumed to be a comparatively recent invention since it is not mentioned at all by al-Badrī, were it not for

[1] Cf. al-Badrī, fol. 16a, and, for the story, again, below, p. 82.

[2] Cf. al-Badrī, fol. 24a.

[3] *Op. cit.* (p. 29, n. 3), II, 307, quoted by Dozy, *Supplément aux dictionnaires arabes*, s. v.

[4] Cf. al-Badrī, fol. 22a, and, for the verses, fol. 47a.

[5] Cf. *Qamʿ*, fol. 274a.

the fact that its connection with hashish is somewhat doubtful and hashish might have been only an occasional ingredient. *Bers* is the form under which it is mentioned in Western literature by P. Alpin, who wrote at about the same time as the author of *Qamʿ*.[1] The etymology of the term is by no means clear.[2] The indications of modern dictionaries vary considerably and may not possess much authority as far as the actual meaning of *barsh* and its relation, or lack of relation, to hashish is concerned.[3] A passage of the *Arabian Nights* speaking of a *ḥashshāsh* refers to his addiction "to opium and *barsh* and his use of the green hashish;"[4] the phrasing could be understood to indicate that *barsh* had nothing to do with hashish, but this would by no means be a necessary conclusion. *Qamʿ* refers, strangely enough, to "a leaf of *barsh*," adding "or *ḥashīsh*," and a few lines earlier speaks of the forbidden character of *ḥashīsh* and that of

---

[1] Cf. his *Medicina Aegyptiorum* (above, p. 21, n. 4), 258, quoted by Silvestre de Sacy, *Mémoire sur la dynastie des Assassins*, 47, 61. Alpin contrasts *bers* and other confections with simple *assis*, but this would not automatically exclude the possibility that hashish was an ingredient in those confections.

[2] It is rather tempting to think of a native Egyptian word. Coptic presents quite a few possibilities, whether one thinks of the first consonant as part of the word or as the Coptic definite article. Particularly intriguing is the entry *erbisi* "hemp" from W. E. Crum's *Coptic Dictionary*, 58a (Oxford 1939), with Crum's accompanying suggestion that the Coptic form may be the result of metathesis in view of *ebra* (53a-b) "seed (of cereals and other plants)." The Arabic term *b-r-sh* in the meaning of *ḥ-r-th* "to plow" attested by al-Maqrīzī (*Khiṭaṭ*, I, 101 f., cf. the ed. of G. Wiet, in *Mém. de l'Institut Français d'Archéol. Or. du Caire*, XXXIII, 1913, 76) could hardly be brought into connection with *barsh*. If the drug originated in other parts of the Muslim world, for instance, in Persia, one could think of connecting it with *parsh* "agitation." The form *berǵ* listed in J. T. Zenker, *Türkisch-arabisch-persisches Handwörterbuch*, 189b (Leipzig 1867-1876), would, as a secondary form of *barsh*, suggest Persian origin, but this is probably not so; *berǵ* may not be *barch* but merely a conflation of *barsh* and *banj*.

[3] Zenker, *loc. cit.*, speaks of "Präparat aus Hanfblättern, deren Genuss Heiterkeit erweckt." A modern Turkish-English Dictionary (by A. Vahid Moran, Istanbul 1945), *s. v. berş*, has "electuary (of hemp leaves, laudanum or opium with syrup)." Hava's Arabic-English Dictionary indicates "opium-paste for smoking." Hava also gives the meaning of *Datura stramonium*, thorn-apple or jimsonweed, for *barsh*, and it should be remembered that daturas include *datura Metel L.*, the much used narcotic *jawz māthil* (see below, p. 114). *Abrash* "speckled" may refer to plants of various colors, but it could be suspected that Hava's plant name is secondary to *barsh* as the designation of a drug. Cf. also the following note.

[4] Cf. *Arabian Nights*, ed. W. H. Macnaghten, II, 66 (Calcutta and London 1839-1842), German trans. E. Littmann, II, 571, cited by Dozy, *Supplément* I, 71b. Dozy here also defines *barsh* as "gomme odorante" of Indian origin also derived from the drug?

barsh, as if he meant to distinguish two different drugs.[1] However, he also alludes to the famous story of the introduction of hashish in the Arab world,[2] which would suggest that cannabis played a role in *barsh*. Much depends on the interpretation of *banj* in the *Qamʿ*'s description of the composition of *barsh*, according to which it consists of pepper *(fulful)*, opium *(afyūn)*, saffron *(zaʿfarān)*, pellitory *(ʿāqirqarḥā)*, *banj*, euphorbia *(afarbiyūn)*,[3] and spikenard *(sunbul)*. The initials of the components arranged in order yield the phrase *fāz ʿAbbās*, meaning something like "ʿAbbās has achieved bliss," and this phrase, we may safely assume, was also a current nickname for the drug.[4] In describing the potencies of the ingredients, the author of *Qamʿ* compares *banj* with opium in its effect and indicates that there are two kinds, a poisonous black species and a desiccative, burning, and destructive species. *Banj* might very well be henbane here, and the *barsh* of *fāz ʿAbbās* would thus contain no hemp preparation. However, *Qamʿ* further speaks of "the accursed *ḥashīshah* and its derivations (*tawābiʿ*),"[5] evidently having in mind preparations of a similar type; thus, there might have been other recipes for the preparation of *barsh* which made use of hashish.

A trade name for a hashish confection widely used for a number of years in Cairo was *ʿuqdah*, as al-Maqrīzī informs us. The word has many meanings. It would seem to mean here "node, knob, lump," thus being another of the numerous words referring to the form in which the drug was consumed. A verse of Abū l-Khayr al-ʿAqqād runs:

> Present the one you love with a pill of *zīh*
> And with two *ʿuqdah*s from the lawful plant.[6]

---

[1] Cf. *Qamʿ*, fol. 276a.

[2] Cf. *Qamʿ*, fol. 274b, and below, p. 53.

[3] Meyerhof, in his ed. and trans. of Maimonides, 15, vocalizes *afarbiyūn* and *furbiyūn* (as in Steingass' *Persian-English Dictionary*). I do not know why it might not have been *afurbiyūn*.

[4] The author of *Qamʿ*, fol. 280a-b, jokes that a better combination of the letters would have been *fasā ʿāzib* "a celibate (or widowed) person has farted" or *ʿz' nfs'*, which I do not quite understand.

Lane, *op. cit.* (above, p. 29, n. 3), II, 41 f., speaks of "hellebore, hemp, and opium and several aromatic drugs," but it is not quite clear whether *barsh* is supposed to contain all or some of these.

[5] Cf. *Qamʿ*, fol. 274b.

[6] Cf. al-Badrī, fol. 16b:

> *wa-hādī man tuḥibbu bi-qurṣi zīhin*
> *wa-min ḥilli n-nabāti bi-ʿuqdatayni.*

The meter *(wāfir)* requires a long *ī* in *wa-hādī*, for *wa-hādi*. It could hardly be something like *haddi'* "quiet."

We also have a reference to a man who sitting in a corner over the gate of the Manṣūrī Hospital in Cairo, would use a pint of sweets *min al-ʿuqdah al-marshūshah al-mubakhkharah al-mumassakah min ʿind Ibn Qayṣar bi-sittah wa-thalāthīn nuqrah lā yuṭʿim minhā li-aḥad ʿuqdah wa-law jāʾah ṣāḥib al-ḥall wa-l-ʿaqd*, which, I think, means: "an *ʿuqdah* wetted[1] and perfumed with incense and musk from the shop of Ibn Qayṣar for thirty-six *nuqrah* (dirham); and he would not give anyone an *ʿuqdah* of it to eat, even if the ruler himself were to come to him."[2] The *ʿuqdah* mentioned by al-Maqrīzī was introduced by a Persian Ismāʿīlī *(min malāḥidat al-ʿajam)*. It consisted of hashish mixed with honey and a number of desiccating ingredients such as mandrake root *(ʿirq al-luffāḥ)*[3] and the like. It had to be sold, so we are told, clandestinely. A story strangely similar but not using the term *ʿuqdah* occurs in al-Badrī.[4]

Of the two lists of nicknames for hashish known so far, the longer one is presented to us as the devil's own. Al-Badrī, who is our authority for it, says that it contains about eighty terms, but they are not quite as many. The seventeenth-century Bakrī also gives the number of eighty or more, no doubt relying on al-Badrī.[5] If he actually quoted them, his text will probably prove extremely helpful for the reconstruction of many of the names. As it is, the ms. of al-Badrī poses quite a few problems of reading and interpretation. The list breaks down into two parts of unequal length. The first one gives the nicknames as used in various countries and cities and nations, the second longer one those used by the various professions, mainly, as we would expect, of the lower and lowest strata of society. The

---

[1] Cf. below, p. 59.

[2] Cf. al-Badrī, fol. 28b.

[3] *Luffāḥ* is also mentioned by al-Badrī, fol. 48b, among the pernicious offspring of the *zaqqūm* tree.

[4] Cf. below, pp. 133 f.

[5] The list appears in al-Badrī, fol. 9a-b, and may possibly have been derived by al-Badrī from Ibn an-Najjār's *Zawājir*. My knowledge of the *Kawākib as-sāʾirah fī akhbār Miṣr wa-l-Qāhirah* of Ibn Abī s-Surūr al-Bakrī goes back to Silvestre de Sacy's *Chrestomathie arabe*, 2nd ed., I, 281 f. For al-Bakrī, cf. *GAL*, 2nd ed., II, 383 f., *Suppl.*, II, 408 f.; the introduction of the ed. of his, or his father's, *al-Qawl al-muqtaḍab*, ed. I. al-Ibyārī and as-Sayyid I. Sālim (Cairo, n. y. [1962]); M. A. Enan, *Mu'arrikhū Miṣr*, 169-176 (Cairo 1388/1969).

No attention has been paid here to modern nicknames not attested in the older literature. I do not know whether any substantial lists of them have been compiled. An article by F. Kerim, in *L'Hygiène Mentale*, XXV (1930), 95, lists a very few Turkish nicknames such as *nefes* "whiff, breath," *minare gölgesi* "shade, shadow of the minaret," and *davul tozu* "drum dust." Note, however, that modern Arabic *nafas* also means (a draw on the) water pipe.

schematic arrangement does not inspire great confidence in the list's truthfulness. The first four items, in particular, strike us as pure fancy. However, *asrār*, for instance, is no doubt correctly associated with the Turks, and there may, in fact, be a goodly number of such correct associations. We are in no position to pass judgment on this. It would also be a waste of effort to indulge in too much speculation on the possible vocalization and interpretation of some of the words. The data are, in fact, "devilishly" difficult at times, and only further comparative manuscript material and a wider knowledge of the social conditions reflected in the list can be expected to be of help.

1. The people of India: *as-s-k-y-n-h*
2. The people of Sind: *as-s-y-w-s-h*
3. The people of China: *as-s-n-d-s-h*
4. The people of Ethiopia: *ad-d-r-h (?)*[1]
5. The people of Persia: *al-bankā "banj"*
6. The people of the Yemen: *al-khaḍrā'* "the green one"
7. The people of Baghdād: *bint al-jirāb* "daughter of the bag"
8. The Turk people: *asrār "esrār"*

9.-10. The people of the ʿIrāq: *al-kaff* and *jamāl az-zayn*[2]

11. The people of Mosul: *ibnat al-ʿ-k-r-m-y*[3]
12. The people of Diyār Bakr: *al-ghubayrā'*

13.-14. The people of Anatolia: *al-ʿ-z-k-y (?)* [4] and *aẓ-ẓ-f-r*[5]

15. The Kurds: *kh-w-y-n-h*[6]
16. The people of Aleppo: *al-k-r-m-w-m*[7]
17. The people of Antioch: *ra's al-qiṭṭ* "cat's head"
18. The people of Hama: *al-muḥammaṣah* "the toasted one"[8]

---

[1] This might be "durrah," but the ms. itself indicates an uncertain reading by the addition of a dot underneath the first letter.

[2] Hardly to be corrected to Jamāl-ad-dīn "Beauty of the Religion." *Az-zayn* may, however, refer to an individual known as Zayn-ad-dīn.

[3] The reading is uncertain. Whether we might read *al-ʿaskarī* "daughter of the soldier"??

[4] Perhaps, what is meant, is *al-frky*, to be connected somehow with the rubbing or husking (*f-r-k*) done in preparing hashish (see below, p. 60).

[5] *Aẓ-ẓufr* "fingernail" (cf. below, p. 173), rather than *aẓ-ẓafar* "victory," but cf. also the spelling *aṭ-ṭ-f-r-y* in al-Badrī, fol. 8b (below, p. 58).

[6] I. e., *khuwaynah* or *ḥuwaynah* "little tavern"??

[7] The first *m* might possibly be a hook, but the meaning indicated for *kurtūm* ("small stones, stony tract") in the *Wörterbuch der klassischen arabischen Sprache* (letter *K*), 118b, is hardly applicable. Whether it could be *kurkum* "saffron, turmeric"?

[8] The ms. indicates *ḍ* for *ṣ*. The indicated reading seems preferable.

19. The people of Syria: *aṣ-ṣaḥīḥ*[1]
20. The people of Egypt: *az-zīh*
21. The people of the West *(al-gharb)*: *ibnat al-qunbus* "daughter of cannabis"
22. The people of Homs: *al-mubahhijah* "the one that cheers"[2]
23. The people of the Coastal Plains *(as-Sawāḥil)*: *maʿdin az-zumurrud* "emerald mine"[3]
24. shadow players[4]: *al-b-t-n*
25. hermits[5]: *al-maʿlūm*
26. mendicants[6]: *al-luqaymah* "little morsel"
27. *ḥullah* wearers (?)[7]: *shajarat aṭ-ṭarab* "shrub of emotion"
28. caftan wearers (?)[8]: *shajarat al-fahm* "shrub of understanding"
29. bums *(juʿaydīyah)*[9]: *maʿlūm al-fuqarāʾ* "*maʿlūm* of the poor (the Ṣūfīs)"

---

[1] Again, the ms. indicates *ḍ* for *ṣ*, but see above, pp. 28 f.

[2] The reading is not fully clear. Perhaps, rather, *al-muhayyijah.*

[3] Al-Badrī, fol. 11b, speaks of *maʿādin az-zumurrud wa-l-yāqūt*, apparently with reference to hashish and pomegranates. The use of emerald, for simple green, is common in the poetry on hashish. Cf. also below, p. 77.

[4] For *mukhāyilīyah*, cf. Dozy, *Supplément*, I, 418b. In fact, a low-class and fraudulent mendicant fraternity may be meant, like those following here. Perhaps, we should read *at-tibn* "straw." Turkish *tütün* "smoke" seems excluded, in view of the lack of evidence for the smoking of hemp (cf. below, p. 65).

[5] This is the likely meaning of *mutajarrid* in this context. For the meaning of *maʿlūm*, see above, p. 27.

[6] For *al-jawlaqīyah*, cf. Steingass, *Persian-English Dictionary*, 379a: *jōlakhī*. For the "little morsel," cf. no. 46 and below, p. 92. Ibn Taghrībirdī (below, p. 142, n. 3) speaks of "the little morsel of the poor, the green one."

[7] The interpretation of *al-ḥlʾtyyh* is a mere guess, suggested by the possible meanings of the next two professions. It might be "sweetmeat makers," ordinarily *ḥalāwātīyah*, or again a type of beggars.

[8] *Al-muṭaylasah*, rather than *al-muṭaylisah* "caftan makers." The assumption is that a group of beggars and frauds distinguished by the type of garment they wore is meant, but this remains uncertain.

[9] Cf. Dozy, *Supplément*, I, 197b; W. M. Brinner, in *EI*², *s. v.* ḥarfūsh. For *juʿaydīs* as hashish eaters, cf. the two anecdotes in al-Badrī, fol. 11a-b: (1) A *juʿaydī*, noticing a lighted candle in a house, calls "fire," people come and pour water over the wall of the house until he finds himself swimming in a puddle of water, shouting, "help, I am drowning." (2) One of two *juʿaydīs* who had eaten hashish and become thirsty leaves the house to fetch water. Meanwhile, a seller of pizzas *(manqūshah)* passes by and sells the other *juʿaydī* a pizza, which sticks to his face. His companion upon returning thinks that he has turned into an *ʿifrīṭ*. "Bum" would seem hardly a very satisfactory translation of *juʿaydī* in view of the situations presupposed in these stories, but nothing very specific was presumably meant by it.

30.-31. merchants *(tujjār)*: *al-wuṣūl* "arrival" or "receipt" (?) and *rāḥat al-bāl* "peace of mind"
32. lantern bearers[1]: *ʿashīrah* "family" or "girl friend"
33. spongers *(ṭufaylīyah)*: *al-muhaḍḍimah* "the one that facilitates digestion"
34. crossbowmen *(bunduqānīyūn)*: *t-r-z-y-d as-s-f-'-q-y*
35. Gypsies *(zuṭṭ)*: *r-ḍ-w-y* "the pleasing one" (?)
36. (Ṣūfī) shaykhs *(mashā'ikh)*: *ziyārat al-Khiḍr al-akhḍar* "visit of the green Khiḍr"
37. Ṣūfīs: *mūṣilat al-qalb* "the one that connects the heart"
38. veterinarians *(bayāṭirah)*: *ḥ-n-h*[2]
39. travelers[3]: *zuwwādah* "provisions"
40. barber-surgeons *(jarā'iḥīyah)*: *lazqah* "adhesive bandage"
41. dancers (? *rāqiṣah)*[4]: *al-ʿuknah* "belly wrinkle" (?)
42. leather workers[5]: *tashmīʿ al-khayṭ* "the waxing of the thread"
43. water carriers[6]: *mishʿal* "lantern"
44. cooks *(ṭabbākhūn)*: *ḥimmaṣah* "chick-pea"
45. songstresses *(maghānī)*: *aghṣān as-saʿādah* "branches of bliss"
46. philosophers (?)[7]: *luqaymat al-fikr* "thought morsel"
47. astrologers *(munajjimūn)*: *saʿd b-l-ʿ*[8]
48. rope-makers and porters *(fattālūn* and *ḥammālūn)*: *al-mukhaffifah* "the one that lightens (the load)"
49. builders *(bannā'ūn)*: *dawā'* "medicine" (?)
50. architects *(miʿmārīyah)*: *q-r-b-t-h*[9]

---

[1] Or "lantern makers" (*al-mashāʿilīyah*).

[2] *Ḥannah* "wife" (??), or, perhaps, to be corrected to "henna" with which hashish was compared (below, p. 63)? Presumably, however, a technical term of veterinary medicine is to be looked for here.

[3] *As-sf'rh*, to be equated with *safarah* or *suffār*.

[4] If "belly wrinkle" is the right interpretation, "dancers" seem to be meant. *Rāqiṣ* and *rāqiṣah* are used by al-Badrī (fol. 86a) for male and female dancers, but *rāqiṣah* is a strange form for the plural required here. Even "Qarmatians" (no. 60) does not quite permit us to assume that "extremist sectarians" (*rāfiḍah*) could be meant. "Mason" (*raqqāṣ*) is also unlikely.

[5] *Al-'dmy(ūn)*, from *adam* "leather" as usual, rather than from *udm*, *idām* "condiment, dessert." The nickname for hashish would seem to be a technical term used by leather workers, tanners, or leather merchants.

[6] This is the likely precise meaning here of *suʿāh* "runners."

[7] The ms. has *al-mtgh/flsh*, hardly to be connected with the root *f-l-s* "bankrupt." The following "astrologers" invites the correction suggested here to *al-mutafalsifah*. Cf. no. 26.

[8] Possibly, *saʿd balagh* "fortune has arrived," but there may very well be some other astrological allusion concealed here.

[9] *Qarībah* "near one" could have been an architectural term. Or is *qarīnah* "wife" or the like meant?

51. misers *(bukhalā')*: *al-m-y-l-y-s-h*[1]
52. washers of corpses[2]: *al-quds* "Holy Jerusalem"
53. grave diggers *(ḥaffārūn)*: *as-sukkarī* "sugary" (?)
54. beggars *(ḥarāfishah)*: *bunduqah* "pill"[3]
55. brokers *(dallālūn)*: *al-malīḥah* "the pretty one"
56. druggists *('aṭṭārūn)*: *safūf* "medicinal powder"[4]
57. makers of electuaries *(ma'ājīnīyah)*: *diryāq* "theriac"
58. *al-kh-m-y-'-t-y-h*:[5] *khuḍārī* "wild duck" (with a play on "green")
59. *at-t-q/f-ṭ-y-s-h*: *dhanab aṭ-ṭā'ūs* "peacock's tail"
60. Qarmatians[6]: *qurrat al-'ayn* "consolation"
61. homosexuals *(m-ḥ-'-n-t-h,* read *makhānithah, makhānīth)*: *ash-shumay'ah* "little wax candle"
62. *al-ḥ-d-'-y-th-y-h*: *al-muhanni'ah* "the one that causes good appetite"
63. procurers *(qawwādūn)*: *mulayyinat aṭ-ṭibā'* "the one that softens the temperaments"
64. *al-m-'-r-ṣ(ūn)*[7]: *jāmi'at ash-shaml* "the one that brings the party together"
65. narcotizers (?)[8]: *malūf* "moist"
66. falconers *(bazādirah)*: *layānah (?)*[9]
67. importers *(jallābah)*: *al-'uwaymilah* "the little agent"
68. manufacturers *(ṣunnā')* of hashish: *al-bishbīshah (?)*
69. sellers *(bā'i'ūn)* of hashish: *kuḥl* "antimony"
70. Satan and his cohorts: *al-mutaṣayyidah* "the huntress"

---

[1] Hardly, *al-mulaysā'* "the little one easy to swallow."

[2] *Mughassilū* (ms. *mf/ghlsyn*) *al-amwāt*. My inference that the nickname refers to Jerusalem is somewhat gratuitous. Again, it is possible that some technical use of *quds* in the profession is meant.

[3] Cf. below, pp. 61 f.

[4] The root *s-f-f* "to eat dry," is commonly used in connection with hashish, see below, p. 57, etc.

[5] Hardly, *al-ḥummayātīyah* "specialists in the treatment of fevers." This, and the following profession (where the reading is even more uncertain), may have something to do with the snaring of fowl.

[6] *Al-qarāmiṭah* may be here a nickname for some low-class group held in contempt. See above, no. 41.

[7] Steingass, *Persian-English Dictionary*, 1271a, lists *mu'arriḍ* as "circumciser of boys," which would make good sense here. A correction to *mu'ris* "one who gives wedding parties" cannot be rejected out of hand.

[8] *Al-marāqid* may be the plural of *murqid*. For "moist," see below, p. 59.

[9] The ms. is smudged and the reading is completely uncertain. One should not think of *lubābah* (above, p. 31). "The soft one" is not impossible.

The other list appears in connection with an amusing anecdote on the fly-leaf of an Istanbul ms. of an undetermined date.[1] One of the local hashish users *(ḥashshāshīyah,* later on also referred to as an *ḥashā'ishī)* imported and sold hashish, thus spreading ruin in the city and corrupting the young Muslims living there. He was often caught and punished, but no punishment had any deterrent effect on him. He always returned to his evil ways of pushing dope. Eventually, however, he was brought before the judge and forced to accept an agreement under oath *(qasāmah)* that he would no longer import either wine or hashish or, if he did, he would be liable to a fine of 500 dīnārs. Now, in administering this oath, the judge tried to be very specific and to avoid leaving any conceivable loopholes. He therefore enumerated by name some twenty different kinds of hashish. The pusher, quickwitted as he was, immediately pointed out that he had not the least bit *(qirāṭ)* of knowledge about any of these kinds, and he suggested that the judge would do better to administer the oath to himself–implying, of course, that if the judge knew that much about the different kinds of hashish and the popular names for them, he must have plenty of experience and probably be a user himself. The clever comeback pleased all those present very much. The pusher was given the opportunity to repent of his evil ways, which he did,[2] and he led afterwards a blameless life. The motif of the defendant turning tables in this manner on the judge is not uncommon.[3] In fact, in an almost identical story, the judge shows himself conversant with all the low-class places in and around Cairo where wine was consumed.[4] But the list of supposed nicknames for hashish is interesting, even if both reading and interpretation in most cases remain highly doubtful:

1. *s-b-y (?)*
2. *ṣafadī* "from Ṣafad"
3. *iṣbahānī* "from Iṣfahān"

[1] The main texts contained in the Istanbul Ms. Feyzullah 1587 are dated, respectively, in Rabīʿ I 556/March 1161 (scribe: Muẓaffar b. Asʿad al-ʿImādī) and in 582/1186-87. The note is found on fol. 191a. The *adab* work from which it was no doubt derived remains to be traced.

[2] For "repenting" in connection with the use of drugs, cf. below, p. 97.

[3] Cf. F. Rosenthal, *A History of Muslim Historiography*, 2nd ed., 367 (Leiden 1968), in the translation of as-Sakhāwī, *Iʿlān*. The story involves the Ṭabbālah estate, known as a drug center in Mamlūk Cairo (cf. below, p. 137).

[4] Cf. al-Badrī, fol. 132a.

4. *ṣihyawnī* "from Zion" (Ṣahyūn in Northern Syria)
5. *qurn* "pill" (?)[1]
6. *muʿanbar* "amber-scented"[2]
7. *bizr* "seed"
8. *akhḍar* "green"
9. *b-s-m-w-q-y (?)*[3]
10. *b-s-m-w-t-y (?)*
11. *kibāsh* (of doubtful meaning, see above, pp. 29 f.)
12. *q-l-y-ʿ/f-t-y*
13. *jabalī* (probably referring to some mountain or locality)
14. *m-h-*. . . (perhaps, *miṣrī* "Egyptian" ?)
15. *gh-y-r ṣ-'(?) '-l-w-n(?)-y*[4]
16. *dubb al-hīsh*[5]
17. *tuffāḥī* "apple-colored (scented, flavored)"
18. *ḥamātī-bayrūtī* "from Hama and Beirut"[6]
19. *s-r-ṭ-b-'-w-y (?)*
20. *qalandarāwī* (see above, p. 25, n. 8)
21. *ḥ-w-'-l-f/q-y (?)*

The preponderance to place names mentioned would suggest a Syrian locale for the list, uncertain though this must be. The genuineness of the nicknames should be rated much lower than that of the other list, though, again, this is merely an impression that cannot be substantiated. It is remarkable that both lists are totally different, another testimony to the great variety of nicknames and the constantly changing pattern of their use, or to the inventiveness that went into thinking them up.

---

[1] Cf. below, p. 62. Perhaps, *quran*, pl. of *qurnah*, is meant (?).

[2] Cf. above, p. 25.

[3] Nos. 9, 10, and 12 look like names derived from localities, in the first two cases, Syrian localities beginning with *b-* (the shortened form of Aramaic house).

[4] A combination with *ghubayrā'* seems hardly possible. A checking of the ms. may yield some better reading.

[5] The vocalization of *hīsh* is confirmed by the occurrence of this combination in a *zajal*, where it rhymes with *ḥashīsh*. The author of the poem quoted by al-Badrī, fol. 56b, was Burhān-ad-dīn al-Miʿmār (cf. below, p. 66, n. 2). It begins: "I repent my use of hashish as long as I live" *(tāyib anā ʿan al-ḥashīsh—ṭūl mā aʿīsh)*, but much in the poem remains doubtful, including, in particular, the line referring to *dubb hīsh*.

[6] The ms. seems to have an *n*, for *t*, in Ḥamātī, but Hama is clearly meant. Possibly, *wa-lā* should be supplied between the two words so that we would have here two brands of hashish.

All these nicknames served as shibboleths by which the members of an exclusive club recognized each other. But it should not be forgotten that the employment of more or less private words is also the common custom of social outcasts who thereby express their solidarity among themselves and their feeling of rebellion against restrictions imposed upon them by society. The nicknames are thus not only of lexical interest. The more we can learn about them, the better will be our understanding of the attitude of Muslims toward the use of drugs.

2. The History of the Use of Hashish

Whatever the name under which it was known, certain presumed pharmacological properties of hemp were known to physicians in the Muslim orbit as early as there was a scientific medicine in Islam. However, then and later, little was made of this knowledge by medical writers.[1] The quotations brought, for instance, by Ibn al-Bayṭār and al-Maqrīzī can be considered as quite representative. Hashish might also have been used here and there for "pleasure and enjoyment," but we have no evidence to this effect from the first four or five centuries of Islam. Any speculation that the use of the drug for this purpose might have occurred only in the eastern portions of the Muslim world close to India could also not be verified at present.

Later jurists never failed to remark on the fact that hashish is not mentioned in the Qur'ān or the old Prophetic traditions, nor were they able to find any express reference to it in the name of the founders of the four legal schools. When such ancient authorities as the Shāfiʿite al-Muzanī (d. 264/878) or the Ḥanafite aṭ-Ṭaḥāwī (d. 321/933) are cited as having pronounced themselves against the use of narcotics,[2] we can be quite certain that the term *ḥashīsh* was not used by them; it is also most probable that they did not employ any other term specifically denoting hemp preparations, unless it was *banj* understood to mean hemp. In connection with a late commentary on the famous legal compendium of the Ḥanafite al-Qudūrī (d. 428/1037), we hear about *ḥashīsh*, but the basic text does

[1] Cf. Meyerhof, in his ed. and trans. of Maimonides, 174; M. Levey, in *EI*², *s. v.* ḥashīsh.

[2] Cf. *Risālah fī ḥurmat al-banj* (above, p. 18). In the statement reported to go back to an-Nasafī (below, p. 48), these references were taken seriously as evidence for the history of the use of hashish.

not contain the word.[1] In his *Mabsūṭ*, Khwāharzādeh (d. 483/1090) evidently employed only the ambiguous *banj*.[2] It is tempting to assume that az-Zarkashī, in his brief reference to a work by Abū Isḥāq ash-Shīrāzī (d. 476/1083) entitled *at-Tadhkirah fī l-khilāf*, meant to imply that it contained an express mention of the word *ḥashīsh*.[3] In this case, ash-Shīrāzī, who spent his life in Shīrāz and Baghdād, would be our oldest source for the actual use of the term. Since law books are not known for ready acceptance of newly coined slang, it could be assumed to have been around for some time and hashish was already even at that time considered a social and legal problem. Unfortunately, it is unlikely that ash-Shīrāzī employed this or any other specific term denoting hemp. We still lack the unambiguous reference—just one would suffice—that could be decisive.

From around 1123 comes the first attestation of the designation *Ḥashīshīyah* in connection with the Neo-Ismāʿīlīyah. In the *Īqāʿ ṣawāʿiq al-irghām*, which is a reply to Nizārī critics of the Mustaʿlian *al-Hidāyah al-Āmirīyah*, we find this term used twice with reference to the Nizārīs.[4] Hashish has been much discussed in Western literature in connection with the Assassins, beginning with the great discovery by Silvestre de Sacy of the true derivation of their name. However, very little that might be helpful for the history of the use of hashish has come of it. It has been pointed out that hashish does not have the properties that would ordinarily make it a serviceable stimulant for anyone being sent on a dangerous mission of assassi-

---

[1] Cf. al-Fanārī and al-Qudūrī, *Mukhtaṣar*, 73 f. (Delhi 1267). The commentator is al-Ḥaddād(ī) (d. 800/1397), apparently in his *Sirāj al-wahhāj* (*GAL, Suppl.*, I, 296).

[2] Cf. al-Fanārī. See also Ḥājjī Khalīfah, 1580.

[3] Cf. az-Zarkashī, below, p. 181. Az-Zarkashī (below, p. 187) has a reference to the *Baḥr al-madhhab*, apparently the work of ar-Rūyānī (d. 502/1108, cf. *GAL, Suppl.*, I, 673), possibly through ar-Rāfiʿī. The term employed in this connection is not indicated. Ar-Rūyānī's work is preserved in Cairo, but without consulting it, we can merely guess that the plant may have been named *qinnab* or *shahdānaj*. In a later quotation from ar-Rūyānī (below, p. 196), *banj* occurs.

[4] Cf. the edition by A. A. A. Fyzee, *al-Hidayatu'l-Amiriya*, 27, 32 (Oxford University Press 1938, *Islamic Research Association* 7), and, for the date, S. M. Stern, in *JRAS*, 1950, 20-31.

Ash-Shahrastānī, *Milal*, ed. W. Cureton, 202 (London 1842-1846), trans. T. Haarbrücker, II, 3 (Halle 1850-1851), mentions *ḥashīshīyah* as misguided ancient religious thinkers, among eternalists (materialists), physicists, and metaphysicians. Since ash-Shahrastānī died in 548/1153, this could be another quite early attestation of the use of the word to designate hashish eaters, meaning, possibly, confused thinkers. However, the reading may be incorrect, and *ḥiss* "sense perception" may be involved.

nation.[1] The famous and widespread story of the paradisiacal garden at Alamut can be brought into connection with hashish only most vaguely and indirectly;[2] nothing in the story points to hashish in preference to other drugs. The few instances where use of narcotic drugs is implied for the sectarians may have been the result of hostile speculation spun out of their name rather than factual occurrences. It is worthy of note that attacks on the Neo-Ismāʿīlīyah accusing them of being hashish eaters were apparently not made very often, although this would have been an effective verbal slur.[3]

As has been suggested recently, the reason for the choice of the term *Ḥashīshīyah* might have been in the first place the low and disreputable character attributed to hashish eaters, rather than the sectarians' devotion to the drug.[4] Now, if the term was in common use around 1123 so that it could appear in a kind of official document and required no explanation whatever, this would indicate that it was by then familiar and had been known for some time. And if it indeed refers to the use of hashish, it can serve as concrete evidence for the existence of the drug's nickname in the early twelfth century. If, moreover, it was already used at that time metaphorically for low-class rabble, it must have been well established in general use for some time at least; no modern means of rapid communication are necessary to give quick currency to a slang expression, but it may be assumed that in medieval times it took a little while for such an expression to be widely accepted. There are many ifs here, of which the most crucial is the one implying doubt as to whether the name of the Assassins is really to be connected with the meaning "hashish" among the many possible connotations of the Arabic word. It remains plausible, however, that this was indeed the case. Thus, the nickname, and with it, the drug's extended use, appear to have surfaced during the late eleventh century, and both may have been promoted by the real or alleged use of cannabis by sectarians who were engaged in spreading a vast network of open and secret influence over the Muslim world, extending to the area from Egypt to Iran, and beyond. Assuming that this is so, the question of the

---

[1] Cf. M. G. S. Hodgson, *The Order of Assassins*, 134 (The Hague 1955).

[2] See below, p. 93.

[3] No importance in this respect, I believe, should be attached to the fact that later fifteenth-century hashish confections were said to have been introduced by Ismāʿīlīs, cf. above, p. 34, and below, pp. 133 f.

[4] Cf. B. Lewis, in *EI*², *s. v.* ḥashīshiyya, and *idem*, *The Assassins*, 11 f. (New York 1968).

place of origin, whether it was Syria or Egypt or some more eastern region, is still left unanswered.

Once hashish consumption had become a widespread and debated custom, there was much discussion among Muslim scholars and other interested parties about its history. This discussion contains nothing to contradict the statements just made. The theories put forward range from the fanciful to the strong semblance of historical fact. They all add up to the impression that here was an urgent situation that needed understanding and historical perspective so that it could be handled intelligently. The samples preserved in literature make us suspect that there once was much more which went unrecorded and that the legal and political struggle over the drug was accompanied by arguments derived from history favoring one side or the other.

It was quite sensibly argued that the properties of hemp had been known continuously since the most ancient times, indeed, it is said, "since God brought the world into being. It existed in the time of the Greeks. Proof of that is what the physicians in their books have to say about the temper of the drug and its useful as well as harmful properties on the authority of Hippocrates and Galen." This statement of al-Maqrīzī begs, however, the question of the use of hashish for play and pleasure, nor does it say anything about the time it started to become a social problem in Islam.

The Indian connection of the plant, attested by the descriptive adjective attached to its name, was utilized in a legend about an Indian shaykh who "lived in the time of the Sassanian kings and saw the coming of Islam."[1] His name appears in al-Maqrīzī as something like Bīr Raṭan, but in al-Badrī, the second *r* is replaced by the connected hook *(b/t/th/n/y)*.[2] I have no explanation for the name, unless perhaps, *Bīr-*, if this is the reading intended, is meant to be Persian *pīr* = *shaykh*. Al-Maqrīzī indicates as his informant a certain Qalandarī shaykh, Muḥammad ash-Shīrāzī. Al-Badrī is more detailed in his report. It would seem that the source he claims to follow was a *Kitāb Riyāḍ al-ʿārif* by a certain Naṣrallāh aṭ-Ṭūsī, whose

[1] The text in al-Maqrīzī adds rather incongruously, "and became a Muslim." It may not be a mere coincidence that the (fictitious?) Indian about whom we hear in the thirteenth century, who claimed to have met the Prophet, was called Shaykh Ratan (with *t*, not *ṭ*), cf. adh-Dhahabī, *Mīzān*, II, 45 (Cairo 1382/1963); al-Kutubī, *Fawāt*, I, 324-327; Ibn Ḥajar, *Lisān*, II, 450-455 (Hyderabad 1329-1331).

[2] In addition to the occurrences on fols. 4a and 5a, al-Badrī refers back to the story on fols. 8b and 48b.

identity remains to be established. Al-Badrī, fol. 5a, also refers in this connection to a Shaykh an-Naṣr (= Naṣr-ad-dīn), who may be the same person. Moreover, he also cites a *History* by a certain Manbijī, as well as "the author of the *Kharīdah*," as further authorities,[1] and he interrupts his report by giving details of the phenomenal success of hashish in Egypt.

The avowed purpose of this story is to contradict another story, soon to be discussed, that attributes the introduction of hashish to a certain Shaykh Qalandar or to the founder of the Ḥaydarī fraternity, Shaykh Ḥaydar, for it is prefaced by remarks praising the piety of both these figures who, it is claimed, never ate hashish in their lives. The use of the drug became common among Ḥaydar's followers only years after his death. Therefore, the Khurāsānians ascribed the introduction of the drug to him who was completely innocent of it.

According to al-Badrī, the Indian shaykh was from Bengal, and with the dropping of the final *-lah* of Bangālah, the drug was called *bang*.[2] Before his time, the Indians were not acquainted with hashish. Once when he was worshiping his idol, Satan spoke to him from the interior of the idol and introduced him to hashish and taught him how to prepare it.[3] The use of hashish spread through India, China, and Ethiopia, and then to the West. In what seems to be another version, conflated by al-Badrī with that of Naṣrallāh aṭ-Ṭūsī, it is more sensibly claimed that it spread from Iran to the land of the Turks and the land of the Khiṭā (China). In Iraq, it became known only in 628/1230-31, and from there spread westward, as is also stated in the report of al-Maqrīzī.[4] Somewhat naively, it is suggested that verses playing with the term "Indian (maiden)" *(hindīyah)* for hashish[5] could serve as a confirmation for the historicity of the story, while, in fact, the poets merely drew upon the known botanical fact of the Indian provenience of the plant.

Turning now to the Muslim views of the history of the drug within

---

1 Al-Manbijī is quite clearly written, but I do not know who this Manbijī might be. One might think that the *Kharīdah* could be the *Kharīdat al-ʿajāʾib* of Ibn al-Wardī from the first half of the fifteenth century (*GAL, Suppl.*, II, 162 f.), but the text as printed does not contain any reference to the history of hashish.

2 *Bangālah* and *Bang* were names of Bengal, cf. A. H. Dani, in *EI*², *s. v.* Bangāla.

3 Cf. below, p. 59.

4 Cf. below, pp. 52 f.

5 Cf. below, p. 153. Al-Badrī adds another poem (see below, p. 57, n. 2) in which *hindīyah* is used for hashish, but without any allusion to Indian girls.

Islam proper, we would consider it almost inconceivable that at some point of the discussion, Muslim scholars would have foregone the temptation to ascribe traditions condemning hashish to the Prophet himself. There were quite a few, and expectedly, they were modeled after certain stereotypes common in *ḥadīth* literature:

"The greatest destruction at the end of time will result from eating the green hashish."

As-Samarqandī on the authority of Maʿmar: "The Prophet said, May God curse one who seeks intoxication by means of a liquid or a dry (substance)."

ʿAlī: "The Prophet said, Beware of the wine of the non-Arabs (= the Persians), for it will make you forget the confession of faith. (The Prophet's statement attributed it to the Persians, because coming from their country, it then spread further. It is nothing else but hashish. He called it wine because 'all wine is intoxicating, and everything intoxicating is forbidden.' This tradition makes it obvious that hashish is intoxicating and forbidden.)"

Abū Hurayrah: "The Prophet said, Beware of the green one, for it is the greatest wine."

Ḥudhayfah b. al-Yamān: "I went together with the Prophet into the countryside. He saw a tree and shook his head. I asked him why he was shaking his head, and he replied: A time will come upon my nation when they will eat from the leaves of this tree and get intoxicated, and they will pray while intoxicated. They are the worst of the worst. They are the *birāʾ* of my nation, as God has nothing to do with them *(minhum bariʾ)*."[1]

We also find references to the *zaqqūm* tree from the Qur'ān (37: 62/60, 44: 43/43, 56: 52/52) and the *ghubayrāʾ* in contexts suggesting that they are a kind of cover names for hashish. The Berlin Ms. of Ibn Ghānim, in a passage missing in the Princeton Ms., treats the reader to a *ḥadīth* reported by Surāqah about a Bedouin who appeared before the Prophet in rather poor physical condition. He explained that he had been searching for some camels for five days and was greatly suffering from hunger when he came across "a *ḥashīshah* consisting of five and six fingers,[2] notched (?) at the top,

[1] All the foregoing quotations from al-Badrī, fols. 55b and 54b. Which Maʿmar may be meant is not certain, nor is the identity of the Samarqandī mentioned.

[2] Al-Badrī, fol. 48a-b, who has the same story, has "seven." Al-Badrī, following the *Zawājir* of Ibn an-Najjār, describes the *zaqqūm* in some fanciful detail and quotes from "al-Ghazzālī and others" the statement that it is the

smelling clean and having red-colored wood. I ate some of it, and I swooned, as you can see, staggering (but) not as the result of some inner commotion (?)."[1] The Prophet had the explanation. It was the *zaqqūm* tree which does not sate those eating from it, who can expect to be condemned on the Day of Judgment.[2] The *ghubayrā' ḥadīth*, cited by Maḥmūd al-Muḥammadī,[3] has the Prophet state solemnly in phrases occurring in numerous traditions that "there is a tree called *ghubayrā'*, an accursed tree. It will appear at the end of time. Those who eat from it do not belong to us." The author continues that this tradition can be used as an argument for the prohibition (of hashish) in three ways, namely, on the strength of the phrases "accursed tree," "appearing at the end of time," and "not being one of us if one eats from it," as he is aware of the forbidden character of *ghubayrā'*, this being documented in a Qur'ān commentary entitled *'Ayn al-ma'ānī*.[4] Scrawled between lines of this passage in the Berlin Ms., we meet with an expression of strong disapproval: "This is a *ḥadīth* which is not recognized and absolutely does not exist in the books. This man made a useless effort trying to use it as an argument." Whether the person who wrote these words had a personal stake in the matter when he got so incensed about the citation of a dubious anti-hashish tradition?

Serious scholars would, of course, not be taken in by fabrications of this sort. Even less so would they have been ready to give credence to frauds committed for the benefit of hashish. In fact, it was hardly more than a mere joke to pretend that the Qur'ān itself indicated that hashish was constantly consumed by the blessed in Paradise, for what else could the reference to "green" in Qur'ān 18:31/30 ("green garments of *sundus*") signify? Needless to say, making such a remark foreshadowed a bad end for the addict who soon found his brain dried up and who was reduced to beggary *(taḥarfasha wa-tasarṭana wa-tafarwasha)*.[5] It could even happen that a student,

origin of forty-nine different plants such as *shahdānaj barrī*, *dāthūrah*, and many others, all narcotics and intoxicants.

[1] The text is somewhat corrupt: *fa-laqītu ḥashīshatan wa-hiya bikhamsati aṣābi'a wa-sittati aṣābi'a maḥrūrata (leg. maḥzūzata?) r-ra'si dhakīyata r-rā'iḥati ḥamrā'a l-'ūdi fa-akaltu minhā fa-'m (leg. fa-ghumiya) 'alayya kamā tarā amīlu min ghayri hawan.* "Swaying without wind" would be entirely out of place here, unless an allusion to the plant is intended.

[2] For hashish being described as overpowering the *zaqqūm*, cf. the poem from the Gotha Ms., below, p. 171, but see also note 5 to that page.

[3] See above, p. 17.

[4] Possibly, the work of as-Sajāwandī (*GAL, Suppl.*, I, 724)?

[5] The quotations in this paragraph are from al-Badrī, fols. 50a and 49a.

deranged from too much hashish and having exchanged the garment of Ṣūfīs with that of beggars *(ḥarāfishah)*, would be inspired by Satan to transmit the following statement as a tradition ascribed to the Almighty Himself: "When God created this plant and called for it to appear before Him, it went to Him, and He said to it: By my might, majesty, splendor, and perfection! I have not created a plant nobler and finer than you are. Nowhere else have I let you dwell but in clean minds and the clean stomachs of my servants."

It was also highly unsatisfactory for any Muslim to have to admit that the primary legal authorities did not furnish sufficient evidence to determine the proper attitude toward the use of hashish. We have already seen that it was believed that some general remarks concerning the prohibition of unspecified narcotics could be credited to al-Muzanī and aṭ-Ṭaḥāwī.[1] The Shāfiʿite, al-Muzanī, was much the older of the two, and this was certainly not very agreeable to those Ḥanafites who were fighting the use of hashish in their time. It is in this light that we have to view the sketch of the history of hashish, in the framework of the legal effort to suppress its use, which appears in the Gotha Ms.[2] A *Commentary* of at-Timirtāshī is said to be its source. The authority quoted by that author is Ḥāfiẓ-ad-dīn an-Nasafī (d. 710/1310).[3] An-Nasafī, in turn, reports a reply to a query addressed to Shams-ad-dīn al-Kurdī.[4] Now, this query is unequivocally stated to have concerned "the *ḥashīsh*, that is, the leaves of hemp." The text may be corrupt in the Gotha Ms., but after making due allowance for textual corruption, it remains principally noteworthy for the unbelievable confusion it exhibits: "No text on hashish being either permitted or forbidden has been reported on the authority of Abū Ḥanīfah and his colleagues, since it was not yet used in their time. It remained under cover *(mastūr)*. Thus, it retained its state of being basically permitted like all other plants.[5]

The addict in the first case is said to have been al-Khaffāf, apparently identical with Shihāb-ad-dīn Aḥmad al-Khaffāf ad-Dimashqī mentioned by al-Badrī, fol. 12b, below, p. 80. Cf. also below, p. 59. The reading of the words *tasarṭana* and *tafarwasha* is clear. The meanings applicable here escape me. *Tasarṭana* could hardly be intended as "being affected by cancer." Dozy, *Supplément*, I, 648b, indicates meanings such as "being stupefied."

[1] Cf. above, p. 41.

[2] Cf. above, p. 18.

[3] Cf. *GAL, Suppl.*, II, 263.

[4] I have no identification for him unless he is not al-Kurdī but al-Kardarī (d. 624/1244) (*GAL, Suppl.*, I, 653 f.).

[5] Cf. below, p. 112.

Also, no statement of its being either permitted or forbidden has been transmitted from any of the ancients after their time, till the time of the Imām al-Muzanī, the disciple of ash-Shāfiʿī. The harmfulness (of the use of hashish) became first apparent in the Arab and the non-Arab Iraq. The Imām al-Muzanī was living in Baghdād.[1] When the *fatwā* of the Imām[2] declaring hashish forbidden reached Asad b. ʿAmr, the disciple of Abū Ḥanīfah, who was living in the non-Arab Iraq, he said that it was permitted. But when the use of hashish became general and widespread everywhere with all its terrible harmful consequences...[3] the Imāms of Transoxania all agreed upon the legal view expressed by al-Muzanī that eating hashish was illegal and the consumption of hashish to be declared forbidden. They issued a *fatwā* calling for the burning of hashish despite its great value (?) *(maʿ khaṭar qīmatih)*.[4] They demanded that the sellers of hashish be chastised *(ta'dīb)* and the eaters be severely punished *(taʿzīr)*..." The historical view expressed here is that hashish was commonly used in the Muslim east since the ninth century and already about this time was dealt with as a great danger to society by both Shāfiʿites and Ḥanafites. Obviously, all this is pure fancy and dictated by professional self-interest, although for all we really know it just might have been true in substance.

We come much closer to historical fact with the famous story of the discovery and propagation of the use of hashish by Persian Ṣūfīs. According to az-Zarkashī, it was widely believed that Ḥaydar, elsewhere with the *nisbah* az-Zāwajī, from Zāwah in the province of Nīsābūr, the founder of the Ṣūfī fraternity named after him, discovered hashish around the year 550/1155.[5] Others, however, az-

---

[1] This is quite untrue.

[2] The context requires that this should be al-Muzanī, but Asad b. ʿAmr lived long before his time. He died in 188/804, or in 190.

[3] There is an omission in the ms.

[4] Or could this mean, "with the loss of its price," that is, "without recompensation"? Cf. below, p. 135.

[5] Cf. below, p. 176. One ms. has the date 505, but even in 550, Ḥaydar must have still been very young if he was indeed already born by then. According to al-ʿUkbarī (al-Maqrīzī), the discovery of hashish took place in 608, ten years prior to Ḥaydar's death (below, p. 52).

Al-Badrī, fol. 2a, quotes a profusion of further dates from various authorities, but unless they can be traced back to the original sources, they are quite suspect. He states that hashish made its appearance around 600 or, according to another source, in 505. He cites an unnamed author of an *Awā'il* work as giving the date as the turn of the sixth century to the seventh century, "when the Tatar rule made its appearance." The dates 620, 650, before 700 (read

Zarkashī adds, connected the introduction of hashish with a certain Aḥmad as-Sāwajī,[1] a Qalandarī Ṣūfī apparently originating from a town called Sāwah.[2] We hear about a rather prominent Qalandarī, Jamāl-ad-dīn as-Sāwajī, who is said to have been in Damascus around 1210 to 1225 and who thereafter settled in Damiette.[3] It is possible that he was supposed to be identical with the Qalandarī who is credited with the introduction of hashish. With respect to his relationship to Ḥaydar, the Qalandarī may represent a second stage of the story, or he may have been put up as a rival to Ḥaydar to satisfy some particular faction interested in hashish aetiology.

Az-Zarkashī's version of the Ḥaydar story is brief and thereby invests it with some kind of quite beautiful and poetic sensitivity: "Ḥaydar went out in a state of depression because he felt like withdrawing from his companions. He came across this *ḥashīshah* and noticed that its branches were swaying although there was no breeze. He reflected that this must be so because of a secret contained in it. He picked some of it and ate it. When he returned to his companions, he told them that (the plant) contained a secret, and he ordered them to eat it."[4]

Az-Zarkashī was not the first to report this story. It was already told at length by al-ʿUkbarī about a century earlier. Az-Zarkashī may, in fact, have derived his information from al-ʿUkbarī, although in his time the story was no doubt circulating in many versions.

"before the seventh century"?), and the beginning of the 700s (*ʿalā ra's as-sabʿ mi'ah*) (!) are attributed to, respectively, the Ḥāfiẓ al-Yaghmūrī, Ibn ʿAsākir, Ibn Kathīr, and Ibn al-Athīr. On fol. 56a, al-Badrī attributes to Ibn Kathīr the statement that he had said before derived from an *Awā'il* work. Strange as it is, Ibn ʿAsākir could hardly be anyone but the historian of Damascus who lived before the date indicated, and although there were other Ibn al-Athīrs and the seven hundreds must be corrected to the six hundreds, the famous historian appears to be meant and he lived too close to that date to be seriously considered. The information of al-Bakrī, *Kawākib*, certainly goes back to al-Badrī. It has the addition that a Shaykh Qarandal at the beginning of the 600s introduced the drug. [The "700s" ("500s," below, p. 53) can hardly mean "seventh (fifth) century."]

[1] Note, however, that all the Zarkashī mss. (except B), as well as the quotation from az-Zarkashī in al-Badrī, fol. 3a, have *r* for *w* (al-Badrī: al-Masārijī).

[2] Yāqūt places the town midway between ar-Rayy and Hamadhān, whereas the first edition of *EI*, *s. v.*, locates it at a distance of twenty-two *farsakh*s from Qazwīn and nine *farsakh*s from Qumm.

[3] Cf. the first edition of *EI*, *s. v.* Ḳalenderiyya, and Ibn Baṭṭūṭah, I, 61 ff. The date is given in H. A. R. Gibb's translation, I, 37, n. 108, without an indication of its source.

[4] Cf. below, pp. 176 f.

Al-ʿUkbarī is cited by al-Maqrīzī and al-Badrī.[1] The latter knew al-Maqrīzī's *Khiṭaṭ* and quoted them elsewhere in his work (fol. 4b), but he does not depend on al-Maqrīzī since he inserts, quite plausibly, a certain Abū Khālid, described as a steward *(naqīb)* of Shaykh Ḥaydar, between the latter and the informant of al-ʿUkbarī; no mention is made of this Abū Khālid by al-Maqrīzī, at least not in the text available in print, which reads in translation:

"In *as-Sawāniḥ al-adabīyah fī (l-)madā'iḥ al-qinnabīyah*, al-Ḥasan b. Muḥammad (al-ʿUkbarī) said: I asked Shaykh Jaʿfar b. Muḥammad ash-Shīrāzī in the city *(baldah)* of Tustar[2] in the year 658/1260 why this drug was discovered and why it reached the poor (the Ṣūfīs) in particular and then spread to the common people in general. He (in fact, not Shaykh Jaʿfar but the just mentioned Abū Khālid) told me that his shaykh, the Master Ḥaydar, practiced much mystical exercise and exertion and used little food, excelling in asceticism and pious worship. He was born in Nishāwur in Khurāsān, and he lived on a mountain between Nishāwur and Zāwāh where he had acquired a small monastery.[3] A number of Ṣūfīs were in his company. He withdrew to a certain spot within (the monastery) and remained there for over ten years, never leaving it nor having anyone come in except me to serve him. He continued: The Shaykh then one day went up into the countryside alone by himself. During midday, the heat became oppressive, but when he returned, his face radiated energy and joy, quite a contrast to his usual appearance as we knew it from before. He let his companions come in and talked to them. When we saw the Shaykh so sociable after having been withdrawn and alone for such a long time, we asked him about it, and he said: In my isolation, I suddenly got an urge to go out into the countryside all by myself. When I came out, I noticed that every

[1] Although al-Badrī elsewhere in his work correctly identifies the author of the *Sawāniḥ* as al-ʿUkbarī, here, apparently through homoioteleuton omission, he makes al-Ḥasan b. Muḥammad ash-Shīrāzī the author of the work. This, however, does not invalidate the genuineness of the insertion of Abū Khālid.

[2] Al-Badrī seems to have a similar but different name.

[3] Silvestre de Sacy identified the place with Nīsābūr, but the use of the unusual form of the name here is puzzling. Cf., however, Yāqūt, *Muʿjam*, *s. v. Naysābūr*, who gives Na/ishāwūr as the vulgar form, and the fourteenth-century Meccan scholar, ʿAfīf-ad-dīn an-Nishāwurī (d. 790/1388, cf. Ibn Ḥajar, *Durar*, II, 300-302), whose original connection with Nīsābūr is remembered in Ibn al-ʿImād, *Shadharāt*, VI, 313 (Cairo 1350-51).

The edition of al-Maqrīzī has Mārmāh, and Silvestre de Sacy, Rāmāh, but al-Badrī's Zāwāh (no diacritical dots) = Zāwah would seem to be correct.

plant was completely quiet and showed not the slightest motion because there was no wind and the summer (heat) was oppressive. But then, I passed by a plant with leaves and noticed that in this weather it was gently swaying and moving without any force (being exercised upon it from outside), like someone who is inebriated. I started to pick a few of the leaves and eat them. Thus it happened that I was filled with this restful joy you have observed in me. Now, let us go, and I shall show you the plant, so that you can recognize its shape. He continued: We went out into the countryside, and he showed us the plant. When we saw it, we said that it was the plant known as hemp *(qinnab)*. He told us to take a leaf and eat it, which we did. Then, we returned to the monastery, finding in our hearts an irrepressible joy and gladness. When the Shaykh saw us in this condition, he told us to guard this drug, and he made us take an oath not to tell anyone of the common people about it. On the other hand, he exhorted us not to conceal it from the Ṣūfīs. His words were: 'God has granted you the privilege of knowing the secret of these leaves. Thus, when you eat it, your dense worries may disappear and your exalted minds may become polished. Therefore, keep their trust and guard their secret!' Shaykh Jaʿfar (read: Abū Khālid) continued: After we had become acquainted with this secret, I grew hemp in the monastery of Shaykh Ḥaydar while he was alive, and he told us to plant it around his tomb after his death. Shaykh Ḥaydar lived for ten years after that. I was in his service all the time, and I never saw him stop eating it day in and day out. He told us to take little food and (instead) eat this *ḥashīshah*. He died in (6)18/1221 in the monastery on the mountain. A big cupola was built over his tomb. Many votive gifts were offered to it by the Khurāsānians. They venerated his power, visited his grave, and showed great respect to his companions. At the time of his death, he exhorted them to show this drug and its secret to the refined and the great among the Khurāsānians, and they used it.—He continued: Hashish continued to spread in Khurāsān and Fārs. The people of Iraq were not acquainted with its use until there came to them the ruler of Hurmuz and Muḥammad b. Muḥammad, the ruler of al-Baḥrayn,[1]

[1] According to the Paris Ms. of al-Badrī, Muḥammad was the name of the ruler of Hurmuz. In fact, the ruler of Hurmuz at the time was Sayf-ad-dīn Abū Naḍar, but no precise information is readily known to me about these minor rulers in connection with the incident mentioned here. For the political situation in general, cf. J. Aubin, *Les Princes d'Ormuz*, in *JA*, CCXLI (1953), 80 ff.

kings of the shore adjacent to Fārs during the reign of al-Mustanṣir, in 628/1230-31. Their entourage carried hashish along with them and showed the people how to eat it. The result was that hashish became known in Iraq. Knowledge of it reached the Syrians, Egyptians, and Anatolians, and they used it."[1]

Verses quoted by al-Maqrīzī and other authors that refer to hashish as "the wine of Ḥaydar" and bring it otherwise into connection with him do of course not confirm the story of Ḥaydar's discovery of hashish, as medieval authors were inclined to believe, but they show that it had rapidly become accepted and was considered to be true. The fine aetiological tale telling how the plant itself reveals its incredible and beautiful power to the inspired seeker after spiritual release reflects a highly favorable attitude toward hashish, and it is therefore somewhat strange to find it repeated with seeming approval by later scholars such as az-Zarkashī and al-Maqrīzī who had been taught to hold quite different views concerning the effects of hashish. The character of the Ḥaydar story as a literary motif underlines its legendary character. However, the use of hashish by Ṣūfī fraternities and their presumably large role in the spread of hashish use can be accepted as a fact in view of all the later evidence pointing in this direction. Ibn Taymīyah's great concern with the problems of hashish was certainly connected with its use by Ṣūfīs and largely fostered by his animosity against them. The author of *Qamʿ* also probably had in mind the story of the mystical discovery of hashish and thought of the Ṣūfīs when he remarked that the accursed *ḥashīshah* "was originated by some group around the five hundreds" *(aḥdathahā baʿḍ fi'ah fī naḥw qarn al-khams mi'ah)*.[2] The word *fi'ah* "group" is used here for the sake of the rhyme and

[1] The quotation, it seems, from al-ʿUkbarī continues: "This was the year in which the (silver) dirhams appeared in Baghdād (to replace) the *qurāḍah* (snippets of gold pieces) people used to spend." The year meant would seem to be 628, but in fact, as Silvestre de Sacy has shown, it was 632, cf. also the *Ḥawādith al-jāmiʿah* (wrongly attributed to Ibn al-Fuwaṭī), 70 f. (Baghdād 1351). There is no apparent connection of this remark with the hashish story. It seems to have been added as an aside, but why this was done is not stated.

Whether some or much of the following material in al-Maqrīzī was also derived from al-ʿUkbarī is hard to say. It may be noted that the verses quoted are favorable to hashish and therefore could easily have been used by al-ʿUkbarī. Furthermore, they also occur in al-Badrī, whose source quite definitely was not al-Maqrīzī. If Ibn al-Aʿmā (d. 692/1292) was in fact the poet of some of them (cf. below, p. 154), we would have to assume that al-ʿUkbarī used material of a contemporary, which, however, is not excluded.

[2] Cf. *Qamʿ*, fol. 274b. [For "five hundreds," see p. 49, n. 5.]

thus may very well mean Ṣūfīs, rather than sectarians or soldiers. However, it is not the inclination of Ṣūfī organizations toward the use of hashish that is at issue but the precise data suggested by the Ḥaydarī-Qalandarī report. They can be neither proved nor disproved. The "discovery" of hashish was certainly not due to these people, but in addition to propagating its use, they might have also found some special way of preparing it for use that was little known before. By and large, the story leaves us with the impression that at any rate the general circumstances and the approximate time are correctly reflected in it.

The Ṣūfīs were not the only group blamed for the destruction caused by hashish. The fabled Ḥaydar was an older contemporary of Chingiz Khān, and about the time of Ḥaydar's death, the Mongols were poised to invade the lands of Islam. Blaming moral and material ills of any kind upon the machinations of foreigners and enemies is a common human trait. Thus, the Mongols were a natural target for those searching for an explanation of what brought about a social evil assumed to have reached dangerous proportions in their time. It may be tempting to assume that it was Ibn Taymīyah himself who invented the Mongols' guilt concerning the spread of hashish, but it is much more likely that he merely reiterated something that was a current rumor during the thirteenth century before his own time. Ibn Taymīyah is rather vague on occasion, saying that "the eating of hashish originated in the last years of the twelfth century or about that time," without any reference to the Mongols.[1] Or he would state that it "made its appearance among the people no earlier than roughly about the time of *(qarīban min naḥw)* the appearance of the Tatars (Mongols); hashish went forth, and with it, there went forth the sword of the Tatars."[2] But he also states flatly that "it was with the Tatars that it originated among the people,"[3] and it is obvious that he meant to make a causal connection between the appearance of hashish and the Mongol invasion, somehow implying that hashish was used by the enemy as an additional weapon to bring the Muslims to their knees. Later authors, such as adh-Dhahabī (?) and az-Zarkashī,[4] leave the same impression in a more distinct manner.

---

[1] Cf. Ibn Taymīyah, *Siyāsah*. Adh-Dhahabī (if he really is the author of the *Kabā'ir*, see above, p. 9) omits the date and the reference to the Tatars.

[2] Cf. Ibn Taymīyah, *Fatāwī*, IV, 312.

[3] Cf. Ibn Taymīyah, *Fatāwī*, IV, 311.

[4] Cf. below, p. 177.

Az-Zarkashī cites Ibn Taymīyah as having stated with great precision that hashish "appeared at the end of the twelfth century and the beginning of the thirteenth century when the Tatars came into power," and he cites another, unidentified source as having said that "it was an evil restricted to[1] Persia, until the Tatars gained control over its inhabitants. Then, it moved on to Baghdād when the evil effect it had upon its people was already known."[2]

The apparent sudden increase in the use of hashish at the period indicated might have been quite unconnected with the coming of the Mongols. In reality it would seem to antedate that event. However, it could also be that the Mongol invaders were driving in front of them refugees who took the drug habit along and spread it westward. Nor can we discount the possibility that in the wake of the disastrous happenings at the time, the resulting climate of fear and unrest caused an upsurge in the use of narcotics. All these factors might have existed and combined to produce the result whose precise cause or causes even an impartial sociologist living then might have found difficult to trace. The paucity of our information makes it still more so for us.

An attempt to pinpoint the further westward movement of hashish has been made by M. al-ʿAbbādī with reference to a statement of Ibn Saʿīd, the well-known Spanish historian of the thirteenth century.[3] Ibn Saʿīd criticized the prevalence of the use of hashish in Egypt, which aroused his curiosity since, he says, hashish was not known at the time in his own country. Al-ʿAbbādī combines this statement with the seemingly first occurrence of verses on hashish in Spain early in the fourteenth century. In particular, he also adduces a passage from Lisān-ad-dīn Ibn al-Khaṭīb dating to about the year 1360 which described the widespread use of hashish by the low classes as well as the leading families in Granada in many special hideouts all over the city at the time of the usurper Abū Saʿīd Bermejo. According to al-ʿAbbādī, all this leads to the necessary

[1] This seems to be the intended meaning.

[2] Below, p. 177: *wa-qad ʿulima mā jarā ʿalā ahlihā min qabīḥi l-athar* (var. *fatḥ at-Tatar* "what happened to its people as the result of the Tatar conquest"). I do not think that this means that it is known what an evil fate befell the people of Baghdād. Rather, by the time hashish reached Baghdād, it was known how greatly the Persians had suffered from it. In this passage, "its people" hardly refers to "users of hashish," although this would not be impossible.

[3] Cf. al-ʿAbbādī, in his edition of Lisān-ad-dīn Ibn al-Khaṭīb, *Nufāḍat al-jirāb*, intro., 20 f., text, 183 (Cairo, n. y. [1968?]), Spanish trans. by al-ʿAbbādī, in *Revista del Instituto de Estudios Islámicos en Madrid*, XIII (1965-1966 [rather, 1968]), 79.

conclusion that hashish established itself in the Muslim West only during the (later) thirteenth century. This may very well have been the case. As an additional argument in favor of this theory, it may be recalled that about a generation before Ibn Saʿīd, Ibn al-Bayṭār had this to say: "There is a third kind of *qinnab,* called Indian hemp, *which I have seen only in Egypt* where it grows in gardens and is also known to Egyptians as *ḥashīshah.* It is very intoxicating if someone takes as little of it as a dirham[1] or two. Taken in too large doses, it may lead to lightmindedness *(ruʿūnah)*. Some users were affected by mental disorder and driven into insanity; it may also kill..." Ibn al-Bayṭār again stresses that he himself was personally able to observe the effect of this kind of hashish and that it was unknown to him from his own country, Spain. It is true that Ibn al-Bayṭār was probably not older than about twenty years when he left Spain, and therefore may not have had sufficient information about the situation there, but it is a likely assumption that when he made a statement like that he had never seen the particular kind of hemp cultivated in Egypt anywhere else and had not been aware of the use of hemp as a hallucinogenic drug, he relied upon research as solid as he was able to make it. On the other hand, the reported occurrence from mid-fourteenth-century Granada is more dubious evidence. It implies that Bermejo's chief of police had no knowledge of the extensive use of hashish in the area under his jurisdiction and had to be made aware of it by his ruler who thus taught him what as a policeman he should have known by himself but did not. It might be argued that if the use of hashish went on without the police knowing of it, scholars such as Ibn Saʿīd and even Ibn al-Bayṭār might very well have had no information as to the situation in their native country, but being abroad, they learned about things about which they had no experience at home. The use of hashish was clearly very open in Egypt at that time, no doubt much more so than farther west. But it remains indeed possible that it took some time for it to reach Spain on its westward march.

3. The Preparation of Hashish and the Manner of its Use

It is quite likely that there once existed short treatises describing in accurate detail how hashish was prepared and consumed, but such

[1] For the weight of this unit, cf. below, p. 73, n. 2.

treatises would have had only a very small chance to survive and to become available to us. Thus we must be satisfied with the comparatively little and often rather blurred descriptions that turn up in various sources and contexts.

Ibn al-Bayṭār has some valuable and quite precise information based upon his own observations in Egypt. He tells us that he "saw himself Ṣūfīs *(fuqarā')* use hemp in various ways. Some thoroughly baked *(ṭ-b-kh)* the leaves, then rubbed *(d-ʿ-k)* them carefully by hand until they formed a paste *(ʿ-j-n* V), and rolled them into pills *(aqrāṣ)*. Others dried the leaves slightly, toasted *(ḥ-m-ṣ* II*)* them, husked *(f-r-k)*[1] them by hand, and mixed them with a little husked *(maqshūr)* sesame and sugar, put that dry into the mouth (*s-f-f* VIII) and chewed *(m-ḍ-gh)* it for a long time."

Less clear, in particular with respect to the use intended, is al-Maqrīzī's quotation of some physician(s) prescribing that "the eater of hemp (seed) or hemp leaves must eat it together with almonds or pistachios or sugar or honey or poppy (seeds) and drink afterwards oxymel to ward off the harm that may be caused by it. Roasted *(q-l-w)* it is less harmful. Therefore it is customary to roast it before eating it. When it is eaten unroasted, it is very harmful. Human tempers differ with regard to (the preferable manner of) eating it. Some cannot eat it mixed with something else. Others add to it sugar, honey, and other sweets." Mixing hashish with honey, in particular, was considered, it seems, as ordinary as mixing wine with water.[2] Already the great Ḥunayn is credited—unhistorically, no doubt—with the remark that it was best to have hemp leaves ground with sugar and almonds and to swallow the mixture dry *(s-f-f)*.[3]

Al-Badrī (fols. 8a-9a) gives a good number of additional details, but he somewhat impairs his credibility by including a scatological recipe, which was presumably a malicious invention. However, the methods described as employed in Egypt and Syria may very well be authentic. The method he considers as close to the one in use in Egypt consists of taking seven parts of mature leaves of cultivated hemp *(waraq ash-shahdānaj al-bustānī)* to one part of leaves of uncultivated *(barrī)* hemp, (the latter) to serve as a kind of ferment; roasting

[1] Cf. below, p. 60, for the applicable meaning of *f-r-k*.

[2] As in a very corrupt verse from a poem cited in al-Badrī, fol. 5a, which, he says, was recited by "the preacher of Baghdād" to his son, Jamāl-ad-dīn al-Ahwāzī, and he appears to have derived it from the *Kharīdah* (above, p. 45, n. 1).

[3] Cf. al-Badrī, fol. 7a.

(ṣ-l-q) them in water until they boil over the fire; placing them in large closed clay jars and depositing these in a humid place for about six weeks until the leaves start to decompose *(ta'fīn)*; leaving them in place for another week soaked (in water?) *(maghmūr)*; pulverizing them and blending them thoroughly; then forming the mixture into some kind of pills *(k-b-b* II*)* and leaving them in the shade for the air to dry them and for them to gain potency.

The best method, according to al-Badrī, is that of the Syrians. They let the hemp leaves dry and toast *(ḥ-m-ṣ* II*)* them over the fire in a copper kettle for about three hours. Then, when they want to form pills, they mix the mass with honey (or date syrup, *dibs*).

Some Indians substitute for the uncultivated hemp some other very potent substance.[1] Or they (apparently, still the Indians) use the same combination of leaves of cultivated and uncultivated hemp (as the Egyptians); place them in stone mortars; pulverize them finely; soak *(gh-m-r)* them in salted water for seven days of fermentation; leave the mortars exposed to the sun so that the sun will cause the humidity to evaporate (*ṭ-y-r* II) and the mass becomes pungent and salty; and, when the mass is close to being dry, form pills and pellets from it *(yukabbibūnahā ṭābāt)*.

Al-Badrī may have derived the preceding information from Ibn an-Najjār's *Zawājir*. This is not certain but he states so expressly with respect to a method described as producing the hashish of the Anatolians *(Rūm)* called *ṭ-f-r-y* (?):[2] "When at the end of autumn and in the winter, one can find only dry leaves of uncultivated hemp whose properties have weakened because of the evaporation of humidity, they add to each nine parts of leaves of cultivated hemp, which has been kept fermenting (?) *(mukhammar)* for a while, one part or more of cow dung to serve as ferment in place of the leaves of uncultivated hemp. They say: 'If we put the cow dung in the mass for fermentation, it comes out light, hot, and very potent *(shadīdat as-saṭlah)*. If it does not contain any dung, it comes out heavy, crude, and uneven.' They then ferment it with urine and soak it in it until it starts to decompose and worms are generated in it. If the worms are slow in coming, they squeeze out rags[3] with menstrual blood, and if they do not find any, they take spilled blood *(dam ṣabīb)* and

[1] *Waraq al-bizr al-hindī adh-dhakar*, lit. "the leaves of the male Indian seed (?)."

[2] Cf. above, p. 35, n. 5.

[3] Apparently, *khiraq*. The following *khrwq* may be a mistake for *khiraq*.

leave it there for a week until it swarms[1] with worms. They then pulverize it for a complete blending of the parts. Then they sift the mass. Others do not sift it but form it into pills and leave it in the shade until it dries." Al-Badrī is happy to report that this was also the method recommended by Satan to the Indian Bīr Raṭan.[2] As an additional Satanic trick, he ordered his son and his cohorts to put their urine on all intoxicating plants without people seeing them do it so that hashish was defiled by Satanic human urine openly and by Satanic jinn urine secretly.

In addition to terms such as *ḥammaṣa* and *ṣalaqa* already mentioned, quite a few others had their place in the production of hashish and its immediate preparation for use. *Ṣ-ḥ-n* "to grind" is one of them.[3] There is the amusing story of two hashish eaters, one of them thin and the other thick, and both having protuberances in front and in back. Fortified with *zīh* and pomegranates, the thin one leaves for the bath. There a jinnī in the form of an elephant appears, removes both of his protuberances, and affixes them to the wall. The other *ḥashshāsh* wants to rid himself of his protuberances in the same manner, but upon leaving the bath, he ends up with four instead of his former two. At the time the first *ḥashshāsh* entered the bath, we are told, he retired to some lonely spot and began grinding *(ṣ-ḥ-n)* it (apparently, the hashish) upon the marble (floor). He left aside the stubble *(qashsh)* and tended (the hashish) with wetting *(taʿāhadahā bi-r-rashsh)*.[4]

Commonly we hear about the "killing" *(q-t-l)* of hashish, an expression marvelously suited for the exercise of poetic ingenuity. Thus, a poet of *mawālīyā (mawwāl)*, Aḥmad al-Khaffāf, sang:

> They said: The medicine?[5] I replied: The transplanted son of cannabis.
> My rope he has untwisted. As long as I turn away from him, I am twisted.
> How many a person killed by him has returned home dragged by force.
> It is remarkable how he kills us, being himself "killed."[6]

---

[1] The reading of the ms. seems to be *yabqul*.

[2] See above, p. 44.

[3] Cf. al-Badrī, fols. 11b and 57a. See also below, p. 100.

[4] For the "wetting," cf. also above, p. 34.

[5] The *dawā'* "medicine" is suggested but then rejected as the cause of the poor condition of the person addressed. It is not the disease (*dawā*) that is inquired about.

[6] Cf. al-Badrī, fol. 6a:

qālū d-dawā qult ibn al-qinnab al-mashtūl
ḥablī naqaḍ nā ʿannū mā ('a)nthanī maftūl

The "killing" of hashish is interpreted as a cruel action resented by the maltreated hashish, as in these rhymes by ʿAlā'-ad-dīn ʿAlī b. Aybak ad-Dimashqī (728-801/1327(8)-1398):

They have toasted it in the fire till they burned it.
They have "killed" it by chewing till they made it good.
They have broken it into pieces, enabling it to cause drunkenness to settle in them.
It strangled them for their having strangled it.[1]

Thus, hashish takes its revenge. It kills the user as the user before killed it, according to verses by ʿAlī b. Sūdūn al-Bashbughawī and others.[2] And it was certainly considered very witty to have hashish complaining about being "killed" with reference to Qur'ān 81 : 9/9:

Hashish implored—Its Lord and asked humbly,
Stretching out its palms—"For which sin it was killed."[3]

The "breaking" *(k-s-r)* of hashish appears to be another of the customary procedures, and the just mentioned removal of the stubble seems also to be meant by *f-r-k* "to husk," mentioned by Ibn al-Bayṭār[4] and in this *mawālīyā* poem by a certain ʿAlī al-Qayrawānī:

They said: Hashish tires your liver. Give it up!
Why do you always toast and "husk" it?

---

kam lū qatīl ilā baytū rajaʿ maʿtūl
wa-dā ʿajab kayf yaqtulnā wa-hū maqtūl.

Perhaps, in the first line, *mastūl* = *masṭūl* "hashish intoxicated" is meant instead of *mashtūl* "transplanted" whose precise significance is not quite clear to me. In the second line, the ms. has *n' wʿnw*. Possible, *nā* = *anā* is to be deleted.

The meaning of "untwisted" and "twisted" here is "weak" and "strong." I have no information on the poet, unless he is identical with the aforementioned Khaffāf (above, p. 47, n. 5), which is doubtful.

[1] Cf. al-Badrī, fol. 18a:

ḥammaṣūhā bi-n-nāri ḥattā ('a)ḥraqūhā
qatalūhā bi-ḍ-ḍarsi ḥattā ('a)nʿamūhā
shaqqafūhā (?) tumakkinu s-sukra fīhim
khanaqathum bidāla mā khanaqūhā.

For *shaqqafūhā*, the ms. seems to suggest *shaffafūhā*, and it is possible that "to thin out" is the intended meaning. A combination with *s-f-f* is out of the question. Cf. *shaqfah kabshīyah*, above, p. 30.

For Ibn Aybak, whose date of death is also given as 803, cf. as-Sakhāwī, *Ḍaw'*, V, 194 f.

[2] Cf. al-Badrī, fol. 18a, and below, p. 91.

[3] Cf. al-Badrī, fol. 18a:

inna l-ḥashīsha ḍḍaraʿat—li-Rabbihā wa-btahalat
bāsiṭatan akuffahā —"bi-ayyi dhanbin qutilat"

[4] Cf. above, p. 57.

I replied: It contains meanings which your minds (ordinarily)
Cannot perceive, (but) were imagination to push them, it would move them.[1]

Popular forms of poetry use a verb *lāṭa* in connection with hashish, which may merely refer to the eating of it. However, since "to plaster" is one of the many meanings associated with this root, it may not be entirely excluded that it means the preparation of hashish for use by an admixture of some sort of clay as attested elsewhere (below, p. 83). One of the two available occurrences is cited below, p. 69, n. 1. The other is to be found in the following *mawālīyā*:

Always enjoy yourself and eat hashish.
"Plaster" (?) it and drink of *banj* the full bowl.
If someone importunes you for eating your *kaff* dry, say:
Sir, why do you annoy me so much when I am high?[2]

The form in which hashish was usually consumed is designated by a variety of terms, all meaning pill or pellet, such as *qurṣ*, *ṭābah*, and, in particular, *bunduqah* (originally, "hazelnut").[3] There are such

---

[1] Cf. al-Badrī, fol. 24b (in connection with his discussion of *kirshah*):
qālū l-ḥashīshah tutʿib kabdak utrukhā
fa-mā ant dāim tḥammiṣhā wa-tafrukhā
fa-qult fīhā muʿaynī (?) laysa tudrikhā
ʿuqūlkum law lakazhā l-wahmu ḥarrakhā.
The reading of *muʿaynī* as a diminutive of *maʿnā* is uncertain. Since the word seems to be used in the context as a feminine noun, a correction to *maʿānī* may be considered, but there may be other explanations. The antedecent of "them" could be the minds but quite possibly, and perhaps preferably, the meaning(s).

I have no information on ʿAlī al-Qayrawānī.

[2] Cf. al-Badrī, fol. 22a:
dāwim masarrtak dayman wa-l-ḥashīshah kūl
luṭhā wa-shrab min al-bankā malā l-kajkūl
wa-in laḥḥ lāḥḥīk fī saffak li-kaffak qūl
ay sīdī kam tufajjiʿnī wa-(ʾa)nā masṭūl.
Kajkūl, also *kashkūl*, from Persian *kachkūl*, is the beggar's bowl.

[3] Cf. above, p. 38. *Bunduqah* is of very frequent occurrence in al-Badrī. Among the verses on it he quotes on fol. 16a, we have, for instance, those by Badr-ad-dīn Fulayfil (b. ʿAbdallāh al-Muhtadī) about whom I have no further information, if, indeed, the form of his name is correctly given here:

Hashish, good youth,
Rises on my eye's horizon.
Thus leave wine alone as an ill omen
And cast off worries with a *bunduqah*.

inna l-ḥashīshata yā fatā
fī ufqi ʿaynī mushriqah

phrases as *bandaqa bunduqah* "to make a pill"[1] or *kabbaba ṭābāt.*[2] The noun *kubbah* "lump" appears as a pun in verses by Burhān-ad-dīn al-Miʿmār, addressed to a neighbor who was an addict and ate hashish even while the plague *(kubbah)* was raging:

I said to the man occupied with hashish:
Woe unto you! Do you not fear this grain?
People are dying of a plague that has appeared.
He replied: Let me live eating the lump.[3]

Fūlah "bean" is also clearly used for hashish pills slipped to an unsuspecting young boy by someone wishing to seduce him,[4] and it seems to be used this way, perhaps as a double entendre, in connection with the stinginess ascribed to addicts.[5] *Qurūn* (read *quran* ?) *az-zīh*, with the singular *qurnah* (vocalization?), may also refer to the pill form of hashish, rather than a kind of container for it.[6] The same word possibly occurs in the first verse of the long poem of Abū l-Khayr al-ʿAqqād:

Substitute two pills (?) for wine
And bring down the rain cloud with less than the two bottles.[7]

---

fa-daʿi ṭ-ṭilā mutaṭayyiran
wa-rmi l-humūma bi-bunduqah.

The third line may have to be corrected to *fa-daʿi ṭ-ṭilāʾa taṭayyuran.* I doubt whether any allusion to "shooting with a crossbow" *(qaws bunduq)* was intended as an additional poetical finesse.

[1] Cf. al-Badrī, fol. 11b, in the story just cited (above, p. 59).

[2] Above, p. 56.

[3] Cf. al-Badrī, fol. 32a:

qultu li-man bi-l-ḥashīshi mushtaghilun
wayka a-lam takhsha hādhihī l-ḥabbah
fa-n-nāsu mātū bi-kubbatin ẓaharat
fa-qāla daʿnī aʿīshu bi-l-kubbah.

The rhyme would seem to indicate the vocalization *kabbah*, for the *kubbah* of our dictionaries. A play on the word *ḥabbah* seems to be intended in verses by al-Miʿmār when his children want "grains" (= food) from him, and he replies, referring to his destitution, that he does not own a grain *(qālū nurīdu ḥubūban —wa-lastu amliku ḥabbah)* (al-Badrī, fol. 23b).

[4] Cf. al-Badrī, fol. 30b.

[5] Cf. below, p. 79, n. 9.

[6] Cf. al-Badrī, fol. 28a-b, in the story of Muslim al-Ḥanafī, below, p. 144. Cf. also above, p. 40.

[7] Cf. al-Badrī, fol. 16b, above, p. 33, n. 6:

taʿawwaḍ ʿan mudāmika qurnatayni
fa-danni l-muzna dūna l-qullatayni.

"The two bottles" constitute the legal separation between purity and impurity in liquids. If the translation of the second line is right, it would seem to mean that a much smaller quantity of hashish is needed than that required of beneficial rain producing grapes and wine (?).

However, the reading of the Paris Ms. of al-Badrī: *qirbatayn* "two skins" also makes sense, indicating that the proper beverage should no longer be wine but water (from water skins) drunk after the consumption of hashish; the parallelism with "two bottles" would favor this reading but would not make it absolutely necessary.

The finished product looked deceptively like henna to the inexperienced eye, as Ibn Baṭṭūṭah tells us.[1] And this is also exactly how al-Bakrī, in the *Kawākib*, described it: "They beat the leaves until they are like a salve, then they soak them in water until they are like henna." Hashish possessed a distinctive smell which was poetically described as "exciting and stimulating"[2] or as superior to musk and any other perfume, as in these verses of divers attribution:

My friend asked me when there emanated from it
A smell that put to shame the smell of perfume:
Is it musk? I replied: It does not come from
Musk but from *Kāfūrī* hashish.[3]

For the containers in which hashish was carried by the user a variety of words were used, such as *ḥuqqah* "small box." There was the purse *(kīs)* for carrying it around, and this was most important for poets because it enabled them to play constant minor variations

[1] Cf. Ibn Baṭṭūṭah, II, 351 f., trans. Gibb, II, 467. For the way henna was prepared as a cosmetic, cf. G. S. Colin, in *EI*², *s. v.* ḥinnā'.

[2] Cf. al-Maqrīzī, II, 25, in a verse by a certain Zayn-ad-dīn Abū ʿAbdallāh Muḥammad b. Abī Bakr b. ʿAbd-al-Qādir al-Ḥanafī, quoted by al-Maqrīzī from the Ḥāfiẓ al-Yaghmūrī. As in the following example, the hashish here is *Kāfūrī* hashish.

[3] Cf. al-Maqrīzī, II, 25, and al-Badrī, fol. 5a, as well as already an-Nuwayrī, *Nihāyah*, XI, 30, who, like al-Maqrīzī, has two additional verses. An-Nuwayrī's quotation is anonymous. Al-Maqrīzī attributes the verses to Nūr-ad-dīn Abū l-Ḥasan ʿAlī b. ʿAbdallāh b. ʿAlī al-Yanbuʿī, who appears to have lived in the first half of the thirteenth century, since al-Maqrīzī refers in this context to the historian, Ibn ʿAbd-aẓ-Ẓāhir (d. 692/1293). Although al-Badrī had just referred to al-Maqrīzī and might be therefore assumed to have derived these verses from him, he nevertheless attributes them to a certain Shihāb-ad-dīn Aḥmad b. al-Ḥusayn al-Miṣrī aṣ-Ṣūfī.

At the beginning of the second half-verse, al-Badrī has a different wording *(arajun yazdarī)*, a further indication that he probably did not quote the verses from al-Maqrīzī. At the end of the first half-verse, he has "me" for "it." But this apparently merely suggests that the smell of hashish emanated from the poet who carried it; it does not indicate mouth odor after the consumption of hashish or the like.

Al-Bustān al-Kāfūrī was a park in Cairo named after Kāfūr al-Ikhshīdī and famous or infamous for the hashish grown there, cf. further below, p. 135.

on the theme that wine required a cup *(ka'/s, kās)* whereas the *kīs* made it so much easier to transport hashish. It could be kept in the pockets *(jayb(ah)*, pl. *jiyab)* of one's dress, in the wide sleeve, or, quite generally, in garments *(thiyāb)*.[1] There always was the handkerchief *(mandīl)* to keep it in,[2] and it might also be wrapped in paper.[3]

From all that has been said here, it is apparent that hashish was consumed in a solid state form. It is almost always described as being "eaten." In comparison to wine, it was, for Ibn Taymīyah, like faeces as compared to urine.[4] Where the use of hashish was favored over wine, a poet could wittily remark that the ritual ablution with sand *(tayammum)* was obligatory for a person who was unable to find the necessary water for it.[5] When hashish was poetically described as if it were wine and called, for instance, the wine of Ḥaydar or the wine of the bankrupt (the Ṣūfīs), it does not mean that it was a liquid like wine, but the *tertium comparationis* was its quality as an intoxicant. However, Ibn Taymīyah also states expressly that hashish may be dissolved in water and drunk.[6] Legally, he considers it important to note that hashish could be consumed in a solid state as food *(jāmid, maṭʿūm)*. Yet, he acknowledges that people also make a distinction between its solid or dry *(jāmid, yābis)* form and its liquid *(mā'iʿ)* form.[7] The process that gives hashish its potency, called "toasting" *(taḥmīṣ)* and "roasting" *(ṣalq)*, may be compared

---

[1] Cf. al-Badrī, fol. 49a, in verses by the chief *naqīb* of the Iraq, Ḥusayn Ibn al-Aqsāsī (d. 645/1247) (cf. L. Massignon, *Cadis et Naqibs Baghdadiens*, in *WZKM*, LI, 1948-1952, 106-115 = *Opera Minora*, I, 264 [Beirut 1963]), cf. also below, p. 92, n. 5.

Thiyāb could, however, mean "pieces of cloth," corresponding to *mandīl*.

[2] Cf. al-Isʿirdī, verse 13, below, p. 164, cited by F. Rosenthal, *Four Essays on Art and Literature in Islam*, 87 (Leiden 1971, *The L. A. Mayer Memorial* 2).

[3] Cf. Ṣafī-ad-dīn al-Ḥillī, below, p. 173.

[4] Cf. Ibn Taymīyah, *Fatāwī*, IV, 303.

[5] Cf. al-Badrī, fol. 46b.

[6] Cf. Ibn Taymīyah, *Siyāsah*, and adh-Dhahabī, *Kabā'ir*.

[7] Cf. Ibn Taymīyah, *Siyāsah*, and adh-Dhahabī, *Kabā'ir*. In *Fatāwī*, II, 304, while Ibn Taymīyah speaks expressly of the dry and liquid forms of hashish, it is not quite clear whether he might not have thought rather of intoxicants in general.

I do not know precisely what kind of drink was sold by the *şerbetciyan-i beng-i bāde*, mentioned by Ewliyā Čelebī in the seventeenth century. "Sellers of henbane drink," as translated by G. Baer, may be somewhat too narrow, but anyway it appears to have been a liquid containing the one or other narcotic, cf. Baer, *Egyptian Guilds in Modern Times*, 36, 174 (Jerusalem 1964, *Oriental Notes and Studies* 8).

to the fermentation of wine *(ghalayān)*,[1] still, it refers to stages in the preparation of hashish for use as a solid paste.

In our souces, hashish is never described as having been smoked. The procedure of smoking is nowhere explicitly mentioned. The verb "to drink," which in more modern times often doubles for "to smoke," is never applied to hashish in a way that would suggest smoking.[2] The smell of hashish can, of course, not be understood to be the smell of its smoke. It has been stated that the smoking of hashish "was practiced in the east before the use of tobacco."[3] If so, any concrete evidence for it seems to be still lacking, and it would seem to remain true that the smoking of hashish was a custom that developed after the introduction of tobacco and continued side by side with the consumption of hashish in various solid preparations. In the story from the seventeenth century related by al-Mīlawī,[4] the eating of hashish and the "drinking" of tobacco were done simultaneously by two men. The point of the story requires smoking, but the hashish is eaten, and its consumption is distinguished from the smoking that was going on at the same time.

The eating of hashish could be accompanied by eating particular foods. Sweets and fruits were especially favored.[5] Pomegranates seem to have had some specific function in the ritual of hashish consumption.[6] The combination of wine and hashish was quite often attempted, although it must have been a luxury not accessible to the ordinary addict of the lower classes who chose hashish because it was cheap.[7] A respectable scholar found nothing wrong in using both wine and hashish on the same occasion.[8] The combination was

---

[1] Cf. az-Zarkashī, below, p. 191.

[2] This no doubt also applies to the verses in al-Aqfahsī which refer to the "drinking" of hashish without any allusion to wine, cf. above, p. 12.

[3] Cf. M. Meyerhof, in *EI*, *Supplement*, 85a, *s. v.* ḥashīsh. I wonder whether the negation "not" might not have been omitted by accident from Meyerhof's article. B. Laufer, *Tobacco and its Use in Asia*, 27 (Chicago 1924, *Field Museum of Natural History*, *Anthropology Leaflet* 18), knew of no evidence for the theory that the intricate water pipe pre-existed in Persia (for smoking hashish) because it made its appearance so soon after the introduction of tobacco. Cf. also B. Laufer, W. D. Hambly, and R. Linton, *Tobacco and its Use in Africa*, 13 (Chicago 1930, ... *Leaflet* 29), for the eating of hemp by sixteenth-century Kafirs.

[4] Cf. below, p. 129.

[5] Cf. below, pp. 78 f.

[6] Cf. al-Badrī, fols. 11b-12a and 15b-16a, cf. above, p. 59, and below, pp. 77 and 95.

[7] Cf. below, p. 131.

[8] Cf. al-Badrī, fol. 14a-b, below, p. 146.

praised as engendering at the same time "the laziness of hashish and the energy of wine."[1] Similarly, Ibrāhīm al-Mi'mār (d. 749/1348),[2] called in this connection "master of the craft" *(shaykh aṣ-ṣinā'ah)* (not of architecture, with which he does not seem to have had anything to do, but of poetry), might wonder about the extraordinary effect of wine plus hashish:

> He mixed hashish with wine
> And died of intoxication and became confused.
> He became quarrelsome on the spot,
> And I asked: What is this unexpected occurrence?
> When he was sober (again), he answered me, saying:
> Be kind to your brother when he mixes.[3]

However, the combination was considered as particularly sinful and therefore is often described as being characteristic of the revels of homosexuals.[4] It may be a contest between the boy who prefers wine, and his lover who prefers hashish and finally succeeds in persuading the boy to try hashish. Usually, though, bad boys try to attract men by tempting them with the combined use of wine and hashish as the resulting stronger intoxication would help to overcome any moral scruples.

The locale of hashish use was no doubt often dingy, and the act furtive, whether it was done in company or by oneself.[5] Pro-hashish sentiment loves to conjure up an idyllic setting at murmuring brooks or "in gardens where greyish pigeons coo."[6] But after all, one of the supposed advantages of hashish was that it could be taken anywhere, in the open streets[7] and even in mosques. Scurrilous stories happening when one of the worshipers in the mosque was under the

---

[1] Cf. Ṣafī-ad-dīn al-Ḥillī, below, p. 174.

[2] Cf. *GAL, Suppl.*, II, 3. Al-Badrī very frequently quotes al-Mi'mār or Burhān-ad-dīn al-Mi'mār. Whether or not he is identical with Ibrāhīm al-Mi'mār could be decided, perhaps, on the basis of Ibrāhīm's preserved *Dīwān*. O. Rescher, in describing the Istanbul Ms. Fatih 3793, calls him Jamāl-ad-dīn. The epithet "master of the craft" is also applied to Abū Nuwās (cf. al-Badrī, fol. 119a).

[3] Cf. al-Badrī, fol. 45b:

> *khalaṭa l-ḥashīshata bi-n-nabī-*
> *dhi fa-māta sukran fa-khtalaṭ*
> *wa-ghadā yu'arbidu fī l-makā-*
> *ni fa-qultu mā hādhā l-falaṭ*
> *fa-ajābanī idhā ṣaḥā*
> *sāmiḥ akhāka idhā khalaṭ.*

[4] Cf. al-Badrī, fols. 45a-46a, and below, p. 158 (n. 5).

[5] Cf. below, pp. 137 ff.

[6] Cf. al-Badrī, fol. 5b: *bayna r-riyāḍi wa-naghmati l-warqā'i.*

[7] Cf. Ṣafī-ad-dīn al-Ḥillī, below, p. 173.

influence of hashish can be suspected to reflect the not uncommon reality of the presence in the mosque of men in a state of hashish intoxication, which as a rule might not have been noticeable to the inexperienced, and therefore it did not cause any real offence when a hashish eater mingled among the crowd assembled in prayer.[1]

The public bath appears to have been a particularly convenient place for taking hashish.[2] In fact, the public bath, one of the most enduring material legacies of Graeco-Roman Antiquity, offered both privacy and companionship within its ample facilities. It was nothing unusual for those who had the time to spend the better part of the day in it. Going there in the morning, a person might still be found there in the evening.[3] It was a place of relaxation where members of many different social strata could meet and enjoy a certain freedom from their daily chores and worries—something to which hashish was believed by many to be able to make a further contribution. The description of things that allegedly happened to hashish eaters in public baths furnishes lively vignettes of this aspect of life in medieval Islam. At times, it reads like the scenario for a burlesque play, and it may, in fact, have served this very purpose. Thus we hear of an addict who in the company of his friends entered a bath and "killed" and used hashish in front of them. His friends apparently were non-users. Upon leaving they met a handsome boy about to go into the bath. The hashish eater turned around and, claiming that he was following the dictates of hashish which he was unable to control,[4] re-entered the bath and seated himself opposite the boy. His sexual excitement made itself felt and started a chain reaction of mischief. One after the other in succession, the head bath attendant *(ballān)*, a customer, the watchman *(ḥāris)*,[5] and, finally, the bath owner *(ḥammāmī)* with his cash box *(ṣundūq)*, all came to grief. The wild disturbance that ensued caused considerable amusement among those observing what was going on.[6] The role of hashish in this farce is rather limited and could very well have been dispensed

[1] Cf. al-Badrī, fols. 11b, 14b-15a, and 49b, cf. below, pp. 80 and 143.

[2] Cf. al-Badrī, fols. 11a-12a, 15a-16a, 29a-30a, 32a, and 33b, above, p. 59, and below, p. 134.

[3] Cf. al-Badrī, fols. 15b-16a, in the story of Aḥmad b. Barakah, below, p. 95.

[4] Cf. also below, p. 75, n. 3.

[5] Some minor functionary, possibly in charge of guarding the bathers' belongings and similar tasks, cf. the following story and A. Louis, in *EI*², III, 145a, *s.v.* ḥammām. For the cash box, cf. *Arabian Nights*, IV, 482, trans. Littmann, VI, 168. [For the medieval bath, cf. now H. Grotzfeld (Wiesbaden 1970).]

[6] Cf. al-Badrī, fol. 32a-b.

with entirely, but it occupies the center of the stage in another most vivid and entertaining story. A certain al-Jayshī al-Ḥakwī (?) took hashish and went to the al-Fāḍil Bath at Bāb Zuwaylah. Sitting in the bath under the influence of the drug, he was told by someone that he should come out and listen to al-Māzūnī at the wedding of ash-Sharābī (?).[1] Wearing only a bath towel *(fūṭah)*,[2] he left and walked along. When he reached al-Khurunfish,[3] he overheard someone telling his friend that he should accompany him to the al-Baysarī Bath.[4] He followed those people in, continued his bathing as if he had never interrupted it, had his head shaved, and then went to the locker room *(maslakh)* to look for his clothes. When he could not find them there (as they were still in the other bath), he looked for them all over the place. He asked the watchman what might have happened to them, but then, the bath attendant *(ballān)* noticed the markings *(ʿalām)* of the al-Fāḍil Bath on the towel and wondered about it. People started shouting, "Bravo, hashish!," and they all moved in procession to the al-Fāḍil Bath with al-Jayshī naked, dancing with lascivious gestures *(tamakhlaʿa)*, and singing:

By God, bravo hashish! It[5] stirs deep meanings.
Do'nt pay attention to those who blame it.
Refrain from the daughter of the vines
And do not be stingy with it.
Eat it dry always and live! By God, bravo, hashish!

[1] I would guess that al-Māzūnī was a singer performing here at a (wedding) procession (*zaffat ash-Sharābī*).

[2] According to *EI*², *loc. cit.*, *fūṭah*, in modern Tunis, is the loin-cloth, which, as shown here, accurately describes its use. It was furnished by the bath.

A story of the Hoja Nasreddin leaving the bath naked under the influence of hashish is one of the few Near Eastern items included in G. Andrews and S. Vinkenoog, *The Book of Grass* (New York 1967).

[3] This is no doubt the nearby street and quarter mentioned by W. Popper, *Egypt and Syria under the Circassian Sultans*, 31 and map 9 (Berkeley and Los Angeles 1955, *University of California Publications in Semitic Philology* 15). Al-Maqrīzī refers to the al-Khurunfish Arcade *(qabw al-Kh.)* in *Khiṭaṭ*, I, 458, stating that it was formerly known as Bāb at-Tabābīn. Elsewhere, the printed text of al-Maqrīzī (II, 27 f., 49, 54, 69, 96, 109, 197) has the form *al-Khrshtf*, once also *al-Khrnshf*. It may be "The Arcade" mentioned by as-Sakhāwī, *Ḍaw'*, I, 163, as the haunt of *juʿaydīs*.

[4] Cf. al-Maqrīzī, *Khiṭaṭ*, II, 69. Baysarī, without the definite article, is the usual form of the name of the amīr, but al-Baysarī is found, for instance, in adh-Dhahabī, *ʿIbar*, V, 387 (Kuwait 1960-66), *anno* 698/1299, the year of Baysarī's death. Neither bath is mentioned in al-Maqrīzī's discussion of public baths in Cairo. Al-Fāḍil may be the Qāḍī al-Fāḍil al-Baysānī who left a considerable mark on Cairine topography.

[5] It could hardly be the second person, addressing hashish, as hashish is used here as a grammatical feminine.

It is above pure wine.
When noble men use it,[1]
Eat it and agree, young man.
Eating it revives the dead. By God, bravo, hashish!

It gives the stupid, inexperienced, dull person
The cleverness of the straightforward sage.
I do'nt think I can escape from it.
. . . .[2] By God, bravo, hashish![3]

The places where hashish could be eaten were many, and so were no doubt the ways in which users tried to obtain the desired results. For some, it was a sort of religious ritual, making the place where it was consumed equivalent to a mosque. The Ṣūfī poet al-Yanbuʿī said of his enjoyment, in pleasant company, of hashish that "my salon is a mosque, and my drink is the green one," meaning apparently not that he was eating his hashish in a mosque but that he felt that the sacred act of eating hashish turned his living room into a place of worship.[4]

A highly idealized description of an elaborate hashish eating ritual is presented to us in al-Badrī (fol. 2a-b) as a fictitious exhortation of an equally fictitious "Shaykh Qalandar": "You must know that it behooves the intelligent, educated, virtuous, and sophisticated

---

[1] On *lāṭa*, see above, p. 61.

[2] "My load is . . . a feather" (?), but *rīsh* has many possible meanings. If the reading is *al-ghazzāl* "spinner of cloth," it may refer to the fact that he is naked, his load of clothing being light as a feather (?).

[3] Cf. al-Badrī, fol. 15a-b:

wallāhi ṭayyib yā ḥashīsh—ghawāmiḍa-l-maʿnā tujīsh
daʿ qawla man fīhā yalūm
wa-usmu (?) ʿan bint al-kurūm
wa-lā takun ʿanhā laʾūm
wa-staffihā dāʾim wa-ʿīsh—wallāhi ṭayyib yā ḥashīsh

tasmū ʿalā ṣafw al-mudām
waqtan yalūṭūhā l-kirām
kulhā wa-wāfiq yā ghulām
fa-l-mayt idhā (ʾa)kalhā yaʿīsh—wallāhi ṭayyib yā ḥashīsh

tuʿṭī l-ghabī l-ghirra l-balīd
nabāhata-l-ḥabri s-sadīd
mā (ʾa)ẓunnu lī ʿanhā maḥīd
ḥ-m-l-y m-n ʾ-l-gh-z-ʾ-l rīsh—wallāhi ṭayyib yā ḥashīsh.

Wa-usmu (ms. *w-ʾ-s-m*) seems doubtful. An eighth conjugation of *s-m-m* or *sh-m-m* yields no suitable sense here. A correction to *wa-shtamir* appears excluded by the meter. For *wa-staffihā*, the ms. shows different diacritical dots. *Ghulām* lacks the dot over the *gh*, but *ʿallām* "expert" is unlikely and does not fit the meter. For *al-ghzʾl*, the dots in the ms. admit also the reading *al-qrʾl*.

[4] Cf. al-Maqrīzī, above, p. 63, n. 3, and also below, p. 148.

individual, who wishes to use this drug which has the advantage over wine of being lawful, to cleanse his body of impurity and his garments of stains and to adorn himself with the acquisition of the virtues and to discard the commission of the vices. He must ask for it someone who knows its secret and disapproves of keeping it concealed (?),[1] and eat it in his place and not partake of it in the company of non-users. He must hold it in his right, not in his left, and say:

'In the name of God, the Lord of the last world and the first, who brought forth the pasturage (Qur'ān 87: 4/4), created and then formed (87 : 2/2), provided and gave, destined and guided (87 : 3/3), and taught the secret and disclosed (it). May God pray for Muḥammad, the prophet of right guidance, and his companions, the leaders in piety! (I know) that You have deposited wisdom in Your creatures and created usefulness in the things You have made. You have shown their specific properties to those with whom You are pleased, and revealed their secrets to those whom You have chosen. You have managed this plant with Your wisdom, brought it forth with Your power, and made it a nourishment for many of Your creatures by Your decision, volition, power, and will. Thus I am asking You by Your generosity that encompasses[2] the elite and the common people, to let me succeed in using it in obedience to You and with avoidance of any disobedience to You, that You remove from me the desires with their hindrances, the doubts with their consequences, and the troubles with their disturbances, that You let me see the existent things as they really are, and that You provide me with its benefits and ward off from me its harmful results, You who has the power over everything and sees every situation!'

He then puts it into his mouth, grinds *(s-ḥ-q)* it very strongly (with his teeth), drinks (something to go) with it,[3] moves his jaws, and sends it down into his guts. Then he praises God for His kindness. He cleanses his mouth of its remnants, washes his face, and raises his voice in song *(nagham)* for the Creator of beauty, for (beauty) provokes hashish intoxication *(saṭlah)* and rest. He rubs antimony on his teeth so that coarser souls *(al-akhshān)* will not

[1] The text is doubtful, possibly *wa-yunkir* (ms. *wa-yskr* ?) *sutratah*??

[2] The ms. seems to have *al-ʿāmm li-l-khāṣṣ wa-l-ʿāmm*, but possibly *at-tāmm* "Your perfect generosity for ..." is meant.

[3] This would seem to be the intended meaning, provided the reading of the ms. *(wa-yashrab ʿalayh)* is correct.

notice what the matter is with him, and he braids the hair of his beard. Cheerfulness(?) does not leave his mind, and he is restful (?)[1] in the way he walks and in his commands and prohibitions. He uses the most delicate food and the noblest of sweet speech. He gazes at beautiful faces and sits in the most pleasant[2] of places. He stays near where water is murmuring, and keeps company with experienced friends. He turns to reflecting about cause and the thing caused, about doer and the thing done, about event and result, about speaker and the thing spoken, and about agent in sweetness (?) and the thing caused by action. In this condition, (enough) of the eternal knowledge of God and His universal grace emanates upon him to let him perceive the views and their meanings and to show him the things with their contents. He notices the hearts with the eyes and controls the eyes with the hearts. He separates from his idea of humanity and joins his idea of divinity. The name by which the poor are known *(nisbat al-fuqarā')* becomes lawful for him in reality, and he reaches the degree of divine success *(tawfīq)*."

"The Shaykh Qalandar" concludes with a warning against the improper use of hashish and against divulging its benefits to the common people, instead of sharing it with fellow Ṣūfīs. Remote from reality as it is, the ritual is a good reflection of the dream world constructed by faithful cultists. Even in this dream world, dissimulation was considered necessary in order to throw the uninitiated off the user's scent, and even in the company recommended as proper, the user is depicted as withdrawing into himself and into his supposed lonely communion with the divine.[3]

4. The Reported Effects of Hashish

It is to be expected that Muslim authors cannot shed very much light on the "origin" of hashish use. Perhaps, we should also not be greatly disappointed if we have little concrete data about the technical side of hashish preparation. We might think, however, that our

---

[1] The word, seemingly ending in *-ḥf* may possibly be *qaṣf (wa-lā yazūl* [*yuzawwil*?] *al-qaṣf min* [read *'an*?] *dhihnih)*. This is followed by *wa-yatarannaḥ* "and he is unsteady," which to my mind would make sense only if the earlier negation were also to apply to it. Perhaps we should read *yatarayyaḥ* and translate as suggested above.

[2] *Anzah* is to be understood in this sense, and does not mean "most isolated (or the like)," connecting it with *munazzah*. Cf. also the passage from al-'Ukbarī's *Sawāniḥ*, below, p. 78, n. 3.

[3] Cf. also below, pp. 139 f.

sources would be able to give us a good deal of solid information on the effects of the drug. We do indeed hear rather much about the manifold ways in which hashish affects the user, but truth and fiction are hard to disentangle. We have no first-hand report of bona-fide hashish eaters setting down their experiences in writing with clinical detachment. Many reports give the impression that their narrators might possibly have been addicts themselves. It is even possible that some of the authorities who denounce the use of drugs in the strongest terms were secret addicts or at least had some actual drug experience that informed their judgment. It is, however, much more likely that they relied upon second-hand knowledge. They may have derived their information from the actual observation of users and from what those men told them. Often, they seem to have based themselves upon a kind of generalities compounded by fact, rumor, and fantasy in about equal proportions. The jurists were principally concerned with two aspects, the temporary effect of intoxication and the alleged mind-changing aspects of drug use, considered as more or less permanent. Any other detail found attention by them only if it was giving support to their general outlook on the use of drugs; fact and experience were of minor interest to them. The poets, whether they were praising or attacking the use of hashish, were not necessarily informed by experience, as their first loyalty clearly was to literary convention.[1] Storytellers naturally chose and exaggerated the elements they thought of as most interesting to their audience. Moreover, they also depended a good deal on conventional motifs which they transformed to apply to hashish. It often makes no real difference whether the effects sustaining a given anecdote were those of hashish, or wine, or personal eccentricity, or any similar agent. We merely learn what was *believed* to be likely effects of hashish.

Brief but highly interesting remarks on the difficulty encountered in the past in any attempt to obtain real knowledge about a drug's effects can be found at the beginning of Ibn Ḥajar al-Haytamī's treatise against the use of *qāt*:[2] Information from experience requires a long time to accumulate. Information gathered from users is unreliable and indecisive. There are, for instance, contradicting statements from users with regard to the simple question of whether

[1] Cf. below, p. 151, n. 1. Hashish poetry imitated all the topics of wine poetry, including such things as poems in which the poet asks for hashish, cf. al-Badrī, fols. 18b-19a, who also includes a prose letter on the subject.

[2] See above, p. 11.

the use of *qāt* is harmful or not. Traditional information seems to be the best guide as to how to handle the problem. From our point of view, we would heartily disagree—at least, in principle—with Ibn Ḥajar al-Haytamī's attitude. However, for a Muslim scholar, especially one writing in the waning centuries of medieval Islam, it was only natural to distrust empiricism and to rely upon authority and tradition.

There was no real possibility of any sort of controlled experimentation, even if the idea of using this thoroughly modern technique had ever occurred to medieval scholars.[1] In times past, it would have been completely out of the question to attempt to measure the relationship between amount and effectiveness of drugs such as hashish. It was realized that hallucinogenic drugs could be used in larger or smaller doses and thereby exercised more or less intensive effects. Some extraordinary feat of consumption might occasionally be mentioned. Thus it could be stated that someone was able to consume thirty dirhams weight of nutmeg *(jawzat aṭ-ṭīb)*, or someone else was described as using a daily dose of one ounce (Egyptian) of *k-n/tbābatī*.[2] But hashish in its various forms and, in particular, when it was taken mixed with other ingredients, could have had any degree of potency. It would have served no valid purpose for a medieval author to indicate quantities normally consumed by addicts.

The effects of cannabis were also described in medical terms[3] according to the rules of humoral pathology. They were assumed to be due to the actions of natural heat and the reduction of bodily humidity, leading to "hot" diseases and fevers. But obviously, there was no agreement whether hemp was hot and dry, or cold and dry,

---

[1] As an example of what was possible in medieval times in this respect, we may refer to the unhappy story of the scholars at the Niẓāmīyah who wanted to improve their mental faculties by the use of *balād(h)ur* (anacardia) and asked a physician how to take it and how large a dose a human being could stand, cf. Ibn Khallikān, *Wafayāt*, VI, 91 (Cairo 1948), in the biography of Ibn Shaddād. Among physicians and in medical literature, the general problem of proper dosage was, of course, realized and much discussed.

[2] Cf. al-Badrī, fols. 39a and 47a, see also above, p. 31. The dose indicated corresponds to twelve dirhams or 37.5 grams, somewhat more than an ounce, according to W. Hinz, *Islamische Masse und Gewichte*, 35 (Leiden 1955, *Handbuch der Orientalistik*, ed. B. Spuler, *Ergänzungsband* 1). The standard weight of the dirham was 3.125 grams.

[3] Cf. above, p. 41, and below, pp. 114 f. Cf. also the *Report of the Indian Hemp Drugs Commission 1893-1894*, 174 f., 197 f. (reprinted Silver Spring, Maryland, 1969).

and to what degree.[1] If we can trust az-Zarkashī, the great Rāzī gave this description of the effects of eating cultivated hemp leaves, in an unnamed work of his: "It causes headache,[2] cuts off and dries up the semen, and generates pensiveness *(fikrah)*.[3] The reason is that the humidity of bodies being in equilibrium goes hand in hand with the preservation of living beings. Thus, whatever dries up the body's humidity is harmful and helps to ruin it. It (apparently, the hemp leaves) generates sudden death, mental confusion, hectic fever, consumption, dropsy, and effeminacy."[4] The mixture of medicine and popular beliefs is quite characteristic of the views ascribed to physicians. Experience and experiment would seem to have played a small role in it, even in respect to the information inherited from Graeco-Roman Antiquity. A dubious anecdote knows of evidence for the curative power of hemp leaves in cases of epilepsy *(ṣarʿ)*.[5]

---

[1] Cf. Ibn Jazlah, as quoted by al-Maqrīzī. Since the Yale Ms. L-740 (Catalogue Nemoy, No. 1509), stated to contain Ibn Jazlah's *Minhāj*, contains nothing on hemp proper, I have so far been unable to check Silvestre de Sacy's references to the work and al-Maqrīzī's quotations from it.

[2] Cf. Galen, *De alimentorum facultatibus*, I, 34 (= VI, 550 Kühn): *kephalalgēs*. According to Ibn al-Bayṭār, this was mentioned by Isḥāq b. ʿImrān and by ar-Rāzī, in his *Dafʿ maḍārr al-aghdhiyah*. In the *Dafʿ*, ar-Rāzī further refers to "dimming of the eye," cf. the Yale Ms. L-473 (Catalogue Nemoy, No. 1519), fol. 31b.

The medical authorities quoted by Ibn al-Bayṭār hold views quite similar to those cited here in the name of ar-Rāzī. As they can be easily consulted in the translations of Ibn al-Bayṭār, no further attention has been paid to them here (but see below, p. 114, n. 7).

Al-Badrī, fols. 5b ff., quotes many ancient and Islamic medical authorities, beyond the references in al-Maqrīzī, but when they resist identification in the sources or cannot be traced to the earlier literature, the attributions must be treated with some suspicion.

Ar-Rāzī himself, in the section on simples in the *Ḥāwī*, XXI, i, 124, refers to *shahdānaj* as a medicament for the ear. When consumed in too large quantities, it causes headache and impotence *(q-ṭ-ʿ al-bāh)*. Its leaves are good against dandruff *(ḥazāz)* of the head and the beard. It is not certain whether all this is meant to go back to Ibn Māsawayh, who is cited for classifying hemp as hot in the second degree (whereas al-Badrī, fol. 6a, says that Ibn Māsawayh classifies it as hot in the first degree).

[3] The term here is no doubt meant to have a negative connotation in the direction of worrisome thought. Elsewhere in connection with the effects of hashish, it is something positive.

[4] Cf. az-Zarkashī, below, p. 178.

[5] Al-Badrī, fol. 7b, claims that this effect of the drug is mentioned by ar-Rāzī in the *Manṣūrī*, in the chapter on *ṣarʿ*. This remains to be checked. The anecdote (see also below, p. 152, n. 2) is subsequently reported in the first person, giving the impression that it is also derived from the *Manṣūrī*. However, it deals with a situation from the first half of the thirteenth century.

The principal purpose in using hemp for pleasure was what in present-day language is described as "getting high." Arabic has a special term for hashish intoxication in the root *s-ṭ-l* (also *ṣ-ṭ-l*), listed in the dictionaries, often with the express addition that the meaning "intoxicate" refers to hashish intoxication.[1] *Masṭūl, masāṭīl* "high on hashish" and the verbal nouns *insiṭāl* (and *istiṭāl*) are common in al-Badrī, in al-Bakrī (according to Silvestre de Sacy), and elsewhere. *Musaṭṭil(ah)* is the intoxicating action of hashish as mentioned in al-Badrī and *Qamʿ*. A note in al-Badrī, fol. 47a, explains that the root means "feeling the effects of hashish," and this in connection with a verse in which the portmanteau *saṭlānaj* is coined to provide a rhyme word for *shahdānaj*. The noun *saṭlah* (the vowel of the first syllable is, it seems, not assured by express attestation) is common; in a verse by Ibn Sayyid-an-nās (671-734/1273-1334), it appears next to *sukr* among the six alleged bad qualities of Ṣūfīs, obviously making a distinction between intoxication from wine *(sukr)* and intoxication from hashish *(saṭlah)*.[2] With no further qualification, *masṭūl* signifies "being high on hashish," for instance, in a verse by Ibn al-Wardī, which is followed by another verse saying that "*qunbus* does with me whatever it wants."[3] *Maṣṭūl* is listed separately from *s-ṭ-l* with the meaning of "fool" in H. Wehr's *Arabisches Wörterbuch.* A modern Turkish-English dictionary has the entry *mastor (mastur)* "a drunkard (with hashish), drowsy-headed man." Disciples of a Ṣūfī, ʿImād-ad-dīn Aḥmad b. Ibrāhīm al-Maqdisī aṣ-Ṣāliḥī, are described as *akalah saṭalah baṭalah,* which supposedly means "eaters, hashish eaters (?), and good-for-nothings." However, the form *saṭalah* in this meaning seems to be most dubious and unusual, and may not be correct.[4] While the proper word for

[1] The peculiarity of the meaning once again justifies our asking ourselves what its origin might have been. No answer is as yet readily available. It would be intriguing to note that tenth-century Syriac lexicography knows of *s'ṭl* as an "Indian drug," were it not for the fact that Arabic medical literature speaks of *sh'ṭl,* cf. ar-Rāzī, *Ḥāwī,* XXI, i, 126.

[2] Quoted by al-Kutubī, *Fawāt,* II, 348; al-Maqrīzī, II, 414.

[3] Cf. Ibn al-Wardī, *Dīwān,* 283 (Constantinople 1300), quoted anonymously by al-Badrī, fol. 32a-b. For Ibn al-Wardī's occupation with hashish, cf., further, below, p. 151, n. 1.

[4] Cf. adh-Dhahabī, *ʿIbar,* V, 357. Ibn al-ʿImād, *Shadharāt,* V, 403, in quoting adh-Dhahabī, omits the crucial word, probably because he did not understand it or considered it a mere repetition by the scribe of *baṭalah.* Cf., however, A. von Kremer, *Beiträge,* in *Sitzungsberichte, Akad. d. Wiss, Wien, phil.-hist. Cl.,* CIII (1883), 253, where *s-ṭ-l* is listed in the meaning of "beggar pretending to be blind."

hashish intoxication existed and was widely known and used, a more precise and detailed definition of what the hashish "high" was and how it manifested itself was, regrettably, not given in connection with the root and must be gathered from dispersed indications in the literature.

The effects of hashish are classified as physical, mental, and religious, with the former two as a rule not sharply distinguished from each other. The anti-hashish forces were understandably very expansive in cataloguing the manifold ways in which the drug was believed to cause havoc among users. Occasionally they came up with summary condemnations in the form of aphorisms such as: "There are as many harmful qualities in hashish as there are beneficial qualities in the toothbrush *(siwāk)*."[1] Or, "The only use of hashish is for drying out sores of horses *(n-sh-f ʿaqr ad-dābbah)*."[2] But as a rule, they indicate a variety of details, even if their lists are built around a number of basic data.

The addicts themselves, or rather, those who speak for them and in favor of their habit, are long on emotional lyricism but quite short on concrete facts. For them, hashish is a thing of true beauty. It gives them irrepressible joy and repose and provides them with relief from worries and anxiety. It reveals to them "secrets" and opens up to them new "meanings." It increases their understanding and enlarges their imaginative perceptions. It makes them witty and entertaining company: "By its sublety, it clothes the dull person with frivolous wit so that he becomes smart and a good companion, in contrast to wine which is nasty in its effects and causes fear of being unexpectedly caught by the authorities."[3] It is indeed con-

---

[1] Cf. al-Badrī, fol. 55b, quoting az-Zarkashī (not, apparently, the *Zahr*); *Qamʿ*, fol. 276b. On the authority of al-Aḥnaf b. Qays, it was known even popularly that the *siwāk* possessed seventy-two good qualities, cf. *Arabian Nights*, I, 433 (= trans. Littmann, I, 607).

[2] Cf. al-Badrī, fol. 55b. Until the source of the statement is discovered somewhere in the hippiatric literature, it can hardly be determined precisely which disease may be meant by *ʿ-q-r*. It could be saddle sores or sores in various parts of the horse, but we also find, for instance, a chapter heading *fī l-ʿaqr al-ʿāriḍ fī l-ʿaynayn* in the collection translated into Arabic under the name of Theomnestus and preserved in the Istanbul Ms. Köprülü I, 959, fol. 26a. This corresponds to Greek *peri diakopēs ophthalmōn*, presumably, "rupture (of blood vessels?) in the eyes," cf. *Corpus Hippiatricorum Graecorum*, ed. E. Oder and C. Hoppe, I, 74 (Leipzig 1924-1927). Incidentally, in the same context we hear about the juice of *banj* (fol. 26b), translating *hyoskyamou chylos* (*CHG*, I, 75, l. 27).

[3] Cf. al-Badrī, fol. 5b (see above, p. 45, n. 5):

stantly stressed that wine causes quarrelsomeness, and hashish a kind of languid placidity. It is noteworthy (although the sources themselves rarely comment upon the fact)[1] that no truly violent actions directed against other persons under the influence of hashish are mentioned in any of our stories. The pro-hashish faction has much to say along the general lines indicated here, but it never really comes to grips with the points raised by the attackers. There was no real dialogue, and none was possible, since either side was as a rule committed to its own position and the arguments for it.

An outward effect of hashish on the user was changes in his coloring and complexion. His skin took on a greyish-green complexion, and he looked pale.[2] The most immediate telltale sign of hashish use is the reddening of the eyes.[3] It is an indication that hashish has started to exercise its effect. The phrase *qadaḥat fī ʿayn-* "it has hit the eye..." is commonly used in al-Badrī, who also once (fol. 31a) uses the verb *ṭalaʿat* "went up to the eye..." The reddening of the eyes was another boon for poets, as it enabled them to play around with the concept of emerald (green) hashish turning into a red carnelian *(ʿaqīq)* in the eyes.[4] The same precious stones, incidentally, also served to picture the contrast between green hashish and red wine. With a little greater effort at originality, it was possible for a man like Ibn al-Kharrāṭ (ca. 777-840/1375(6)-1436)[5] to rhyme:

> We have a companion carrying in his hand half a pill
> Resembling a pomegranate tree shining green.
> We bore with him for a while after he swallowed it.
> Then we noticed in his eye its blossom.[6]

---

taksū l-balīda khalāʿatan min luṭfihā
fa-yaṣīru(a) dhā kaysin wa-ḥusni ikhā'i
ḍidda sh-sharābi fa-innahū dhū shunʿatin
wa-yukhāfu fīhī (!) kabsatu n-nuqabā'i.

For the topic of danger from the authorities, cf., for instance, below, p. 164, and for the quarrelsomeness caused by wine, cf. below, p. 110, etc.

[1] Cf. al-Qarāfī, below, p. 110.

[2] Cf. al-Isʿirdī, verse 30, below, p. 165.

[3] Cf. also, in particular, below, p. 128. In addition to the numerous references from al-Badrī, cf. also Ibn ʿAbd-aẓ-Ẓāhir, as cited by al-Ghuzūlī, *Maṭāliʿ*, II, 129, and Ibn Ḥijjah, *Thamarāt*, I, 363 (Būlāq 1286-87, in the margin of ar-Rāghib al-Iṣfahānī, *Muḥāḍarāt*). Wine is constantly described as making the cheeks red, but Abū Nuwās once also adds the eye, cf. his *Dīwān*, 180 (Beirut 1382/1962): *ajdathu ḥumratahā fī l-ʿayni wa-l-khaddi.*

[4] Cf., for instance, al-Badrī, fols. 17a, 18b, 19a.

[5] For Zayn-ad-dīn ʿAbd-ar-Raḥmān b. Muḥammad b. Salmān b. al-Kharrāṭ, the head *kātib al-inshā'* in Egypt, cf. as-Sakhāwī, *Ḍaw'*, IV, 130 f.

[6] Cf. al-Badrī, fol. 22a:

The color changes provoked by the use of hashish also gave rise to a hostile ditty by the "elegant youth," Ibn al-ʿAfīf at-Tilimsānī (660-688/1262-1289), quoted occasionally in slightly different forms:

> Hashish holds no advantage for its eater,
> But he is not turned in the right direction.
> Yellow in his face, green in his mouth,
> Red in his eye, black in his liver.[1]

It was noted that hashish stimulated the appetite. An idealized picture of the situation in this respect was painted by al-ʿUkbarī in the *Sawāniḥ*, as quoted, with disapproval, by al-Badrī (fol. 24b): "Only intelligent and well-to-do[2] people use hashish. When taking it, a person should consume only the lightest of foods and the noblest of sweets. He should sit in the most pleasant of places[3] and bring around the most distinguished (?) of friends.[4] In the end, he will talk about something that was and something that was not.[5] Then he will go on (?) and be concerned with thinking about[6] sweets and food and assume that all this is reality whereas in fact, he is asleep." The reality, al-Badrī notes, was not always as pleasant, and the stories he tells prove it. We hear about individuals always eating hashish alternately with chicken[7] or lamb(?).[8] A user, picked up by Zayn-ad-dīn Ibn al-Kharrāṭ and his friends in Damascus, eats large

---

> *lanā ṣāḥibun fī kaffihī niṣfu ṭābatin*
> *ḥakat shajara r-rummāni lāḥa khḍirāruhā*
> *ṣabarnā ʿalayhi sāʿatan baʿda balʿihā*
> *fa-bāna lanā fī ʿaynihī jullanāruhā.*

An-Nuwayrī, *Nihāyah*, XI, 101, describes pomegranate blossoms as white, red, or rose-colored. They are usually orange red.

[1] Cf. Ibn al-ʿAfīf, *Dīwān*, 29 (Beirut 1885); Ibn Kathīr, XIII, 315; Ibn Taghrībirdī, *Nujūm*, VII, 381; al-Badrī, fol. 7b. In the margin of the Princeton Ms. of al-Aqfahsī, fol. 21a, the verse reads: "green in his hand, yellow (pale) in his stomach *(jawfih)*." The Gotha Ms. (above, p. 18) makes the yellow face and the red eye exchange places, not unreasonably since the reddening of the eye is an early sign.

[2] *Min al-akyās wa-dhawī al-akyās*, playing on the double meaning of the root.

[3] Cf. above, p. 71, n. 2.

[4] *Wa-yastajlib ʿalī* (?) *al-ikhwān* (?).

[5] *Yataḥaddath bi-shay' kān wa-bi-shay' lā* (!) *kān*, a phrase repeated by al-Badrī, fol. 57a, and apparently referring to the hashish eater's spinning of tales while being high.

[6] *Thumma yasrud wa-yahdus fī dhikr*. However, the root *s-r-d* seems to have some particular meaning in the hashish ritual.

[7] Cf. al-Badrī, fol. 19b.

[8] Cf. al-Badrī, fol. 21b *(kharūf)*.

quantities of apricots and then a very substantial meal.[1] When ʿAlī b. Sūdūn al-Bashbughawī ate inadvertently a quantity of *k-n/tbābatī*, he got very hungry, described a full-course meal in verse, and was served it.[2]

In particular, it is sweets and fruits and the like that addicts crave.[3] Those high on hashish *(al-masāṭīl)* pounce upon sweets as greedily as does a lover upon the mouth of the beloved he wishes to kiss, according to a verse by Ibn al-ʿAfīf at-Tilimsānī.[4] The messengers of the *ḥisbah* office in Cairo *(rusul bayt al-ḥisbah)* who went to the bank of the Nile, sat there eating hashish and dates, and finally entered into a lying contest for the last remaining date (thus bringing down upon them the double condemnation of Qur'ān 5: 42/46: "hearing lies, eating what is prohibited [*suḥt*]"), satisfied their hashish-induced craving for sweet fruit.[5] A scurrilous tale of two users who went down to a sugar cane press *(maʿṣirat al-qaṣab)* in Damiette and sat opposite each other, chewing sugar cane and spitting it out with such abandon that finally they could no longer see each other because of the mountain of sugar cane refuse between them also illustrates the sweet tooth stimulated by hashish.[6] The gluttony and uncontrollable desire for sweets and fruits could be expensive and contribute to reducing a user to penuriousness.[7] The stinginess attributed to addicts[8] was also thought to have its roots in their craving for expensive food. Both hunger and stinginess are combined in verses composed by al-Badrī himself:

Once I visited my friends under the influence of *zīh*
In the morning, and hunger made itself felt in the evening.
One gave me a bean, generously,
And another some dessert, meanly.[9]

---

[1] Cf. al-Badrī, fols. 21b-22a.

[2] Cf. al-Badrī, fol. 22a-b, see above, p. 31.

[3] This gave al-Badrī an excuse for a long excursus (see above, p. 14). Cf. also, for instance, above, p. 65.

[4] *Dīwān*, 72 (Beirut 1885); aṣ-Ṣafadī, *Wāfī*, ed. S. Dedering, III, 132 (Damascus 1953, *Bibliotheca Islamica* 6c).

[5] Cf. al-Badrī, fol. 24a.

[6] Cf. al-Badrī, fol. 23b.

[7] Cf. al-Badrī, fol. 22b, and below, p. 158.

[8] Cf. al-Badrī, fol. 17b.

[9] Cf. al-Badrī, fol. 24a-b:

ṣabbaḥtu fī z-zīhi yawman
khullānī wa-l-jūʿu massā
bi-fūlatin jāda lī dhā
wa-dhā bi-nuqlin wa-khassa.

The ms. has *khl'n*, perhaps to be corrected to *khullānan*, but "my friends"

An anecdote told about an originally well-to-do Egyptian addict, no doubt a figment of the imagination of the narrator, combines the supposed characteristics of stinginess, fondness for sweets, and self-illusion: In a hashish dream, he saw and heard a voice telling him that his end was near and that he should give some of his money to his friends among the hashish eaters. He swooned, was carried home, and when he woke up, ordered the sweetmeats bakers to prepare a lot of sweets. He had them carried to al-Junaynah[1] and had them distributed there among his friends, reality becoming like a dream. Then he took hashish again. Now he saw a castle built entirely of various kinds of sweets and other delicacies. He was told by the same voice that such a castle was the reward for one who regaled his friends as he had done. But then he woke up and found that there was nothing there and that his money was all gone. Originally he was a stingy man. However, his hashish habit impoverished him and finally caused him to lose his mind together with his money.[2]

An affinity of the hashish eater to music was occasionally detected. It was not considered to be as normal and expected as the relationship between wine and song of which it could be said, for instance: "Between wine and song there is a relationship under most conditions and a similarity with respect to praiseworthy qualities common to both."[3] But hashish was beautiful music to the sense of hearing,[4] and listening to music increased the pleasure of it. Thus al-Khaffāf was under the influence of hashish when he joined a musical soirée where women on a balcony *(manẓarah)* were looking down, and hashish and music combined to loosen his inhibitions.[5] A user under the influence of the drug is deeply moved by a flutist playing at an amīr's party. He leaves, and not knowing what he is doing, he enters a mosque, mixes with the assembled worshipers without first performing the required ablutions, remains prostrated in prayer when the others have finished and are leaving, is awakened

---

seems preferable. Since *fūlah* "bean" may mean a hashish pellet (cf. above, p. 62), the intended meaning could be that the stingy friends provided the author just with some more hashish and fruit, the latter in small quantity. It would seem, however, that beans are literally meant as a cheap and unattractive kind of food.

[1] See below, p. 95.

[2] Cf. al-Badrī, fol. 24b.

[3] Cf. al-Ghuzūlī, *Maṭāliʿ*, I, 230.

[4] Cf. below, p. 152, n. 5.

[5] Cf. al-Badrī, fols. 12b-13b, and, for the story, also above, p. 29, n. 1, and below, p. 146, n. 5.

and does not know where he is but thinks that he is still listening to the flutist.[1] We have, however, only a single statement to the effect that the use of hashish improved and was indeed necessary for a musician's performance. The singer in question was a certain Thaqīlīyah (?).[2]

Hashish is stated consistently by its adversaries to be something that saps the user's energy and ability and willingness to work. Implicitly, this was considered its greatest danger to the social fabric. With the help of a general Prophetical tradition, this aspect is usually verbalized by the root *f-t-r* (*futūr* and *mufattir*)[3] as well as the common words for laziness and sluggishness such as *kasal* and *fashal*. Hashish has a numbing effect which causes the excessive sleeping done by addicts and the heaviness in their heads when the drug takes possession of their brains.[4] Addicts stagger about and nod and are drowsy. The word *futūr* is in fact also paraphrased as something that causes "numbness *(khadar)*[5] in the extremities," and the root expressing "numbness" is employed generally to refer to narcotics *(mukhaddir)*.[6] *Futūr* is not among the harmful effects of wine; it is an additional evil trait of hashish.[7]

It is largely in this sense that we must understand the described sexual effects of hashish. We encounter the statement that use of the drug entails "the opening of the gate of desire."[8] This, however,

[1] Cf. al-Badrī, fols. 14b-15a.

[2] Cf. al-Badrī, fol. 21a-b. The information is said to be derived from al-Ghuzūlī's *Maṭāliʿ*, which, however, does not seem to contain it. A subsequent quotation from al-Ghuzūlī by al-Badrī, fol. 25b, can be traced to *Maṭāliʿ*, II, 82. The continuation of the story appears also in Ibn Ḥijjah, *Thamarāt*, I, 40, in a shortened version which makes no reference to hashish and, as printed, calls the man Ibn Naqīlah (Nuqaylah). During a serious illness brought on by excessive eating, he was asked by Badr-ad-dīn (Aḥmad b.) Muḥammad b. aṣ-Ṣāḥib (d. 788/1386): "How are you, Thaqīlīyah (Ibn Ḥijjah: How is the Naqīlīyah)?" He replied: "I am very much afraid that it will get buried with a tooth in it (*mā akhwafanī an takūn madfūnah wa-fīhā nāb*)." If the reading and translation are correct, the name may refer to some dish.

[3] The second conjugation is, I believe, more likely than the fourth, used in *Concordance*, s. v.

[4] Cf. al-Fanārī (above, p. 17).

[5] On the medical use of the term *khadar*, one may compare the monograph by Qusṭā b. Lūqā, as quoted by ar-Rāzī, *Ḥāwī*, I, 42, 51 (Hyderabad 1374 ff./1955 ff.).

[6] According to as-Sakhāwī, *Ḍaw'*, II, 111, Aḥmad b. Muḥammad b. Sulaymān az-Zāhid (d. 819/1416, cf. *GAL, Suppl.*, II, 112) wrote on "Intoxicants, both numbing and intoxicating" (*al-Kalām ʿalā l-muskirāt mukhaddirihā wa-muskirihā*). He probably included also hashish in the former category.

[7] Cf. Ibn Taymīyah, *Fatāwī*, IV, 310, and az-Zarkashī, below, p. 186.

[8] Cf. Ibn Taymīyah, *Fatāwī*, IV, 310, also IV, 326 (*infitāḥ shahwatih*, speaking of *ghubayrā'*).

is not meant to refer to increased sexual urges but rather to the presumed addictive character of the drug.[1] On the contrary, it is stated by physicians that "it cuts off the desire for sexual intercourse," and was therefore esteemed by ascetic Ṣūfīs.[2] "Addicts," we are told, "may think that it strengthens (the ability for) sexual intercourse. This may perhaps be so in the beginning, but then it loosens the sinews because of its cold temper."[3] A theoretical foundation was believed to exist for the assumption that hashish had a debilitating effect with respect to sex, for already Galen, as the Muslims knew, attributed to hemp the medicinal quality of cutting off or drying up the semen.[4] On the other hand, according to al-ʿUkbarī's *Sawāniḥ*, hashish enables the user to have splendid sexual experiences *(mubāsharat al-manākiḥ al-bahīyah)*,[5] and among the inhibitions it removes we also find that of sex, as in the story of Abū Jurthūm.[6] Constant drug use is said to have been accompanied by extraordinary sexual activity in Ibn al-Barīdī,[7] but in another story, we hear about a certain Abū l-Khayr al-ʿAqqād who, on his wedding night, was given a *lubābah* by a friend to help him "to relax with his bride," but the drug merely put him to sleep.[8]

What was believed to be the most pernicious effect of hashish as far as the individual was concerned was that it led to effeminacy *(takhannuth)* or passive homosexuality *(ubnah, ma'būn)*.[9] As we read in az-Zarkashī,[10] it makes the best of fine young men effeminate. Inevitably, hashish is mentioned in connection with homosexuality. It is described as breaking down resistance to sexual advances by its power to intoxicate and to weaken the will.[11] Much was made by

[1] Cf. below, pp. 96 f.

[2] Cf. al-Maqrīzī who seems to continue here his quotation from Ibn Jazlah.

[3] Cf. Dāwūd al-Anṭākī, *Tadhkirah*, I, 200, also quoted in Leclerc's translation of Ibn al-Bayṭār.

[4] Cf. Galen, *De simpl. med.* VII (= XII, 8 Kühn); Dioscurides, *loc. cit.* (above, p. 22, n. 9); Paul of Aegina, ed. Heiberg, II, 220. Galen is cited by al-Maqrīzī.

[5] Cf. al-Badrī, fol. 30a.

[6] Cf. al-Badrī, fols. 10a-b and 12a-b, in the story of Abū Jurthūm, cf. below, p. 146.

[7] Cf. al-Badrī, fol. 47a, in connection with *k-n/tbābatī*.

[8] Cf. al-Badrī, fols. 16b-17a, see also above, p. 31.

[9] Cf. Ibn Taymīyah, *Siyāsah*; adh-Dhahabī, *Kabā'ir*; al-Fanārī, from al-Ḥaddād(ī). Also Ibn Taymīyah, *Fatāwī*, IV, 326 (= II, 254, speaking of *ghubayrā'*), and the passage ascribed to ar-Rāzī, quoted above, p. 74 (n. 4), and below, p. 86, n. 5.

[10] Cf. below, p. 187.

[11] Cf., for instance, below, pp. 156 f., and Fuzūlī, 157.

al-Badrī (fols. 30a ff.) of the combination of the use of hashish and homosexuality.[1] Under the drug's influence, addicts go out "hunting" for young boys. There were special localities, such as Bāb Zuwaylah in Cairo or suburban Būlāq, where they hung out to make contacts. However, when drugging is needed for the scabrous custom, called *dabīb*, of attacking youths while they are asleep in public places such as caravanserais, the verb used is *bannaja* "to drug with *banj*."[2]

Verses on homosexuality and hashish are plentiful,[3] from lines of al-Miʿmār such as

> Mix your hashish with the appropriate amount of clay.
> Chew (it) upon the bed and "kill" it leisurely.
> Eat heavily, for eating is an ornament for you,
> And if you get excited sexually, do not have any but anal intercourse,[4]

and other frankly obscene material to the more sensitive if hardly any more appealing verses comparing hashish, with its darkish green color, to the first down (*ʿidhār*) on a youth's face. Ibn al-ʿAfīf at-Tilimsānī, comparing the locks (*ṣudgh*) with hashish and the mouth (*mabsim*) with wine, furnished the model for a comparison by Muḥibb-ad-dīn Ibn al-Athīr al-Ḥalabī of green hashish with the down and red wine with the mouth.[5] There are verses such as those of Ibn al-Wardī:

---

[1] Cf. also above, p. 66, etc. In al-Maqrīzī, I, 368, as well as in the verse cited II, 414 (above, p. 75, n. 2), drug intoxication is a vice immediately followed by keeping company with beardless boys.

[2] Cf. al-Badrī, fol. 43a, quoting Ibn Makānis (745-794/1345-1392) (cf. *GAL, Suppl.*, II, 7). For *tabnīj*, see above, p. 19.

[3] The subject of homosexuality is introduced by al-Badrī with a quotation from al-ʿUkbarī's *Sawāniḥ*, but how much, if any, of the following material is borrowed from the *Sawāniḥ* is hard to say.

Strangely enough, al-Badrī, fol. 42a-b, quotes verses containing a reference to hashish which seem to be ascribed to Abū Nuwās. If God were to grant him his true wish, he would ask to have each day

> A hand full of hashish, a pound of meat,
> A kilo of bread, and the company of a willing boy.

> *kaffa ḥashīshin wa-riṭla laḥmin*
> *wa-manna khubzin wa-waṣla ʿilqin.*

This could have been invented in imitation of some topic introduced by Abū Nuwās, but as it stands, it is apocryphal.

[4] Cf. al-Badrī, fol. 30a:

> *karbil ḥashīshak wāfiqhā min aṭ-ṭīnah*
> *wa-mḍugh ʿalā l-farsh wa-qtulhā ʿalā ḥīnah*
> *wa-blaʿ thaqīl fa-inna-l-balʿa lak zīnah*
> *wa-(ʾi)n qām ʿalayk fa-lā tankiḥ siwā t-tīnah.*

For *sh*, the ms. has *s* in *al-farsh*. The third line refers to the gluttony associated with hashish.

[5] Cf. al-Badrī, fol. 46a. Information on Ibn al-Athīr al-Ḥalabī is not available. Cf. Ibn al-ʿAfīf, *Dīwān*, 38 (Beirut 1885).

There is a pretty one who says openly:
Souls of the people, live[1]
On my down and my spittle—
My wine and my hashish.[2]

Or those by Nūr-ad-dīn ʿAlī b. Bardbak al-Fakhrī (838-872/1434-1468):[3]

The essential composition of the one I love contains the pleasures of love.
Thus, lovers, take your pleasures and live!
A paste of musk is his mole, his spittle provides
Wine, and his cheeks are hashish.[4]

Of a different character, and just possibly of some historicity, is a long story concerning ʿAlam-ad-dīn, the son, al-Badrī says (fol. 51a-b), of Ṣafī-ad-dīn ʿAbdallāh b. Shukr, a well-known personality generally referred to as aṣ-Ṣāḥib (548-622/1153-1225). There can, however, be little doubt that ʿAlam-ad-dīn was in fact Ibn Shukr's grandson, Aḥmad b. Yūsuf b. aṣ-Ṣafī (d. 688/1289).[5] Anyway, the story goes that ʿAlam-ad-dīn was appointed by his father as a lecturer *(mudarris)* in the Mālikite College founded by him.[6] His lectures were very well attended by legal scholars and much appreciated for their high quality. Yet, ʿAlam-ad-dīn affected a "hippie"-type style of dress and grooming,[7] and he constantly used hashish, in utter disregard of all the conventional and official disap-

---

[1] "Live" in the sense of "obtain sustenance."

[2] Cf. al-Badrī, fol. 46a:
wa-malīḥin qāla jahran
yā nufūsa n-nāsi ʿīshī
min ʿidhāri wa-ruḍābī
bayna khamrī wa-ḥashīshī.

[3] For Ibn Bardbak, cf. as-Sakhāwī, *Ḍaw'*, V, 196 f.

[4] Cf. al-Badrī, fol. 46a:
fī dhāti man ahwāhu ladhdhātu l-hawā
fa-taladhdhadhū yā ʿāshiqūna wa-ʿīshū
maʿjūnu miskin khāluhū wa-ruḍābuhū
minhu s-sulāfu wa-ʿāriḍāhu ḥashīshu
Cf., further, below, p. 154.

[5] Cf., in particular, Ibn Taghrībirdī, *Nujūm*, VII, 378-380. The mix-up between son and grandson would seem to exclude al-ʿUkbarī as al-Badrī's source, although he is quoted immediately before for declaring hashish to be legal. As a contemporary, al-ʿUkbarī is not likely to have made this mistake.

[6] For the Madrasah aṣ-Ṣāḥibīyah, cf. al-Maqrīzī, II, 371.

[7] Resentment of such external features is indicated by Ibn Taymīyah's action, with respect to a shaykh who appeared before him accused of hashish use and impiety, of ordering his Ṣūfī garment *(dalaq)* cut up, the thick growth of the hair on his head shaved, and his nails and moustache clipped, cf. Ibn Kathīr, XIV, 33, *anno* 704/1305, referred to by H. Laoust, in *EI*², III, 951b, *s. v.* Ibn Taymiyya.

proval that provoked. When Ṣafī-ad-dīn died, the incumbent chief judge got the idea of depriving ʿAlam-ad-dīn of the administration and control of the *waqf* endowment of the College. To this end, he had an assembly arranged at which he was ostentatiously to ask ʿAlam-ad-dīn for his legal opinion on the use of hashish, thereby trapping him into an open admission of his addiction and of his sentiments in favor of hashish. Now, the judge on his part was suspected of homosexuality, and it was observed that he was constantly surrounded by a large retinue of beardless slaves. So it came about that when he addressed ʿAlam-ad-dīn in the assembly, asking him for his opinion on "eating hashish which is *waraq ash-shahdānaj*," ʿAlam-ad-dīn stared in dramatic silence at the slaves standing behind the judge long enough for everybody in the audience to become aware of what he had in mind. Finally he broke his silence and said that there was no text forbidding the eating of hashish, whereas homosexuality was forbidden by general consensus, and if the judge was out to pick a fight with him, he in turn was willing to pick a fight with the judge. Thus, the discussion turned to the judge and his slaves, and the judge did not accomplish his iniquitous purpose, quite to the contrary.

Al-Badrī has this story followed by his catharsis for the large amount of space given over by him to lewd verses and anecdotes.[1] He discusses the forbidden character of homosexuality, citing, among other authorities, Ibn Qayyim al-Jawzīyah (d. 751/1350) and the *Taḥrīm al-liwāṭ* by al-Ājurrī (d. 360/970).[2] A good deal of the obscene material had been added by al-Badrī for its own sake. It is without any direct relation to the use of hashish.

The assumption that hashish may cause effeminacy is coupled with remarks that it may lead to something called *diyāthah*. Strangely enough, the scribe of the Fanārī Ms.[3] glossed the term in the margin as indicating, generally, "humbleness, lowliness," with reference to the lexicographer, al-Jawharī. In one way or other, humbleness and lowliness are often stated to be one of the social consequences of the use of hashish, and they are also associated with the lack of energy considered characteristic of the drug user.[4] It is, however, obvious

[1] Cf. above, p. 15.

[2] For al-Ājurrī, cf. F. Sezgin, *GAS*, I, 194 f. This identification, I believe, is correct, but I have no reference to a work by him on this subject.

[3] Above, pp. 17 f. However, al-Jawharī, *Ṣiḥāḥ*, I, 133 (Būlāq 1292), adds the explanation of *dayyūth* as lacking jealousy.

[4] Cf. Ibn Taymīyah, *Fatāwī*, IV, 310.

that in the hashish context, *diyāthah* has its ordinary meaning of being a *dayyūth* "cuckold."[1] We also hear it said that hashish may generate a loss of jealousy *(ghayrah)* such as would be intolerable in a real man. It might easily be suspected that what is really meant here is the fact that an addict might not care whether his wife has other men to support her and thus make it possible for himself to devote all his time to his habit.[2] However, those who spoke of *diyāthah* might have thought primarily of the drug's debilitating effect on will power and sexual desire. It would also seem that "cuckoldry" here was understood by and large not so much as a sexual phenomenon but as a general lack of energy and a man's normal physical desires.

A complete summary of the ravages ascribed to hashish may be found in az-Zarkashī who followed some unnamed authority.[3] In the part of it that deals specifically with physical harm, which incorporates certain traditional medical views on cannabis but naturally goes far beyond that, certain personality changes ascribed to the drug are not forgotten. Az-Zarkashī, or his source, spares no pain to bring together in this one place everything he can think of as detrimental to human beings: "It destroys the mind *(ʿaql)*, cuts short the reproductive capacity, produces elephantiasis *(judhām)*, passes on leprosy *(baraṣ)*, attracts diseases, produces tremulousness *(riʿshah)*,[4] makes the mouth smell foul, dries up the semen, causes the hair of the eyebrows to fall out, burns the blood, causes cavities in the teeth, brings forth the hidden disease,[5] harms the intestines, makes the limbs inactive, causes a shortage of breath,[6] generates strong illusions *(hawas)*, diminishes the powers (of the soul), reduces

[1] Cf. Ibn Taymīyah, *Siyāsah*; *Fatāwī*, IV, 326 (= II, 254, speaking of *ghubayrā'*); adh-Dhahabī, *Kabā'ir*; al-Fanārī.

[2] According to the lexical sources used by Lane, *diyāthah* may in fact signify pimping for one's wife. Ibn Ḥajar al-Haytamī, *Zawājir*, II, 150, speaks of the hashish eater's *diyāthah* "against *(ʿalā)* one's wife and womenfolk, let alone strange women." This may have to be understood to refer to pandering. Cf., further, K. Vollers, in *ZDMG*, L (1896), 625, and Ibn Ḥazm, *The Dove's Neck-Ring*, trans. A. R. Nykl, 188 (Paris 1931).

[3] Cf. the Arabic text, below, pp. 178 f.

[4] For the medical understanding of *riʿshah*, cf. the first volume of the edition of ar-Rāzī's *Ḥāwī*. There ar-Rāzī also quotes aṭ-Ṭabarī, *Firdaws*, 194 f.

[5] In a brief treatise wrongly ascribed to ar-Rāzī on "The Hidden Disease," which is preserved in the General Library in Rabat, the expression is used as a euphemism for *ubnah* (above, p. 82, n. 9). For *kryphia* diseases, cf. K. Deichgräber, *Medicus gratiosus*, 101 f. (Mainz 1970).

[6] *Tuḍayyiq an-nafs* could mean "causes anxiety," but *nafas* is required by the rhyme word *hawas*. Cf., for instance, as-Sakhāwī, *Ḍaw'*, I, 77, l. 9: *la-ḍāqat al-anfās* "(I) would run out of breath."

modesty *(ḥayā')*,[1] makes the complexion *(al-alwān)* yellow, blackens the teeth, riddles the liver with holes,[2] inflames the stomach,[3] and leaves in its wake a bad odor in the mouth as well as a film and diminished vision in the eye and increased pensiveness in the imagination.[4] It[5] belongs to the blameworthy characteristics of hashish that it generates in those who eat it laziness and sluggishness. It turns a lion into a beetle[6] and makes a proud man humble and a healthy man sick. If he eats, he cannot get enough. If he is spoken to, he does not listen.[7] It makes the well-spoken person dumb, and the sound person stupid. It takes away every manly virtue and puts an end to youthful prowess. Furthermore, it destroys the mind *(fikrah)*, stunts all natural talent, and blunts the sharpness of the mental endowment. It produces gluttony, making eating (the addict's) preoccupation *(fannah)* and sleep for him a characteristic situation *(maẓannah)*. But he is remote from slumber,[8] driven out

---

[1] A marginal note in the Gotha Ms. of az-Zarkashī calls attention to the fact that the effect of hashish upon *ḥayā'* was mentioned before as one of the effects that hashish shares with wine. The scribe tentatively suggests a correction to *al-ḥīlah* "resourcefulness," or the like. This emendation shares with many others in history the fate of being ingenious but hardly correct.

[2] *N-q-b* seems to refer to ulceration (cirrhosis?) of the liver. Ms. A of az-Zarkashī and the Princeton Ms. of al-Aqfahsī suggest the synonymous *th-q-b*. Ibn Taymīyah, *Fatāwī*, IV, 326 (= II, 254), speaking of the effects of *ghubayrā'*, says that "it makes the liver like a sponge *(sifanj)*." According to al-Badrī, fol. 55a, an experiment by one of the sages tested the pernicious action of hashish by putting some of it on an animal liver and letting it lie there for a while. It made the liver full of holes *(mankhūrah* [?] *mubakhkhashah)* like a sponge.

[3] "Drying out the moisture of the stomach," says Ibn al-Bayṭār, citing Galen, *De alimentorum facultatibus*, I, 34 (= VI, 550 Kühn). The original Greek is *kakostomachos*.

[4] Cf. above, p. 74, n. 3. In his *Takrīm al-ma'īshah*, al-Qasṭallānī mentioned as the ill effects of the use of hashish that it causes headache, darkens the sight, causes constipation, and dries up the semen; it is useful against flatulence and dandruff, cf. al-Aqfahsī, fol. 20a.

[5] The text, from here to the end of the quotation but with the exclusion of the verses, appears in Ibn Ghānim (above, pp. 6 f.). Ibn Ghānim and az-Zarkashī presumably used the same source. On the other hand, al-Aqfahsī, fols. 21b-22a, would seem to have used az-Zarkashī.

[6] The scribe of the Gotha Ms. has a marginal note referring to the Prophetical tradition branding *ju'al* as the creature most contemptible in the eyes of God.

[7] The last three sentences appear in *Qam'* in a different sequence. *Qam'*, fols. 275b-276a, adds rather dramatically: "If you say in front of him: *ṭāq*, he is frightened right away. It is as if he has been burdened with something that is too much for him to carry *(idhā qult bayn yadayh ṭāq inza'aj li-waqtih wa-ka'annah taḥammal mā lā yuṭāq)*."

[8] The rhyming words apparently are *sinah*, *jannah*, and *la'nah*. However, the Princeton Ms. of al-Aqfahsī seems to vocalize *sunnah*.

from Paradise, and threatened with God's curse unless he gnashes his teeth in repentance and puts his confidence in God. It has well been said:

> The smallest physical harm it causes, and there is plenty of it,
> Is immorality, insanity, and mental exhaustion."[1]

This long and somewhat disorganized catalogue mainly of the physical evils of hashish use is preceded by a briefer but no less awesome enumeration of the effects it has on the user's religion, that is, his morality and his attitude toward the religious duties of Islam. These hashish shares with wine, whereas the physical effects are all its own. Nevertheless, they were particularly objectionable according to the standards of Muslim society. Not infrequently we hear about the hashish user becoming lax in the fulfillment of his religious duties such as prayer and fasting and also forgetting the confession of faith *in extremis* when it becomes necessary for him to pronounce it.[2] The often repeated standard formula of the legal adversaries of hashish says that habituation to the drug "bars a person from the remembrance of God and from prayer" *(yaṣudd ʿan dhikr Allāh wa-ʿan aṣ-ṣalāh)*. *Qamʿ* alludes to the dire fate that awaits the drug user in the other world, for he will be unable to remember, when he is on the point of death, the two sentences of the confession of faith and forget the common formula about taking refuge in God.[3]

---

[1] For *nishāf*, no doubt the correct reading, cf. also below, p. 90. "Dryness" leads, as also indicated in Steingass' *Persian-English Dictionary*, to the further meanings of "dryness in the mouth from extreme hunger; folly, thoughtlessness," resulting from the drying out of the brain.

In al-Badrī, fols. 55b-56a, the verse is ascribed to a certain Shihāb-ad-dīn Aḥmad ath-Thaqafī (?). It is preceded by two additional verses:

> May God curse hashish and those who eat it.
> It is as bad as wine is good.
> As it (wine) gladdens, it (hashish) saddens, and it (hashish) pains
> As it (wine) sustains. Its end is foolishness (?).
>
> *laḥā llāhu l-ḥashīsha wa-ākilīhā*
> *la-qad khabuthat kamā ṭāba s-sulāfu*
> *kamā tuṣbī ka-dhā tuḍnī wa-tushqī*
> *kamā tashfī wa-ghāyatuhā l-khirāfu.*

The last line, as in az-Zarkashī, was certainly borrowed by the author from a common source, even if he lived before the time of az-Zarkashī. The same would seem to apply also in case the ascription of the three verses in al-Kutubī, *Fawāt*, I, 9, to Jamāl-ad-dīn Ibrāhīm b. Sulaymān Ibn an-Najjār (590-651/1194-1253) should happen to be correct.

[2] Cf. al-Badrī, fols. 55b and 57a. For disrespect toward the month of Ramaḍān, cf. below, p. 128.

[3] Cf. *Qamʿ*, fol. 276b.

Az-Zarkashī speaks of "intoxication, destruction of the mind *(fikr)*, forgetfulness *(nisyān adh-dhikr)* (in this case, apparently not meaning forgetting to think of God, but forgetfulness in general), the vulgarization of secrets, the commission of evil actions, the loss of modesty *(ḥayā')*, great stubbornness, the lack of manly virtue, the suppression of jealousy, wastefulness, keeping company with the devil, the omission of prayer, and the falling into unlawful activities." Nor is this all. Someone else is quoted as having totaled up the religious and worldly harm done by hashish and to have come up with no less than 120 items.[1] Fortunately, they are not enumerated.

Other, concise descriptions of the frightful consequences of the use of hashish tend to be eclectic, mentioning the one or other presumed effect of hashish on the addict's body, mind, character, and social status. In his large handbook for government officials, al-Qalqashandī (d. 821/1418) thus informs the reader that hashish "ruins the temper by producing the effect of desiccation in it and generating a preponderance of black bile. It ruins the mind *(dhihn)*, forms bad character qualities, and lowers the user's standing in the eyes of the people, in addition to many other blameworthy qualities."[2] Still later, Dāwūd al-Anṭākī, in his *Tadhkirah*,[3] cuts down the list to reporting that after initially causing joy, hashish produces narcosis, laziness, stupor, the weakening of sense perception, foul breath, the debilitation of liver and stomach, dropsy, and the ruination of color and complexion.

After all these sorry tales of dire calamities connected with the use of hashish, it comes as somewhat of a letdown to find that the comparatively early poem of al-Isʿirdī points merely to the greenish-gray complexion of the face as a physical sign of hashish addiction.[4] The long poem by the author of *Qamʿ* is somewhat more specific but also rather restrained. The physical effects produced by *barsh* are the desiccation of the flesh of the face[5] and the withdrawal (?) of the locks *(kh-s-f al-aṣdāgh)*, to which the author adds dryness of the mouth:

---

1 Cf. the statement on the *siwāk*, above, p. 76, n. 1.

2 Cf. al-Qalqashandī, *Ṣubḥ*, II, 146 (Cairo 1331/1913).

3 *Tadhkirah*, I, 200.

4 Cf. above, p. 77.

5 But note what Dozy, *Supplément*, II, 673a, has to say about the metaphorical usage of *nāshif (ar-ra's)*. Still, I do not believe that in this particular instance, something mental rather than physical is meant.

> Their heads have dried up. Thus, there is no good in them.
> The dry elements follow each other all the time in their bodies.
> There is no spittle in their mouths and no freshness (?) in it.
> Their condition has become a fright.
> Their locks are withdrawn (?), turned down,
> Laid bare, eclipsed, sliding (?).[1]

But he also states that hashish has an emaciating effect, and he remarks upon the user's constant drowsiness and apathy:

> They stagger but without the emotion derived from drunkenness.
> They shrink in size and do not appear tall.
> Great God! It is a disease that whenever
> It enters the body, you see (it turning into) a dreadful place.
> They doze. Thus, step upon their necks
> And make their breasts sandals for you.[2]
> They chew on the smelling breath in their mouths.
> Thus, get on top of them, if you wish to be well-off.[3]

If the last lines are understood here correctly, the attitude recommended toward addicts would not just be to show contempt for them but to exploit their self-induced incapacity for one's own advantage. After all, users under the influence of hashish are believed to be amenable to the most bizarre suggestions since the drug has the

---

[1] Cf. *Qamʿ*, fol. 282b:
nashifat ruʾūsuhumū fa-lā khayran bihā
wa-n-nāshifātu bi-jismihim tatawālā
lā rīqa fī fīhim wa-lā rīyan (?) bihī
aḥwāluhum qad aṣbaḥat ahwālā
aṣdāghuhum makhsūfatun mankūsatun
makshūfatun maksūfatun tatazāllā (?).
For *rīyan*, the ms. has something like *'db'*, but *adaban* "proper behavior" seems unlikely in the context. For *makhsūfatun*, the ms. has *maḥsūfatun*, and the reading of *tatazāllā* is uncertain. I do not know what the idiom about the locks means, hardly the thinning of hair, as this would not go well with the rest of the descriptive terms used. Possibly, it refers to holding the head low in shame (?).

[2] Cf. the verse quoted in Ibn Ḥajar al-Haytamī (above, p. 11):
It (the drug) involves contempt by means of sandals and stick
For the stupid and stubborn immoral person.

fīhā l-ihānatu bi-n-niʿāli wa-bi-l-ʿaṣā
li-d-dāʿiri l-mahbūli wa-l-mutaʿabbidi.
For *mutaʿabbid* "stubborn," cf. Steingass' *Persian-English Dictionary.*

[3] *Yatamāyalūna bi-ghayri sukrin muṭribin*
yataqāṣarūna wa-lā yurawna ṭiwālā
Allāhu akbaru innahū dāʾun matā
mā ḥalla fī jismin tarāhu mahālā
yatanāwamūna fa-dus ʿalā aʿnāqihim
wa-jʿal ṣudūrahumū ladayka niʿālā
yatamāḍaghūna r-rīḥa fī afwāhihim
fa-qṣid ʿulāhum in aradta nawālā.
For *wa-lā yurawna*, the ms. has *wlyrwn.*

power to break the will. Thus, as Ibn an-Najjār states in his *Zawājir*,[1] if one were to say to one of them, "Piss!," he would do so at once.

We have already seen that the great potency of hashish stands comparison with killing in its effects, in puns on the term "to kill" used in connection with the preparation and use of hashish.[2] "The murderous hashish eater" *(al-ḥashīshīyu lladhī yaqtulu)* was considered a suitable metaphor for the dangerous attraction exercised by the beloved's locks.[3] This would not seem to refer directly to the murderous propensities of the sectarian assassins but rather to the powerful effects of hashish. It may also embody a play upon the "killing" of hashish, as is apparently the case in a verse stating that "the green one" is "a *ḥashīshah* that makes every man a *ḥashīshī* (assassin) unbeknown to himself."[4] However this may be, there are other verses by Ibn al-ʿAfīf at-Tilimsānī, describing the state of the poor Ṣūfī under the influence of hashish as remote from the land of the living:

> This poor one whom you see
> Like as a chick thrown to the ground featherless
> Has been killed by hashish intoxication,
> Killing being the custom of hashish.[5]

The influence of hashish on the mind, its "mind-changing" and personality-changing quality, is never quite overlooked even in the discussion of its physical and religious effects. It was the most famous and most frightening and tantalizing aspect of hashish use. The drug was often believed to cause insanity in the habitual user. Such in-

---

[1] Cf. al-Badrī, fol. 17b, and al-Bakrī, *Kawākib*. Uninhibited urination under the influence of hashish is mentioned in the story of Abū Jurthūm, cf. al-Badrī, fol. 10b, and below, p. 146. On the other hand, al-Badrī, fol. 49b, quotes a poem by Ibrāhīm b. Asʿad al-Irbilī al-Laqānī which speaks of hashish as eliminating the constant need for urination that comes from drinking wine.

[2] Cf. above, pp. 59 f.

[3] Cf. Ibn al-ʿAfīf at-Tilimsānī, as quoted by aṣ-Ṣafadī, *Wāfī*, ed. S. Dedering, III, 133.

[4] Cf. an-Nuwayrī, *Nihāyah*, XI, 29.

[5] Cf. aṣ-Ṣafadī, *Wāfī*, III, 133. In al-Badrī, the verses seem to be ascribed to the amīr Sayf-ad-dīn ʿAlī b. ʿUmar al-Mushidd (602-655/1205(6)-1257, cf. al-Ghuzūlī, *Maṭāliʿ*, I, 50; Ibn Kathīr, XIII, 197; al-Badrī, above, p. 14, n. 2, wrote a "*Mukhtaṣar* entitled *Naẓārat Dīwān al-Mushidd*") in this form:

> I am the killed one whom you see
> Like as a chick thrown to the ground featherless.
> They killed the hashish unjustly,
> Killing being the custom of hashish.

Here it may be better to translate "being killed," instead of "killing." This, however, is hardly intended in the version of Ibn al-ʿAfīf.

sanity might be assumed to be temporary but by and large was considered to be a permanent personality change. In the most commonly used Arabic words, hashish "changes the mind" *(tughayyir al-ʿaql)*, or it "makes it absent" or "remote" *(tughayyib)*, removing it from reality. Since the *ʿaql* is what distinguishes man from irrational animals, the effect of hashish could in this sense be conceived as turning its users into dumb animals. There can be no doubt, we are told, that taking hashish has the effect of producing transgression *(taʿaddī)* with respect to normal mental processes *(intiẓām)* of word and deed that draw their perfection from the legal and customary activity of the light of the intellect.[1] By dissolving the moist elements in the body and thereby causing vapors to ascend to the brain, the *ghubayrā'* produces pernicious fancies *(khayālāt)*, and by weakening the mind, it opens up the gate of fantasy *(khayāl)*.[2] This was the way in which physicians and those hostile to hashish put it. The self-styled "elite" *(al-khāṣṣah)* who defended the use of it, called it "the morsel of thought and remembrance."[3] They extolled the pleasure hashish exerted upon the imagination *(al-ladhdhah al-wahmīyah)* as one of its chief attractions,[4] and the fancies *(khayāl)* it engendered were poetically described as most soothing and idyllic: "At times, I see the world as castles. At other times, I see it as lands and gardens around me."[5] The mind-distorting effect of hashish was elegantly hinted at in the phrase: "It moves unmoving resolution to the noblest of places,"[6] which a poet addicted to *k-n/tbābatī* paraphrased in these verses:

---

[1] The text of az-Zarkashī, below, p. 185, shows some variant readings.

[2] Cf. Ibn Taymīyah, *Fatāwī*, IV, 325 (= II, 253). Az-Zarkashī's *tabkhīr-hā (tabakhkhur-hā) (fī) ad-dimāgh* has become *taḥayyuz-hā fī d-dimāgh* in the indirect quotation in al-Fanārī.

Galen, *De alimentorum facultatibus*, I, 34 (VI, 550 Kühn), mentions the warm and at the same time *pharmakōdēs* vapor hemp sends up to the head. Before, he speaks of crushed hemp seeds eaten together with other confections. Thus, the "vapor" may possibly allude to narcotic effects.

[3] Cf. Ibn Taymīyah, *Fatāwī*, IV, 312 and 310. In the latter passage, it is "little morsel," presumably the more correct reading. Cf. above, pp. 36 f.

[4] Cf. al-Badrī, fol. 30a, from al-ʿUkbarī's *Sawāniḥ*.

[5] Cf. al-Badrī, fol. 49b, in verses by Ibn al-Aqsāsī (above, p. 64, n. 1). These verses are supposed to be critical of hashish but, except for the concluding line, go all out to list its supposed good qualities.

[6] Cf. Ibn Taymīyah, *Fatāwī*, IV, 312 and 310. In IV, 310, he adds that hashish is considered "useful for the road." This could mean that it serves to mitigate the hardships Ṣūfīs have to suffer in their peregrinations, but it may rather refer to the fact mentioned also elsewhere that hashish can be consumed in the streets without any further ado, in contrast to wine.

In India my heart has developed
A longing for those places.
K-n/tbābatī, light of my eye,
You have stirred unmoving (feelings) in me.[1]

As suggested by Ibn Taymīyah, the phrase was meant to call attention to the help hashish offered to the pious in their religious devotions, but it no doubt aimed at the drug's supposed ability to allow the human mind to go beyond the limitations of reality. The distortion of the mind was, it seems, a kind of religious experience for the addicts. At least, they claimed it to be such as in the verses of al-Isʿirdī speaking of the "secret" of the drug that permits "the spirit to ascend to the highest points in a heavenly ascension *(miʿrāj)* of disembodied understanding."[2] The constant harping upon the increase in understanding associated with hashish at times naturally provoked a strong reaction, as in these bitingly humorous verses by Ibn al-ʿAfīf at-Tilimsānī when his friends wanted him to participate in their hashish party:

If hashish were able to give an increase in understanding,
Donkeys would achieve high rank in their understanding.[3]

The mental changes observable in the addict made him a fool in the eyes of the common people, someone not to be trusted to react rationally in any way. The vast majority of the stories told about hashish harp upon this aspect and the variety of consequences connected with it. The famous report of the Assassins' conditioning to fanatic devotion through the agency of drugs providing a foretaste of Paradise probably found so much attention because being the first circumstantial description of hashish(?)-induced hallucinations, it exalted the alleged mind-changing powers of the drug.[4] The popular appeal of the conceit of almost miraculous mental change is proved, if proof is needed, by the *Arabian Nights* and the

---

[1] Cf. al-Badrī, fol. 47a:
fī l-Hindi aḏḥā fu'ādī
yaṣbū li-tilka l-amākin
k-n/tbābatī nūra ʿaynī
ḥarrakti ʿindī sawākin.
The poet may be Fulayfil.

[2] Cf. below, p. 163, verse 8.

[3] Cf. al-Badrī, fol. 56a, and below, p. 137.
wa-law anna l-ḥashīsha tazīdu fahman
la-nāla bi-fahmihī r-rutaba l-ḥimāru.

[4] Cf. above, p.43.

way the very late stages of the work view hashish. The question, "Are you a hashish eater" *(ant ta'kul al-ḥashīsh)*, is addressed to someone who makes a seemingly incredible statement, suggesting that he is a mere fool.[1] And when the fisherman, Khalīfah, hedges a foolish plan in the middle of the night, it is said that it must be the hashish he has consumed that is speaking to him, even though there is otherwise no indication whatever in the story that he had used the drug.[2] The *Arabian Nights* also speak about the old roué who had spent all his possessions on beautiful boys and girls. Hashish was the only real consolation left to him. So one day he went to the public bath, withdrew to a lonely spot where he could be alone with himself and swallowed a piece of hashish. This provoked in him exciting dreams of glory and sex, depicted in detail in the continuation of the story and illustrating loss of contact with reality.[3] Another very elaborate description of the dreams of hashish *(banj)* eaters no longer entered the mainstream tradition of the *Arabian Nights*, but is found only among some late manuscript material. This is the story of a fisherman who is under the influence of the drug and thinks that a street in the moonlight is in reality a river, and a dog on the street a big fish, which he then attempts to catch. His further adventures involve the town's judge as a suspected participant in drug revelries, once again an illustration of the popular tendency to ascribe to the most visible representatives of the law the vices that they more than anybody else were charged with avoiding and suppressing.[4] ʿAlī b. Sūdūn al-Bashbughawī tells about hashish eaters who imagine the ocean to be sweet syrup, the fish in it peeled bananas, and the nets to catch them in to be made of pancakes.[5] Az-Zarkashī had also already reported that he had been told that a person befuddled by

---

[1] Cf. *Arabian Nights*, I, 173, trans. Littmann, I, 257.

[2] Cf. *Arabian Nights*, IV, 161, trans. Littmann, V, 516. However, O. Rescher, in his discussion of hashish in the *Arabian Nights*, in *Der Islam*, IX (1919), 85 f., points out that the reference to hashish is not to be found in M. Habicht's edition, IV, 330.

[3] Cf. *Arabian Nights*, I, 692-694, trans. Littmann, II, 193-195.

[4] From Ms. Wortley Montague, according to R. Burton's translation. It was used by M. Henning, in his German translation, XXIII, 135-160, and was referred to by O. Rescher, *loc. cit.*

Under the influence of wine, a drinker may think that a moonlit area is a river, cf. Ibn ar-Raqīq al-Qayrawānī, *Quṭb as-surūr*, ed. A. al-Jundī, 391 (Damascus 1389/1969).

[5] From F. Kern, *Neuere ägyptische Humoristen und Satiriker*, in *Mitt. des Seminars für Or. Sprachen, Westas. Studien*, IX (1906), 34, cited by O. Rescher, *loc. cit.*

hashish thought that the moon was a deep pool of water, and he did not dare to go toward it.[1]

The loss of contact with reality, the ordinary world of the senses, "existence" *(wujūd)*, as a result of the action of hashish expressed by the root *gh-y-b*, may be partial, with the addict under the influence of the drug merely forgetting to do what he was supposed to do or doing it wrongly. Thus, we hear about a singer, Abū ṭ-Ṭayyib Karawīyah (?),[2] sent by the littérateur Aḥmad b. Barakah to buy pomegranates and bring them to the bath. He forgets about his task, wanders aimlessly from place to place, and returns to the bath only late in the evening. Or someone, the story goes, went out to buy barley for his mount and grapes for his wife, then gives the grapes to the animal and the barley to his wife.[3] Complete temporary loss of contact with reality is described in a story about people noticing a man on a horse who was riding in the countryside not knowing what he was doing, opening his knapsack, eating, being thrown by the horse, continuing in his sleep, then waking up, bleeding profusely and not knowing where he was.[4]

The user might at times have aspired to this state of unawareness of everything around him and considered it among the most desirable effects of hashish. However, when it became something permanent, it produced an individual useless to society and to himself, graphically described in verses by al-Hā'im (d. 887/1482):

> How many a person killed by hashish is to be found in al-Junaynah
> Who would not wake up, not even at the blast of the trumpet.[5]
> Among its effects the green one has given him
> The ears of a deaf man and the eye of a blind man.[6]

At al-Junaynah ("The Little Garden"), near Bāb ash-Sha'rīyah,[7]

---

[1] Cf. below, p. 181, and also, p. 145.

[2] Cf. al-Badrī, fols. 15b-16a, mentioned above, p. 67, n. 3, and elsewhere. For Ibn Barakah, cf. as-Sakhāwī, *Ḍaw'*, I, 248; al-Badrī, fols. 25a and 121b.

[3] Cf. al-Badrī, fol. 11a.

[4] Cf. al-Badrī, fol. 11a.

[5] That is, the trumpet of the Day of Judgment.

[6] Cf. al-Badrī, fol. 18a:

> *kam bi-l-Junaynati min qatīli ḥashīshatin*
> *lā yastafīqu wa-lā bi-nafkhi ṣ-ṣūri*
> *wahabat lahū l-khaḍrā'u min af'ālihā*
> *ādhāna uṭrūshin wa-'ayna ḍarīri.*

On al-Hā'im, who is often cited by al-Badrī, cf. *GAL*, 2nd ed., II, 22, *Suppl.*, II, 12. Cf. also the verses quoted below, p. 98.

[7] Cf. al-Maqrīzī, I, 383. Al-Junaynah is also described by al-Maqrīzī as being located in the Ṭabbālah estate (below, p. 137). For the Sha'rīyah Gate, cf.

one could see derelicts lying around "like hospital patients" *(kaḍuʿafāʾ al-bīmāristān)*,[1] crazed like the inmates of an asylum and quite oblivious to the world around them.

Devoted to wine as he was, Abū Nuwās was able to sing:

> Give me to drink till you see me
> Think that a rooster is a donkey.[2]

A hashish eater might expect to "see a camel as similar to a gnat."[3] The same idea was phrased much better and more succinctly by the author of *Qamʿ*: Those under the influence of *barsh* have the illusion that "a gnat is a cow" *(an-nāmūsah gāmūsah)*.[4]

5. Habituation to Hashish and its Cure

It was apparently believed quite generally that the user of hashish acquired a constant craving for it and was rarely able to break the habit. Addiction was assumed to grow always more compulsive and eventually lead to complete physical and mental ruin. In addition to "eating" and the like, a number of words were employed for the taking of the drug, among them *akhadha*, *tanāwala*, or, most consistently, *istaʿmala*. Very commonly, however, we also find the term *taʿāṭā* associated with it. In a way, it is merely a synonym of the other verbs in the sense of "to take," but it also has the approximate meaning of "being concerned with (something constantly, also, in a professional manner)." In philosophical usage, it may correspond, for instance, to Greek *melein* as in *taʿāṭī* (also *muʿānāt* which likewise occurs in connection with hashish) *al-mawt* for *meletē thanatou* "the concern or preoccupation with death." *Taʿāṭā* appears to be something like a technical term suggesting constant concern with some habit. It is used in this sense also in connection with wine and many other matters as it is with hashish.

A more concrete hint at the tendency toward addictiveness among hashish users can be seen in the concept of "desire" *(shahwah, ishtahā)*. These unfortunate people "get drunk on (hashish) and desire it as wine drinkers desire wine."[5] A little wine or a small

W. Popper, *Egypt and Syria under the Circassian Sultans*, 24, 32 ff. Cf. also above, p. 80.

[1] Cf. al-Badrī, fol. 18a.

[2] Cf. Abū Nuwās, *Dīwān*, 269.

[3] Cf. al-Badrī, fol. 10a.

[4] Cf. *Qamʿ*, fol. 275b.

[5] Cf. Ibn Taymīyah, *Siyāsah*; adh-Dhahabī, *Kabāʾir*.

quantity of hashish (but not of *banj*) calls for more,[1] thus requiring constantly increased and more frequent doses and, in any case, a continuation of the habit. The desire for hashish is greater than that for wine so that hashish eaters become unable to do without it.[2] A legal distinction is made between things forbidden by the religious law but "desired by the souls," and things which "the souls do not desire." Among the latter, there are, for instance, blood and the meat of animals not ritually slaughtered. Among the former, we must count drugs that cause pleasure such as hashish, as do wine and fornication, but, again, not *banj* the effect of which is of a different sort.[3] The soul's "desire" was usually something that man had a hard time to fight and get rid of, and success, even if he made an honest effort, was rare. With respect to hashish, the soul's desire was easily equivalent to addiction, to a habit hard or impossible to kick.

When the early literature on hashish tells us that Shaykh Ḥaydar ate hashish daily[4] or that, according to al-Jawbarī in the early thirteenth century, there were those who could not stay away from it,[5] this no doubt referred to some kind of addiction. But we also find it stated expressly that the physical and mental changes caused by the drug were believed to provoke a habitual need for it: "Among the greatest physical harm *(dāʾ)* caused by it is the fact that habitual users *(mutaʿāṭī)* of it are hardly ever able to repent of it because of the effect it has upon their temper."[6] The user "cannot separate from it and leave it alone *(lā yufāriq-hā)*." "One of the properties of hashish is that its user cannot give it up."[7] The technical secular term used in this connection is *qaṭaʿa* "to cut." In the religious language of Muslim scholars, it is "to repent" *(tāba)* as indicative of every act involving the renunciation of sin. And *istatāba* is used in connection with "asking someone to give up" the habit of "eating mind-changing hashish."[8]

---

[1] Cf. ar-Rāfiʿī, *apud* az-Zarkashī, below, p. 189. In connection with wine, cf., e. g., as-Sarakhsī, *Mabsūṭ*, XXIV, 3, 9 (Cairo 1324-1331).

[2] Cf. adh-Dhahabī, *Kabāʾir*: *ḥattā lā yaṣbirū ʿanhā*. This phrase does not appear in the text of Ibn Taymīyah, *Siyāsah*.

[3] Cf. Ibn Taymīyah, *Fatāwī*, IV, 304, 312.

[4] Cf. above, pp. 45 and 52.

[5] Cf. below, p. 158, further p. 152, n. 2.

[6] Cf. az-Zarkashī, below, p. 179. The statement follows upon the one quoted above, pp. 86 f. Two mss. have *muʿāniyahā*, for *mutaʿāṭiyahā*.

[7] Cf. al-Badrī, fol. 17b, perhaps continuing the quotation from Ibn an-Najjār's *Zawājir*. Cf. also al-Bakrī, *Kawākib*.

[8] Cf., for instance, Ibn Kathīr, XIV, 33 (above, p. 84, n. 7).

A very vivid description of the situation is given in *Qamʿ*: "The user *(mustaʿmil,* of *barsh)* finds no escape from it and no way whatever to repent and give it up *(at-tawbah minhu)*, nor is he able to obtain any freedom *(infikāk)*. For were his spirit to get to the maw and his soul to the throat, he would think that repentance is what is difficult for him. So he would wish to repair his soul and his breath by saying to those around him: 'Bring me the leaf,' or, 'Bring me the box(es) *(al-ḥuqq)*.'"[1] This, if I understand the text correctly, means that when the addict feels miserable because of his craving for the drug, he has no thought of trying to resist the craving and get off the drug. His only thought is of having some of it given to him to pacify his compulsive urge.

There were those who used hashish around the clock, "at all the prayer times,"[2] with the result that they were completely lost to reality:

> A visitor of *zīh* for whom its people have unceasingly
> Shown humility, prayerful worship, and activity.
> There is nobody among them but forgetful of existence,
> Submerged in the world beyond reality, unceasingly.[3]

An anecdote tells about an addict who under the influence of hashish boarded a boat on the shore of the Nile in Cairo and fell asleep. The sailors, ready to leave, were unable to rouse him. When he eventually woke up, the boat was well on its way to Upper Egypt. The addict began to miss his *zīh* and asked the sailors to set him ashore. He threatened to commit suicide by throwing himself into the river if they would not do it. Thus, they put him ashore, and once there he walked back to Cairo in one day and one night.[4]

For occasional and, presumably, accidental overdoses of cannabis, the medical authorities recommended certain procedures. One of al-Maqrīzī's sources (Ibn Jazlah?)[5] mentioned his observation that "a person who has eaten hashish and notices that its effect is taking

---

[1] Cf. *Qamʿ*, fol. 276b.

[2] Cf. al-Badrī, fol. 18a, elaborating on this subject.

[3] Cf. al-Badrī, fol. 18a:

> *wa-wāridi zīhin lam yazal fīhi ahluhū*
> *khushūʿan rukūʿan sujjadan dāʾimī l-ʿamal*
> *wa-mā minhumū illā ʿan-i-l-kawni dhāhilun*
> *wa-mustaghriqun fī ʿālami l-ghaybi lam yazal.*

Cf. also above, pp. 95 f.

[4] Cf. al-Badrī, fol. 17b.

[5] It is pure fancy to speak of the great Rāzī, as is done by al-Badrī, fol. 7b, who would thereby be credited with the use of the word *ḥashīshah*.

place and he wants to get rid of it pours into his nostrils some drops of olive oil and eats some sour milk." He adds that "swimming in running water breaks and weakens the strength of the drug's effect, and sleep stops it." It is doubtful whether this reported observation was more accurate and true than another observation immediately preceding it and ascribed to the same person that "many poisonous animals such as snakes flee when they smell the smell of hemp." Ibn al-Bayṭār recommended pumping the stomach through vomiting induced by butter and hot water as well as sorrel juice,[1] and Dāwūd al-Anṭākī, in his *Tadhkirah*, also recommended vomiting and purgation by means of laxatives and fruit juices.

However, the cure of addiction was not to be achieved by such simple means which, moreover, presupposed willingness on the part of the user. It could happen at times that lack of means forced the addict to "repent" and give up his habit, but such "repentance of bankruptcy" *(tawbat al-iflās)* was no real cure and as a rule did not last long. There was many a poor Ṣūfī, we are told, who repented of his hashish habit *(taʿāṭī maʿlūmih)* but said that if he only had money, he would not let his friends (and, apparently, himself) go without food and the opportunity to get high *(insiṭāl)*. The true addict, however, would not show himself perturbed by the vagaries of fate and would not consider it enough of an excuse to pretend giving up the habit:

> I am satisfied with a morsel of porridge
> And a round pill of hashish.
> Why should I reproach time from which individual
> Destiny proceeds, by complaining about (lack of) means?[2]

Since hashish was financially within the reach of most, breaking the habit required some miracle or the intervention of some especially holy man. Az-Zarkashī[3] tells us about Shaykh ʿAlī al-Ḥarīrī in

---

[1] On sorrel *(ḥummāḍ)* as a tonic, cf. Meyerhof, in his ed. and trans. of Maimonides, 74.

[2] Cf. al-Badrī, fol. 56a-b:

> *ana rāḍin bi-luqmatin min dashīshah*
> *wa-bi-qurṣin mudawwarin min ḥashīshah*
> *wa-li-mā-dhā uʿātibu d-dahra wa-l-aq-*
> *dāru tajrī minhū bi-dhammi l-maʿīshah.*

The meter *(khafīf)* requires a short second syllable for *anā*. The poet of the verses is said to have been a certain al-Jaʿbarī, reacting to those Ṣūfī complaints.

[3] Cf. below, p. 180. The Ḥarīrī passage was omitted from two of the mss. available, see above, p. 10.

Damascus who considered the habitual use *(taʿāṭī)* of hashish a greater crime than drinking wine, and he held the eater of hashish deserving of the *ḥadd* penalty more than alcoholics. This Shaykh al-Ḥarīrī was the founder of the fraternity named after him, who died on 26 Ramaḍān 645/22 January 1248. Religious scholars took the dimmest view of his orthodoxy in matters of belief and practice. His son, Muḥammad (d. 651/1253), was praised for repudiating the practices of his father's followers.[1] All the more so does az-Zarkashī's testimony to al-Ḥarīrī's aversion for a drug much used by Ṣūfīs in his time and environment ring true. "This Ḥarīrī," az-Zarkashī further tells us, "was very hard on habitual users of hashish. One of his followers sent a messenger to him to upbraid him for (his attitude). The Shaykh said to the messenger: If the man mentioned is one of my followers so that I have to oblige him, let him give up hashish for forty days until his body is free from it, and forty more days, until he is rested from it after having become free. Then, let him come to me so that I shall inform him about it."[2] The Shaykh who exercised a powerful influence over his followers probably thought that his command would provide the user with the necessary will power to stay away from the drug for a prolonged period. Thereafter, he would be willing to listen to the Shaykh enlightening him about the dangers of hashish, and the Shaykh's personal influence would succeed in keeping him off the drug for good. Unfortunately, we are not told how effective this procedure proved in this or other cases.

A plain miracle was ascribed to the "ecstatic saint," ʿAbdallāh al-Miṣrī *al-majdhūb*, who died in 937/1530-31. "He used to grind *(ṣ-ḥ-n)* hashish amidst the ruins of the Ezbekīyah district of Cairo. It was a miracle bestowed upon him by divine grace *(karāmah)* that whoever took some of the hashish prepared by him and ate it repented immediately and never went back to it."[3]

---

[1] Cf. aṣ-Ṣafadī, *Wāfī*, ed. S. Dedering, IV, 183 f. (Wiesbaden 1959, *Bibliotheca Islamica* 6d). Ibn Kathīr has much information on al-Ḥarīrī and his family.

[2] For *ukhbirahū*, read, perhaps, *ujīrahū* "deliver him from it."

[3] Cf. Ibn al-ʿImād, *Shadharāt*, VIII, 221, *anno* 937, quoting ash-Shaʿrānī.

CHAPTER FOUR

THE LEGAL DISCUSSION

1. The General Attitude

There existed no authoritative "text" on the use of hashish.[1] How the pro-hashish faction exploited this acknowledged fact to its advantage was stated by al-ʿUkbarī in these words: "Know that the pure *sharīʿah* has not indicated that the use of drugs that cause joy *(al-ʿaqāqīr al-mufarriḥah)* such as saffron, bugloss, and others whose action is similar to that of this drug (hashish) is forbidden. No indication has come down from the Prophet to the effect that it is forbidden as such *(taḥrīm ʿaynih)* and that a *ḥadd* punishment has been established for eating it. Because there has been no tradition *(inqiṭāʿ al-khabar)* on this matter, people have permitted it and have used it."[2] The argument was constantly repeated. Particular favor seems to have been enjoyed by a verse which even found the attention of stern Ibn Taymīyah, who accepted the claim that it went back to some unnamed jurist.[3] It appears under the name of ʿAlam-ad-dīn Ibn Shukr, but he may not have been its originator:

> Hashish intoxication contains the meaning of my desire,
> You dear people of intelligence and understanding.
> They have declared it forbidden without any justification on the basis of reason and tradition.
> Declaring forbidden what is not forbidden is forbidden.[4]

---

[1] Cf., for instance, above, pp. 46 ff.

[2] Cf. al-Badrī, fols. 50b-51a.

[3] Cf. Ibn Taymīyah, *Fatāwī*, IV, 310.

[4] Cf. Ibn Kathīr, XIII, 314; Ibn Taghrībirdī, *Nujūm*, VII, 380; Ibn al-ʿImād, *Shadharāt*, V, 404, all *anno* 688.

According to al-Badrī, fol. 50a, ʿImād-ad-dīn Ibn ash-Shammāʿ composed four verses, of which the first two run:

> Hashish intoxication contains a hidden secret
> Too subtle for minds to explain.
> They have declared it forbidden without any justification on the basis of reason and tradition.
> Declaring forbidden what is not forbidden is forbidden.
>
> *fī khumāri l-ḥashīshi sirrun khafīyun*
> *daqqa taʿbīruhū ʿan-i-l-afhāmi.*

Obviously, the second verse is here a quotation, as it also probably is in the verses of ʿAlam-ad-dīn. For Muḥammad b. ʿAbd-al-Karīm b. ash-Shammāʿ (629-676/1231(2)-1277), no doubt the person meant here, cf. al-Yūnīnī, *Dhayl*,

ʿAlam-ad-dīn was, in fact, a legal scholar, but his way of life led to his being rejected by the established authorities.[1] The argument, however, had considerable force in Muslim society.

This situation naturally was a grave embarrassment for professional jurists. They had no occasion to talk about hashish unless and until it became a social problem that required legal attention regardless of the lacking sanction of the religious law as transmitted. In the brief introductory words of his treatise, az-Zarkashī hit the nail squarely on the head: "These are points dealing with hashish that require comment at this time because so many low-class people are affected by it and because many people hesitate to pronounce themselves on the legal situation concerning it, having been unable to find a discussion of it by the ancients."

We can consequently assume that the argumentation of the jurists was greatly influenced by their own personal feelings about the social and moral problems involved. Circumstances must often have determined their attitudes. Political pressures and self-seeking considerations cannot be ruled out as sometimes having had their share in shaping the legal reasoning.

It comes hardly as a surprise to find that modern scholars have reached the conclusion that "the attitude of the ʿUlemā towards the use of narcotics was less definite (than that on wine); they disagreed

III, 282 (Hyderabad 1374-1380/1954-1961); aṣ-Ṣafadī, *Wāfī*, ed. S. Dedering, III, 281 (Damascus 1953); ʿAbd-al-Qādir, *al-Jawāhir al-muḍīyah*, II, 85 (Hyderabad 1332); G. Wiet, *Les Biographies du Manhal Safi*, 328 (Cairo 1932, *Mém. de l'Institut d'Égypte* 19). Al-Badrī maliciously remarks that he should not be named ʿImād-ad-dīn but with inversion of the letters, rather *ʿadīm-ad-dīn* "lacking religion." And he approves of the rejoinder by Ismāʿīl b. al-Maʿarrī, described as the *muftī* of the Yemen:

Those lie who say it is permitted
Wherever the action is like that of wine.
It has been declared forbidden on the basis of reason, tradition, and religious law.
Declaring permitted what is forbidden is forbidden.

kadhaba l-qā'ilūna inna ḥalālan
kullamā fiʿluhū ka-fiʿli l-mudāmi
ḥarramūhū (!) ʿaqlan wa-naqlan wa-sharʿan
wa-ḥarāmun taḥlīlu shay'in ḥarāmi.

Both verses appear in the form ascribed by al-Badrī to Ibn ash-Shammāʿ on the title-page of the Istanbul Ms. Murad Molla 1408 of the *Ṣiwān* by Abū Sulaymān as-Sijistānī. Their author is indicated as ʿAlam-ad-dīn, with the remainder not clearly legible on my photostat ("b. Būrī"?) but Ibn Shukr is probably meant. The scribe of the ms. adds another rejoinder, for which see below, p. 150, n. 4.

[1] Cf. above, pp. 84 f.

upon its legality, though most condemned it."[1] This statement was made for the seventeenth century, and it is possible that by then there were scholars who did come out for the legality of hashish in their own legal writings. However, for earlier centuries, it would be quite difficult to prove that when it came to putting his scholarly reputation on the line and expressing himself in writing, any jurist would have dared to be unequivocally in favor of hashish. If this was done, we have no hard evidence for it in the material at our disposal. It is true that the general climate would not have been favorable to the preservation of such documents, but it is more likely that they were never produced, at least not in written form to be preserved for posterity. Stories told by littérateurs must remain suspect in every single instance. At most, they prove that unofficially, and as men of general culture, legal scholars, too, ventured to view a topic of general interest from several sides. Nevertheless, we may safely assume that some, if not many, seriously considered the idea that there was no firm legal basis for forbidding the use of hashish.

Among the known titles of monographs on hashish, only al-ʿUkbarī's comparatively early "Literary Thoughts in Praise of the Qualities of Cannabis" can be assumed to have been written for the purpose of stressing the advantages of hashish use, but the *Sawāniḥ* no doubt was a belletristic work and not a legal essay. It is also by no means certain whether it was all that one-sided or also contained much that was unfavorable to hashish, nor do we have any information on al-ʿUkbarī to show that he possessed any standing in the legal circles of his time. The reply he is said to have provoked from his contemporary al-Qasṭallānī[2] was that of a jurist and presumably informed by religious and social fervor, but since it is also not preserved, we are still at a loss to gauge the possible extent and quality of the legal arguments presented by al-ʿUkbarī; as in the case of al-Badrī, little space might have been devoted to them.

The writing of treatises against the use of hashish, such as those preserved for us, is at times described as something made necessary by the claims advanced by those who declared the drug permissible, among them, quite frequently, certain Ṣūfīs. "Declaring (hashish) permissible or lawful" is not quite the same as using it. As we shall

[1] Cf. H. A. R. Gibb and H. Bowen, *Islamic Society and the West*, I, ii, 204 (Oxford University Press 1957).

[2] Cf. above, p. 8.

see,[1] it was also considered as a grave sin. The decision as to what should be declared lawful and what not was the prerogative of the legal authorities who alone had the knowledge to make it. Those Ṣūfīs might at times have had legal training, but it would seem that when they were involved in the hashish controversy, they did not act as representatives of the legal establishment but as users and sympathizers who, whatever their position in society, were presumably hard pressed to attempt justifying the use of hashish in legal terms as they were the only ones likely to be heard and to be effective. No strictly legal writing was in all likelihood done by them.

At one time we hear that a certain highly respected Ḥanafite judge, Jamāl-ad-dīn Yūsuf b. Mūsā al-Malaṭī, who died, about eighty years old, in 803/1400, issued a *fatwā* permitting the use of hashish. He was teased about it by Muḥibb-ad-dīn b. ash-Shiḥnah (d. 815/1412). Ibn ash-Shiḥnah told al-Malaṭī that he had composed a couple of verses on some unnamed jurist:

> I am surprised to find a shaykh who commands people to be pious
> But himself never heeds the Merciful One or shows piety toward Him.
> He considers it permissible to eat hashish as well as usury
> And (says that) he who studies truly the *Ṣaḥīḥ* is a heretic.

We are asked to believe that al-Malaṭī did not recognize that he was being teased, although it was he himself who had adopted what must have been a rather peculiar attitude toward hashish, usury, and, supposedly, al-Bukhārī's *Ṣaḥīḥ* and thus could hardly have failed to get the point of the poem.[2] It is not explained to us why al-Malaṭī should have declared persistent students of the *Ṣaḥīḥ* to be heretics. In fact, we may have here a joke based on *ṣaḥīḥ* being a nickname for hashish.[3] The verse apparently expresses al-Malaṭī's disapproval of over-indulgence ("true study") in hashish whereas he permitted it in small quantities. Correspondingly, in a way, we are expressly given to understand that he did not, of course, permit usury, which would be unthinkable, but only certain kinds of transactions generally assumed to fall under the heading of usury.

---

[1] See below, p. 126.

[2] Cf. as-Sakhāwī, *Ḍaw'*, X, 4 f., 336; *idem, Dhayl 'alā Raf' al-iṣr*, ed. G. Hilāl and M. M. Ṣubḥ, 409 (Cairo 1966); briefly also in Ibn al-'Imād, *Shadharāt*, VII, 40. The last half-verse is corrupt. The transmitted readings *sami'a* or *yasma'-i (l-wuḥīya)* have been corrected by the editors of as-Sakhāwī's *Dhayl* to read *yastami' li-l-waḥyi*. A more likely reading would be: *wa-man yasma'-i-ṣ-Ṣaḥīḥa ḥaqqan tazandaqa.*

[3] Cf. above, p. 28.

However this might have been, we have no information as to whether the objectionable legal decision of al-Malaṭī was ever put into writing and achieved publication in one form or other. This was probably not the case in this, and all or most instances when hashish was declared permissible with legal arguments.

At about al-Malaṭī's time, al-Aqfahsī seems to have harbored some incidental doubt about the legal situation regarding hashish, to which he is otherwise strongly opposed. He refers to a comment by Sulaym ar-Rāzī (d. 447/1055),[1] from his *Taqrīb al-Gharībayn*, on the tradition transmitted by Abū Dāwūd that the Prophet "forbade everything *muskir* and *mufattir*,"[2] to the effect that this means that what is *muskir* is forbidden, and what is *mufattir* is (merely) disapproved of *(makrūh)*. In the view of al-Aqfahsī, this could mean that the analogy to wine is not applicable and that there should be no punishment *(taʿzīr)* for hashish and *banj* under these circumstances. The difference between wine and hashish would be that "contrary to wine, (hashish) is used as medicine, it is definitely clean, the person eating it is not subject to a *ḥadd* punishment, it is not necessary to throw it away, its purchase is not forbidden, and eating a small quantity of it is not forbidden."[3]

In general, however, we can say that the scholarly legal view laid down in published and preserved writings was against the use of hashish, if in somewhat different degrees. Between the different legal schools, the condemnation of it was, it seems, also unanimous, if, again, as is to be expected, with varying emphasis.

2. Hashish considered as "Intoxicating" and as "Corruptive"

One argument appealed most to jurists in their fight against hashish and was universally cited. That was the argument based upon analogy to *khamr* "wine," whose unlawful character was divinely established. Those licentious persons who at the time of the

[1] Cf. *GAL, Suppl.*, I, 730, where the name is vocalized Salīm. The reading Sulaym is indicated by Ibn al-ʿImād, *Shadharāt*, III, 275. Cf. also McG. de Slane's translation of Ibn Khallikān, I, 584 (Paris 1843-1871), and Fu'ād Sayyid's edition of adh-Dhahabī, *ʿIbar*, III, 213. Ibn Khallikān mentions the author's *Taqrīb*, without the qualifying genitive. Regrettably, adh-Dhahabī's *Ta'rīkh al-Islām* which may contain decisive information could not be consulted as the Yale Ms. L-612 (Catalogue Nemoy, No. 1176) omits a few years, including the year 447.

[2] Cf. above, p. 81.

[3] Cf. al-Aqfahsī, fol. 21a-b. For *ḥadd* and *taʿzīr*, see below, pp. 123 ff.

early spread of hashish through the Muslim world did not hesitate to recommend its use occasionally used it together with wine.[1] They also praised hashish as a substitute for wine. Thus, ʿAlam-ad-dīn Ibn Shukr exhorted himself:

> O soul, turn to amusement,
> For by play does a young man live.
> Do not get fed up with daily drunkenness.
> If it cannot be wine, let it be hashish.[2]

"A dirham of hashish is more effective than pints of wine," ran the praise of hashish by another littérateur, a certain Jalāl-ad-dīn Abū l-Muʿizz b. Abī l-Ḥasan b. Aḥmad b. aṣ-Ṣā'igh al-Maghribī who lived in the first half of the fourteenth century,[3] and indeed, the numerous confrontations of hashish and wine[4] are rather unabashedly based upon a convenient disregard for the unlawfulness of wine. But the jurists were fully convinced that if hashish could be equated with wine, its unlawfulness was clearly proved.

It was recognized of course that hashish differed from wine in the raw material from which it was prepared, in the form or forms of its preparation, and, above all, by virtue of the fact that wine was exclusively a liquid while hashish was predominantly used as a solid. These differences played a certain role in the discussion. It was, however, a very minor role, and it was all but eliminated by the overriding assumption that hashish and wine were equal in the effect of either as being "intoxicating" *(muskir)*. In this respect, scholars had at their disposal the generally attested Prophetical tradition that "every intoxicant is wine, and every intoxicant is forbidden."[5] Clear-cut as this would seem to make the matter, there remained certain problems. In the first place, there is the problem of how "intoxicant" is to be defined and whether the effects of hashish could be described as intoxicating in the same way as those of wine. Then it must be asked whether intoxicating is to be understood as

---

[1] Cf. above, pp. 65 f.

[2] Cf. Ibn Kathīr, XIII, 314; Ibn Taghrībirdī, *Nujūm*, VII, 380.

[3] Cf. al-Maqrīzī, II, 26, as well as II, 25 (citing the same poet). Al-Maqrīzī's immediate source seems to have been the Ḥāfiẓ al-Yaghmūrī. This Ibn aṣ-Ṣā'igh is not identical with Shams-ad-dīn Ibn aṣ-Ṣā'igh who is repeatedly cited by al-Badrī and who appears to be the author mentioned in *GAL, Suppl.*, II, 2. Before al-Maqrīzī, an-Nuwayrī, *Nihāyah*, XI, 29, quoted these verses anonymously.

[4] Cf., for instance, below, pp. 163 ff.

[5] Cf. *Concordance*, II, 491b43-49, and, for instance, Wakīʿ, *Akhbār al-quḍāh*, III, 42-45 (Cairo 1366-1369/1947-1950).

potentially intoxicating or refers only to the actual condition of intoxication; in other words, it is a problem whether or not a small quantity of a potentially intoxicating substance not leading to actual intoxication would be permissible, together with the problem of the possible immunity of certain individuals to intoxicating effects, which is of less significance in practice. And there is a further, related problem, which is also discussed in connection with wine, namely, whether or not under certain special circumstances, such as medical necessity, moderate use should be adjudged permissible.

Jurists as a rule do not waste time and paper upon discussing why and how hashish is to be branded as intoxicating. It is merely asserted that it is and that many legal authorities assume it to be. As is often remarked, this is in contrast to *banj* which is definitely not intoxicating,[1] although it possesses the qualities affecting the mind that make its use unlawful. Some attempts were, however, made to define and clarify what intoxication meant. Thus we read in az-Zarkashī[2] that the effects of hashish agree with the commonly accepted definition of "intoxicated" as referring to "someone whose orderly speech is confused and who spills his hidden secret, or someone who does not know heaven from earth or length from width." The first alternative, which is in rhymed form, is claimed already for ash-Shāfiʿī, as an-Nawawī tells us.[3] The Qur'ān based description of intoxication as a "covering of the mind" *(taghṭiyat al-ʿaql)*[4] is not an exclusive definition of intoxication since it is also applicable to comparable states resulting from other causes.

All the statements of jurists with respect to intoxication share the

---

[1] It may, however, be noted that the supposed Semitic term for henbane was etymologized by I. Löw, *Die Flora der Juden*, III, 359 ff. (reprint Hildesheim 1967), as belonging to the general root signifying intoxication. For Paul of Aegina, ed. Heiberg, II, 31, the mental effect *(parakopē)* of henbane eaten or drunk was similar to that known of the inebriated.

[2] Cf. below, p. 181.

[3] Cf. an-Nawawī's commentary on the *Muhadhdhab* of Abū Isḥāq ash-Shīrāzī *(al-Majmūʿ, Sharḥ al-Muhadhdhab)*, III, 8 (Cairo, n. y. [1966?]). For the confusion of speech, cf. as-Sarakhsī, *Mabsūṭ*, XXIV, 30. These definitions of intoxication are also quoted by al-Aqfahsī, fol. 13b. The second part appears in al-Ghuzūlī, *Maṭāliʿ*, II, 63. A definition focusing on the "disappearance of worries and spilling of hidden secrets" was current in literary circles according to Ibn ar-Raqīq al-Qayrawānī, *Quṭb as-surūr*, 388 (ar-Riyāshī), 396 (ar-Raqāshī). In al-Badrī, fol. 70a, Hārūn ar-Rashīd is credited with it. The famous Muḥammad b. Dāwūd aẓ-Ẓāhirī (d. 297/310) is described as the inventor of a quite similar formulation, cf. al-Khaṭīb al-Baghdādī, *Ta'rīkh Baghdād*, V, 256 (Cairo 1349/1931). Cf. also Wakīʿ, III, 125.

[4] Cf. az-Zarkashī, below, pp. 115 and 184.

description of it as something leading to *n-sh-w*. This commonly used root is hardly anything but a synonym of the other term for intoxication, *s-k-r*. It is indeed difficult to see how *n-sh-w* could be translated differently. But *n-sh-w* was also distinguished as indicating "the beginning and preliminaries" of intoxication *(sukr)*.[1] In this way, it was probably understood to denote in particular the exhilaration that was the initial emotional effect of wine. The root *n-sh-w* is commonly associated with the description of wine as something "desired" *(sh-h-w)*, meaning the addictive compulsion of wanting more once one has tasted it.[2] Both *n-sh-w* and *sh-h-w* are also attributed to hashish and claimed to be characteristic of it, thus marking it as something intoxicating and therefore forbidden.

However, there were some scholars who denied that hashish could be classified as intoxicating. They probably were few in number, but it was certainly not only the Mālikite al-Qarāfī (d. 684/1285) who was the sole exception to the rule, as az-Zarkashī maintains. Even if he knew of al-Qarāfī's views, Ibn Taymīyah had no doubt also others in mind when he argued against the idea of denying to hashish the effect of intoxication.[3] Al-Qarāfī's argument is found in his *Qawāʿid*, as az-Zarkashī calls the work which has been published under the title of *Furūq (Anwār al-burūq)*.[4] While the botanists have stated in their books that hashish is intoxicating,[5] al-Qarāfī on his part had doubts and preferred to think of it rather as *mufsid* "corruptive." He defines still another term, *murqid*, "narcotic," as something that stops the functioning of the five senses. If there is no arrest of sense perception, and the effect is primarily *nashwah*, joy, and a certain feeling of strength and confidence in oneself *(qūwat an-nafs)*, then we can speak of *muskir* "intoxicating." If the effect is not of this type, then we are dealing with something that must be described as *mufsid* "corruptive." Thus the classification of "intoxicating" applies to substances that, like wine and other alcoholic beverages made from various substances and commonly

---

[1] Cf. *Lisān al-ʿArab*, XX, 198 (Būlāq 1300-1308).

[2] Cf. above, pp. 96 f.

[3] Cf. Ibn Taymīyah, *Fatāwī*, IV, 304.

[4] I, 261 f., in the edition Tunis 1302, with the chapter heading: *al-farq al-arbaʿūn bayn qāʿidat al-muskirāt wa-qāʿidat al-murqidāt wa-qāʿidat al-mufsidāt*. For al-Qarāfī, cf. *GAL, Suppl.*, I, 665 f., and for the text of az-Zarkashī's quotation, cf. below, pp. 182 f.

[5] This dubious statement appears in az-Zarkashī's quotation but is not found in al-Qarāfī's text.

discussed by the jurists,[1] "remove the mind" while at the same time generating *nashwah* and joy. "Corruptive" is what befuddles the intellect, without primarily generating joy, which is the effect of substances such as *banj* and *saykarān*.[2] The effect of wine is properly described in the following verse of Ḥassān b. Thābit, the famous poet of the Prophet's time:

> When we drink it, it leaves us kings
> And lions. Battle action does not repel us.[3]

Intoxicants generate increased bravery and cheerfulness, confidence in oneself, an inclination toward violent action and taking revenge on one's enemies, and a heightened effort to outdo others in generosity and nobility of character. This is the implication of the verse just cited that describes wine and the winedrinker. Because this is the well-known effect *(maʿnā)* of intoxicants, the Mālikite judge, ʿAbd-al-Wahhāb b. ʿAlī b. Naṣr (362-422/973-1031), said:

> Winedrinkers think that wine
> Banishes worry and turns away sorrow.
> They are right: It has fun with their minds, and they imagine
> That it makes their joy complete.
> It deprives them of their religion and their minds.
> Do you (not rather) think that anyone lacking these two would be sad?

This was Judge ʿAbd-al-Wahhāb's reply to those who defended the general assumption that wine generates joy and happiness.

Now, using this distinction between narcotic, intoxicating, and corruptive, al-Qarāfī suggests that hashish is to be classified as corruptive, and not as intoxicating, for two reasons. First, hashish is found to stir the juice hidden in the body, whichever it is. Thereby it creates, for each temper according to the individual's particular condition, acuteness in people dominated by the yellow bile, somnolence and silence for the phlegmatic, weeping and restlessness for the melancholy, and cheerfulness for the sanguine. Some are therefore found to weep very much, and others to be silent. In contrast, almost

---

1 Such as *mizr* made from wheat, *bitʿ* (or *bitaʿ*) made from honey, and *sukurkah* made from millet. Az-Zarkashī omits mentioning them.

2 Al-Qarāfī later adds opium. Az-Zarkashī mentions only *banj*. *Saykarān*, also in slightly different forms, is henbane. Possibly, *banj* here is meant to refer to hemp (?).

3 Cf. Ḥassān's *Dīwān*, ed. H. Hirschfeld, 1, No. 1, line 10 (Leiden and London 1910, *E. J. W. Gibb Memorial Series* 13), trans. (O. Rescher), *Beitraege zur Arabischen Poësie*, V, 2 (Stuttgart 1953-54). Cf. also al-Aqfahsī, fol. 5a.

everybody devoted to wine and other intoxicating drinks is found to be exhilarated *(nashwān)* and joyous and remote from the painful sensations[1] of weeping and silence. In the second place, wine is known to cause a strong tendency toward quarreling among drinkers.[2] They go at each other with weapons and are ready to do frightful things they would not do when they are sober. This is meant by Ḥassān b. Thābit's reference to lions and readiness to do battle. Nothing of the sort occurs when hashish eaters are together. In no way do they behave like winedrinkers. On the contrary, they are quiet and somnolent as in a trance. If one were to take away their things, he would not encounter in them the strong violent reaction to be expected from winedrinkers in such a case. (Hashish eaters) are the closest thing to dumb beasts. Therefore, corpses of people who have died a violent death are frequently discovered among winedrinkers but not among hashish eaters. For these two reasons, al-Qarāfī concludes, "I believe that hashish is 'corruptive,' and not 'intoxicating.' I do not consider the *ḥadd* punishment necessary in connection with it, nor do I consider prayer invalid (for someone who has hashish in his possession); it requires *taʿzīr* as a deterrent so that people do not get mixed up with it." In brief, al-Qarāfī's argument is that the different—and, it would seem to us, by and large more positive—effects of wine vitiate the classification of hashish as an intoxicant, without, however, making it any the less forbidden in principle, although the legal consequences are somewhat less severe. This, however, was not the preponderant attitude which, as has been stated, tended toward the view of ascribing intoxicating properties to hashish.

A question more open to debate was that of the use of small versus large quantities. This point also had considerable impact on the discussion of wine for its potential of driving a wedge into the strict attitude toward alcoholic beverages. For someone as strict as the Ḥanbalite Ibn Taymīyah, the quantity made no difference. The prohibition holds, although, he says, large quantities causing intoxication are forbidden by general agreement *(ittifāq)* among

---

[1] The colorless *ṣudūr* "occurrence" of al-Qarāfī's text may be a mistake for *taḍawwur*, as in az-Zarkashī's quotation, which could hardly be (with most mss.) *taṣawwur* "perception."

[2] The *ʿarbadah* of drinkers is illustrated by stories in a special chapter of Ibn ar-Raqīq al-Qayrawānī's *Quṭb as-surūr*, 431-443. The pro-hashish forces often denounce it as one of the disadvantages of alcohol, cf., for instance, below, p. 164, verse 14.

Muslims and must for this reason be viewed more seriously.[1] Not only "the last cup" of intoxicating beverages such as *nabīdh*, beer, or kumiss, is forbidden but any quantity of them,[2] and this no doubt also applies to hashish. Ibn Taymīyah inveighs against the claim made for the Ḥanafites that they considered a non-intoxicating amount of wine or hashish permissible. With respect to wine and other intoxicating beverages, save some possible doubts with regard to beer, it is simply a lie, Ibn Taymīyah contends, to accuse Abū Ḥanīfah of having made any exceptions (nor would he have made any, had he had occasion to deal with hashish). There is the much cited tradition—which, however, is not to be found in al-Bukhārī and Muslim[3]—that the decisive factor is the potential intoxicating quality: "Where a large quantity causes intoxication, a small quantity is forbidden." This, Ibn Taymīyah concludes, decides the question for intoxicating hashish as it does for intoxicating wine.[4]

The Shāfiʿite adh-Dhahabī, if it was indeed he, followed Ibn Taymīyah in prohibiting anything potentially intoxicating on the strength of the tradition just cited.[5] However, the famous Nawawī, commenting on Abū Isḥāq ash-Shīrāzī's *Muhadhdhab*,[6] relied on the assumption that in contrast to wine, hashish, being a plant, was not ritually unclean,[7] and in this case, a little of it not causing intoxication could be lawfully consumed. In reporting this view of an-Nawawī, az-Zarkashī objects to it as being inconsistent with his view that hashish is to be classified as intoxicating, as this rules out any use of it whatever. However, az-Zarkashī also quotes the *Tanbīh* of Abū Isḥāq ash-Shīrāzī to the effect that "everything clean the consumption of which does not cause any harm may be eaten,"[8] and concludes from it that "a small quantity of (hashish) is clean, and there is no harm in eating it." He further discusses the special case of the hypothetical individual immune to hashish intoxication;

---

[1] Cf. Ibn Taymīyah, *Fatāwī*, IV, 311 f.

[2] Cf. Ibn Taymīyah, *Fatāwī*, IV, 326 ff.

[3] Cf. *Concordance*, II, 491a 29-31, and Ibn Taymīyah, *Siyāsah*, in making the case for the soundness of the tradition.

[4] Cf. Ibn Taymīyah, *Fatāwī*, IV, 301-303.

[5] For ash-Shāfiʿī's own view in connection with wine, cf. *Umm*, VI, 130 f., 175 ff.

[6] The first three volumes of the edition available to me do not yet extend to this passage.

[7] Cf. below, pp. 117 ff.

[8] Cf. the edition of the *Tanbīh* by A. W. T. Juynboll, 90 (Leiden 1879). For az-Zarkashī's text, see below, p. 192, and cf. also al-Aqfahsī, fol. 20a.

here the ritual cleanliness of hashish would make its use permissible, in contrast to wine whose ritual uncleanliness makes it forbidden even for the individual immune to its intoxicating effect. In his discussion of the cleanliness or uncleanliness of hashish, az-Zarkashī also shows himself inclined to assume lawfulness for the consumption of small quantities, and in discussing whether vomiting after swallowing hashish is obligatory as in the case of wine, he adopts a distinction between intoxicating quantities, which require vomiting, and non-intoxicating quantities which do not.[1]

The Mālikite al-Qarāfī considered a small quantity of hashish permissible, this, as az-Zarkashī explains, on the basis of his belief that it cannot be classified as intoxicating but must be considered corruptive. Al-Qarāfī specified that opium, *banj*, and *saykarān* are permissible as long as the amount used is not of such a quantity as to exercise an influence upon the mind and the senses. Less than that is indeed permissible.

The Ḥanafite approach was mostly in the direction toward greater tolerance, providing the excuses that addicts were able to use in their own defense.[2] This at least was the way it turned out in practice while the theory was ambivalent.

A brief and somewhat one-sided summary of the attitudes of the four legal schools toward the consumption of hashish, in analogy to their attitudes toward wine, appears in the *Risālah fī ḥurmat al-banj*[3] in the following form: According to Abū Ḥanīfah and Abū Yūsuf, the drinking of wine, if it does not cause intoxication, is permissible because these two Ḥanafite authorities formulated their legal view with regard to the potential final result, which is drunkenness. On the other hand, the third great Ḥanafite authority, Muḥammad ash-Shaybānī, as well as Mālik, ash-Shāfiʿī, and Ibn Ḥanbal, held the view that the forbidden character applied not only to the final result but was generally applicable to the entire process. For the author of the *Risālah*, the situation with respect to hashish is fully analogous. Not having been mentioned by the ancient authorities, *banj* and hashish have remained basically lawful *(al-ibāḥah al-aṣlīyah)* as all other plants.[4] This, for the author, is the crucial flaw in the legal reasoning about hashish, which needs to be corrected. He

[1] For the question of inducing vomiting, cf. also al-Aqfahsī, fol. 19a-b.
[2] Cf. also the story of al-Malaṭī, above, p. 104.
[3] Cf. above, p. 18.
[4] Cf. above, p. 48.

stresses the fact that the view of the Shāfiʿite al-Muzanī and the Ḥanafite aṭ-Ṭaḥāwī[1] outlawing *banj* must be considered legally binding as if it had been expressed by the founders of the legal schools themselves. Consequently, the eating of *banj* and hashish, whether in small or large quantities, is forbidden. "Nobody after their time has ever said that the eating of *banj* and hashish is permissible, especially if they are taken pure for the purpose of becoming intoxicated, amused, or emotionally excited, or because of having eaten too much food (*aw li-kathrat akl aṭ-ṭaʿām*). Woe unto him who eats them, whether it be little or much. Again, woe unto him who eats them for amusement or emotional excitement or anything of the sort." Notwithstanding the strong stand taken by the author of the *Risālah,* it seems obvious that the problem of quantity could be argued either way and was so argued by adherents of all the schools without much distinction.

The question of the possible medical use of hashish was answered in a similar manner since it involved quantities smaller than those that might ordinarily cause intoxication or some other harm. In the view of jurists, the medical authorities apparently did not have too much use for hemp products in the cure of illnesses (see below). Anyhow, the legal authorities spoke mainly of *banj* in this connection, but the assumption is that whatever they said of *banj* applied equally to hashish. Thus al-Fanārī collected some opinions of his older Ḥanafite colleagues such as Khwāharzādeh who, according to the *Sharḥ al-Mabsūṭ* (?), considered the medical use of *banj* lawful unless it led to mental disturbance,[2] in which case it was forbidden. The same opinion was expressed in the *Mabsūṭ* (that of Khwāharzādeh or, rather, that of as-Sarakhsī?).[3] According to the Ḥanafite *Fatāwī al-Khulāṣah,* there was nothing wrong with using *banj* for medication, even if it brought about some mental disorder, but some authorities limited this to exclude possible intoxication in the process.[4] In his collection of *Fatāwī,* the Ḥanafite al-Bazzāzī

[1] Cf. above, p. 48.

[2] *Dhahab,* or *zāl, al-ʿaql.* In the context, some temporary state such as unconsciousness may be meant, and no lasting deep-seated mental disturbance. However, such a distinction is not inherent in the phraseology used. A person whose "mind is gone" is insane.

[3] At least, the statement appears in the *Kitāb al-ashribah* of as-Sarakhsī's *Mabsūṭ,* XXIV, 9. For ash-Shāfiʿī himself, cf. *Umm,* V, 235, in connection with the divorce of the drunkard.

[4] Cf. az-Zarkashī, below, p. 190. I have so far been unable to identify the work (identical with the famous *Khulāṣat al-fatāwī*?).

(d. 827/1424) adjudged the situation similarly.[1] Again, his contemporary, al-Qalqashandī, a Shāfiʿite, citing Judge Ḥusayn al-Marwarrūdhī (d. 462/1069), expressed the same view with respect to *banj, jawz māthil* (datura Metel L),[2] and opium, if the drug was taken by mistake or for medical purposes.[3] The Shāfiʿite author of *Qamʿ* argued against those who claimed for *barsh* the status of a highly effective medicament *(bur' sāʿah)* and, it seems, demanded on this basis that it be cleared for general use. This was, however, he said, a special case, permissible only upon medical prescription for certain diseases under quite restricted conditions. After vigorously stating that the use of *barsh* was ruled out by the religious law and by reason, he had some further thoughts about its medical properties. He contended that southern people such as the Egyptians must never use it, but it might be good for the constitution of people living in the northern, snow-bound regions of the world, not for all of them but probably for some.[4] For the author of the *Risālah fī ḥurmat al-banj*, it was, or should have been, the general consensus that the drug must not be used even as a medicine. He realized, however, that others considered this permissible, and it is not quite clear whether he himself would not have been willing to make an exception, notwithstanding his strong convictions. When he warned against using *banj* or hashish in the case of "having eaten too much,"[5] this would seem, however, to aim at the lawfulness of their use as medicines.

The fullest information on this subject is again to be found in az-Zarkashī. In his chapter on particular legal problems connected with hashish, he speaks of "the permissibility of its use for medical purposes if it is established that it is beneficial (as an ingredient) in some medicines. Thus, it has been stated that it dissolves flatulence and cleans up[6] dandruff *(ibriyah)*.[7] . . . The reason for its effective-

---

[1] In al-Bazzāzī's chapter on *ashribah*, cf. Ms. Yale A-166 (Catalogue Nemoy, No. 888), fol. 380b. Cf. also below, p. 122.

[2] Cf. Meyerhof's edition and translation of Maimonides, 43 f. For the use in Arabic of *dāt(h)ūrah*, cf. above, p. 46, n. 2, and below, p. 134.

[3] Cf. al-Qalqashandī, *Ṣubḥ*, II, 146. For Judge Ḥusayn, as the author of the *Taʿlīq(ah)* (cf. below, p. 121) a much cited authority, cf. *GAL, Suppl.*, I, 669.

[4] Cf. *Qamʿ*, fols. 276b-277a and 279b-280a.

[5] Cf. above, p. 113.

[6] Rather than *tanfī* "removes."

[7] "Flatulence" goes back to Galen, *De simpl. med.* VII (XII, 8 Kühn): *aphysos*. "Dandruff" was mentioned by Isḥāq al-Isrā'īlī. Both he and Galen

ness in this respect is the heat and dryness it contains. It is necessary to decide upon permissibility.[1] For saffron, scammony, and other drugs which in large quantities are deadly can by general agreement be taken, if needed, in small quantities. I have seen (the Shāfiʿite) ar-Rūyānī (d. 502/1108), in the *Baḥr*, state this openly.[2] He said: It is permissible to use it for medical purposes, even if it leads to intoxication, whenever it cannot be avoided. He continued: Something which is not intoxicating by itself but is so in combination with something else, if it is of no use in another medicine, must not be eaten. If it is of use, its use as medicine is permissible. Ash-Shāfiʿī has expressly stated that the theriac made of various snake meats may be eaten only in the case of a necessity of a kind that would make the consumption of carrion permissible."

Az-Zarkashī also pays attention to the question of whether hashish may be eaten in order to still one's hunger. He decides that this may be done, for in contrast to wine which does not quench a person's thirst but rather increases it, the consumption of hashish does not cause more hunger. This, it may be noted, contradicts the frequently observed fact that the use of hashish stimulates the appetite.[3] However, az-Zarkashī may be right inasmuch as he starts out with a situation in which hunger is present, in which case the effect of hashish would be to alleviate the pangs of hunger. As he puts it, the most hashish does is "to cover the mind." In the context, the phrase must clearly be understood in the sense of hashish being credited with a narcotic effect producing a kind of anaesthesia. Anaesthesia produced by drugs is permissible for medical purposes such as the amputation of a gangrenous hand, az-Zarkashī remarks. Consequent-

---

were quoted by Ibn al-Bayṭār. Other beneficial medical uses mentioned by Ibn al-Bayṭār and al-Maqrīzī on the authority of Galen and others are those of a diuretic, of cleaning the brain, of soothing pain of the ears, and of being good for digestion (although it also said to be difficult to digest and bad for the stomach, cf. below, p. 164, n. 5). See above, pp. 73 f.

[1] Ms. A, in contrast to the other mss., adds a reference to the use of small quantities, which according to an-Nawawī are forbidden, "if there is an absence of need." From this, it follows that in the case of need, the use of small quantities is permissible. The situation is different with regard to wine. See above, pp. 110 f.

[2] For the *Baḥr*, cf. *GAL*, *Suppl.*, I, 673. Again Ms. A has a fuller text, referring to ar-Rūyānī's view that the use of small non-intoxicating quantities of wine is permissible for medical purposes and that the use of plants for medication is absolutely permitted.

[3] Cf. above, p. 78. The view on wine is that of ash-Shāfiʿī, cf. as-Sarakhsī, *Mabsūṭ*, XXIV, 28.

ly it is lawful to eat hashish in the case of hunger or of medical necessity for the purpose of preserving life.

Az-Zarkashī sums up his findings with respect to the circumstances under which the use of hashish could be considered lawful and permissible, stating that they are five: (1) If it is the question of a small quantity, but this is so only according to an-Nawawī; (2) if the user is immune to the intoxicating effect of hashish; (3) if it is consumed for medical purposes; (4) if it is consumed to produce anaesthesia in connection with an amputation; and (5) if it is consumed to still great hunger.[1] The overriding concern of all legal scholars was the abuse of hashish for "enjoyment and pleasure." To this they were unanimously and irrevocably opposed, as far as our knowledge goes.

It is not only the intoxicating effect of hashish but also, as we have already seen, its effect upon mental and physical health and upon religious and moral attitudes that provides the jurists with a strong argument. The law does not permit self-destruction or causing harm to one's body in any way,[2] and that is just what hashish is supposed to do. The physical and mental incapacitation, rather than the transgression of the law, of the addict is mainly held responsible for the harm that may come to his religion, adding another, even more frightening aspect to the devastation the addict brings upon himself.[3] As stated by az-Zarkashī,[4] there is general agreement among all the religious groups in the world that the preservation of mental health is imperative, and, as stated by Ibn Taymīyah[5] and others, it is recognized by all Muslim scholars that anything leading to the destruction of the mind is forbidden. The assumption adopted by all those who were against the use of drugs was that they corrupt the mind and the physical constitution, thereby placing them beyond the pale of accepted custom. If this served only as a second-line argument against hashish, to be used principally by those who were not clear in their minds about its intoxicating effect, the reason was that Muslim religious tradition furnished the more clear-cut legal situation with respect to intoxication, but

[1] Cf. the text, below, p. 195. The concluding words: *wa-tajibu in lam nujawwiz al-istislām*, mean: "and they are necessary (and not merely permissible) if we do not consider submission (to self-destruction) permissible."

[2] Cf. M. Rodinson, in *EI*², II, 1068b, *s. v.* ghidhā', with reference to drugs.

[3] Cf. above, pp. 88 f.

[4] Cf. below, p. 185.

[5] *Fatāwī*, IV, 310.

the argument from self-destruction existed and was compelling.

The jurists who attempted to stem the use of hashish had powerful weapons in these two arguments. However, it ought to be realized that theirs was not a completely impregnable position. It depended neither upon firm authority and upon precedent of the kind generally admitted nor upon the intrinsic character of hashish which was a plant and therefore basically permitted for use, but it had to rely exclusively upon the drug's presumed effects, and they were hard to prove objectively.

3. The Ritual Cleanliness or Uncleanliness of Hashish

Muslim law makes much of the distinction between ritual cleanliness and uncleanliness *(ṭāhir-najis)*, and there is more practical significance to this than would seem to be the case at first glance. Contact with an object classified as unclean necessitates ritual washing and failing that would, for instance, invalidate prayer. Internal use, such as the consumption of hashish, complicated matters. As Ibn Taymīyah saw it, the proper ritual ablution would not be enough since hashish is like wine which invalidates prayer for a certain period.[1]

Quite divergent views were expressed on the status of hashish in this respect. As a plant, we have seen, hashish clearly falls outside the established categories of unclean objects. According to Ibn Taymīyah, its uncleanliness in its quality as an intoxicant most definitely derives from the fact that it acquires its intoxicating effect already during the process of turning from its non-intoxicating state into its intoxicating state *(bi-l-istiḥālah)*, as does "raw wine," *i.e.*, must. *Banj*, on the other hand, is, as repeatedly stated, not intoxicating in the proper sense, and other drugs such as nutmeg become intoxicating only after the completion of the process.[2] In this way, hashish is distinguished from other plant-derived narcotics and closer to wine with its firmly established unclean character. However,

---

[1] Cf. Ibn Taymīyah, *Fatāwī*, IV, 323. In the parallel passage, I, 129, Ibn Taymīyah speaks of cleansing the mouth.

[2] Cf. Ibn Taymīyah, *Fatāwī*, IV, 304. In connection with nutmeg, Meyerhof states in his edition and translation of Maimonides, 38 f., that it was used as a stimulant in modern Egypt after the suppression of the traffic in hashish and other narcotics. Ibn Ḥajar al-Haytamī, *Taḥdhīr ath-thiqāt*, fols. 8b-10a, goes into some detail concerning the legal situation with respect to it, quoting Ibn Daqīq-al-ʿĪd.

even Ibn Taymīyah, convinced as he was of the need for considering hashish as unclean and of the correctness of doing so, had to admit that even among the Ḥanbalites themselves as well as among the representatives of the other legal schools there was no unanimity in this respect. There were those who thought that it could not be regarded as unclean. Others thought of it as clean in its solid state but as unclean if it was in a liquid state. Others fortunately professed what Ibn Taymīyah considered the right opinion, namely, that hashish is unclean just as wine is.[1]

The Shāfiʿite az-Zarkashī graphically shows the vacillation that prevailed on this point. In the brief fifth chapter of his treatise, he begins by stressing the uncleanliness of hashish, only to end up, after citing his authorities, by being not at all sure about the situation. His chapter offers a good illustration of the difficulties facing the legal authorities in their battle against the drug and therefore deserves translation here in full:

"The problem of the cleanliness or uncleanliness of hashish must be discussed on the basis of the earlier discussion of its intoxicating character. Analogical reasoning requires that those who pronounce it intoxicating must also pronounce it unclean. Aṭ-Ṭūsī[2] has expressed himself in this sense in his *Miṣbāḥ* when he says: Hashish is unclean if it is established that it is intoxicating. However, Shaykh Muḥyī-ad-dīn (an-Nawawī) said that it was intoxicating but not unclean, and he did not refer to a contradicting view in this respect. He is supported by the definite statement that it is clean, made by Taqī-ad-dīn Ibn Daqīq-al-ʿīd in what he has written on the *Furūʿ* of Ibn al-Ḥājib.[3] He referred to the general consensus in this respect, saying: Opium, the milk of poppy, is stronger in its effect than

[1] Cf. Ibn Taymīyah, *Fatāwī*, IV, 311, also IV, 304, and *Siyāsah*; adh-Dhahabī, *Kabā'ir*. It may be noted that in the systematic discussion of uncleanliness in the first volume of his *Fatāwī*, Ibn Taymīyah makes no mention of hashish. This is probably due to the fact that in the traditional treatment of the topic, hashish naturally did not have a place. Addicts are also unlikely to have consulted a *muftī* on this problem.

[2] ʿAbd-al-ʿAzīz b. Muḥammad aṭ-Ṭūsī, whose *Miṣbāḥ* is a commentary on the *Ḥāwī* of al-Qazwīnī, died in 706/1306, or 707 as indicated in *GAL, Suppl.*, I, 679. Since I was unable to consult the work, I am not sure as to how far the quotation extends. It possibly included the quotation from an-Nawawī but hardly that from his contemporary Ibn Daqīq-al-ʿīd, although this is not entirely excluded.

[3] For the legal work of the famous grammarian Ibn al-Ḥājib (d. 646/1249), cf. *GAL, Suppl.*, I, 538. Ibn Daqīq-al-ʿīd (d. 702/1303) is listed in *Suppl.*, II, 66.

hashish because a small quantity of it produces strong intoxication, and the same applies to henbane *(saykarān)* and nutmeg. Nevertheless, the general consensus considers them as clean. With respect to the general consensus in this connection to which he lays claim, there is some discussion, as will be reported on the authority of al-Qarāfī in connection with the question of prayer.[1]

In an old commentary on the *Wajīz*, we find that its author[2] said that he had heard two views reported orally on the uncleanliness of hashish.

Ibn al-ʿAṭṭār[3] says: Hesitation has been shown with respect to declaring it unclean if it is (in its solid state).[4] If it is mixed with water and drunk, it is more properly called unclean in the view of those who pronounce wine unclean.

In his *Fawāʾid ar-riḥlah*, Ibn aṣ-Ṣalāḥ mentions as transmitted by the author of the *Taqrīb*[5] an opinion to the effect that a plant is unclean if it is a deadly poison and that this was objected to on the basis of the text of ash-Shāfiʿī.[6] But analogical reasoning requires cleanliness for hashish. We have no plant whatever that is unclean *per se*, except plants that are watered with uncleanliness. They are unclean *per se* according to aṣ-Ṣaydalānī.[7] They went so far as to say

---

[1] See below, pp. 120 f.

[2] Al-Badrī, fol. 53a, has the following statement: "If not literally in these words, then at any rate according to the sense, it was said by al-Adhraʿī (708-783/1308-1381, cf. *GAL, Suppl.*, II, 108) in his book, *at-Tawassuṭ wa-l-fatḥ bayn ar-Rawḍah wa-sh-Sharḥ*: I have seen in a fragment of *Sharḥ al-Wajīz qadīm* that hashish is intoxicating, unclean, and its eater subject to *ḥadd*." It would seem that the *Wajīz* was the famous work by al-Ghazzālī. "Its author" is obviously the author of the commentary, and not al-Ghazzālī. Al-Ghazzālī himself states in chapter 1, section 1, of the book on *al-ḥalāl wa-l-ḥarām* of the *Iḥyāʾ*, II, 83 f. (Cairo 1352/1933) that plants that cause mental disorder (*muzīl al-ʿaql*, above, p. 113, n. 2) such as *banj* are for this reason unlawful, but only "intoxicating" plants are also unclean. This excludes, for instance, *banj* which causes mental disorder but is not intoxicating. The inherent uncleanliness of intoxicants is an additional deterrent against using them.

[3] ʿAlī b. Ibrāhīm (d. 724/1324), cf. *GAL*, II, 85, *Suppl.*, II, 100. According to *GAL, Suppl.*, I, 686, he was the editor of an-Nawawī's *fatwās*. The paragraph referring to Ibn al-ʿAṭṭār is to be found only in Ms. B of az-Zarkashī.

[4] This renders the drift of the discussion, but the text is not quite clear.

[5] The famous *ḥadīth* scholar Ibn aṣ-Ṣalāḥ died in 643/1245, cf. *GAL, Suppl.*, I, 610 ff., and J. Robson, in *EI*², *s. v.* Ibn al-Ṣalāḥ. His "Travel Notes" are listed in Ḥājjī Khalīfah, 1297. The *Taqrīb* appears to be the work of the Shāfiʿite Abū Shujāʿ al-Iṣfahānī (d. 593/1196), cf. *GAL, Suppl.*, I, 676 f.

[6] Cf. above, p. 115.

[7] As-Subkī, *Ṭabaqāt ash-Shāfiʿīyah*, IV, 31 (Cairo 1324), mentions Abū Bakr aṣ-Ṣaydalānī, apparently the person meant here, a pupil of al-Qaffāl, who

about poison that is a plant, that it is clean although it is more harmful than hashish. The statement that hashish is to be declared unclean is not to be considered acceptable, even if (hashish) were intoxicating, for proof comes only in connection with wine, and something other than wine does not correspond to it in all aspects. It is agreed that it is permissible to consume a small quantity of hashish. If it were unclean, this would not be permissible."

Thus, doubts existed, and while those who felt that hashish ought to be outlawed thought it useful to brand it as unclean with all that this involved, it seems that the legal situation was not easily reconcilable to such an approach. The obvious result was another small loophole for the drug.[1]

4. Prayer and Divorce

At the beginning of az-Zarkashī's seventh and last chapter, the question is raised whether carrying hashish on one's person and having it in possession during prayer renders his prayer invalid. This is felt to depend on whether hashish is clean or unclean. Al-Qarāfī reports the answer of an unnamed Egyptian jurist[2] that before the hemp is toasted and roasted, it has no effect upon the validity of prayer because in that state it is nothing but green leaves. Only after it has gone through that process does it acquire its mind-destroying qualities, and its possession then invalidates prayer. Al-Qarāfī—who still seems to be meant rather than az-Zarkashī himself—inquired with a group of people involved with hashish *(mim-man yuʿānīhā)*[3] whether this distinction made sense to them. He found them divided in their opinion. Some accepted it as justified. Others, however, claimed that the efficacy of hashish was absolute and that the toasting process merely served the purpose of improving its taste and producing a better balanced quality. Al-Qarāfī himself,

---

thus lived around 1100. He wrote a commentary on the *Mukhtaṣar* of al-Muzanī (see Ḥājjī Khalīfah, 1636), cited by al-Aqfahsī, fol. 14a.

[1] For the comparison of "dirty" wine with "clean" hashish, cf. below, p. 155. This has nothing to do with the question of ritual cleanliness and uncleanliness, although it was at times combined with it.

[2] Al-Badrī, fols. 53b-54a, says that it is an-Nawawī, and the inquirer is "ash-shaykh," probably still an-Nawawī. However, al-Badrī may merely be quoting from az-Zarkashī, in spite of small textual variants, and his additional data need therefore not be considered.

[3] Cf. above, p. 96, but here the word may also be meant to include "experts" on the subject in addition to addicts.

it will be recalled, considered hashish as "corruptive" and therefore as clean and having no effect upon the validity of prayer, as opposed to "intoxicating" substances.

Another question that was raised concerned the functioning of addicts as prayer leaders. Ibn Taymīyah was convinced that an addict must not be appointed to the leadership of public prayer if a better person is available. A prayer performed behind a prayer leader who is "wicked" *(fāsiq)* is legally classified as disliked *(makrūh)*. There is general agreement on this point. On the other hand, it is more debatable whether a prayer performed under such circumstances is valid or not, with Abū Ḥanīfah and ash-Shāfiʿī lining up in favor of validity, and Mālik and Ibn Ḥanbal being according to one tradition for it, and according to another against it. Appointment of a known addict to lead the prayer is, at any rate, quite out of the question.[1] We do not know how great the practical need was for dealing with this problem, but it certainly was something to worry about, even if tales such as the one about a hashish eater dressed like a legal scholar who was pressed into service as prayer leader and spoiled the prayer by his irrational behavior throw no real light upon the actual situation.[2]

According to the chapter on the prayer of travelers from the *Taʿlīq(ah)* of Judge Ḥusayn al-Marwarrūdhī, a person who missed prayer or fasting while his mind was affected by *banj* or other drugs is required to make up for what he missed after recovery, as is also required of drunkards.[3]

Next to the problems of prayer, those of divorce were closest to the hearts of medieval Muslim jurists and found the most attention in the law books. As in the case of wine,[4] it was a matter of debate whether a divorce pronounced under the influence of hashish was binding or not. A basic question here is whether or not a sin *(maʿṣiyah)* is involved. According to the *Ḥāwī*, possibly that of the Shāfiʿite al-Māwardī (d. 450/1058),[5] the law is the same for the drug

---

[1] Cf. Ibn Taymīyah, *Fatāwī*, IV, 322-324 (= I, 128-130).

[2] Cf. al-Badrī, fol. 11b, and above, pp. 66 f.

[3] Cf. az-Zarkashī, below, p. 197. For the general problems of missed prayers for reasons of temporary insanity and intoxication, cf., for instance, an-Nawawī, *Majmūʿ (Sharḥ al-Muhadhdhab)*, III, 7 f.

[4] Cf., for instance, D. Santillana, *Istituzioni di diritto musulmano malichita*, I, 258 (Rome, n. y.). For ash-Shāfiʿī, see *Umm*, V, 235.

[5] Al-Māwardī's name is not mentioned, but since the quotation is preceded by another from the *Baḥr* of ar-Rūyānī (d. 502/1108), which is a commentary on al-Māwardī's *Ḥāwī*, it seems likely that his *Ḥāwī*, rather than that of

user as it is for the winedrinker, according to one view, but according to another view followed by Abū Ḥanīfah, the divorce is not binding, even though (the addict) is a sinner. According to the *Shāfī* of al-Jurjānī,[1] drinking wine voluntarily or drinking *banj* intentionally for emotional excitement,[2] so as to cause mental disorder, is a sin; consequently, the divorce is binding. According to the Ḥanafite *Fatāwī* of al-Marghīnānī (d. 593/1197),[3] the actions of a person intoxicated by *banj* would not be binding (and this then would include the declaration of divorce).

Among Ḥanafites expressing their opinion on the problem was az-Zaylaʿī (d. 743/1342).[4] Citing ash-Shaybānī as his authority, he maintains that the divorce pronounced by a person under the influence of *banj* is ‹not?› binding like that of the winedrinker. Al-Bazzāzī (d. 827/1424)[5] quotes ʿAbd-al-ʿAzīz b. Khālid at-Tirmidhī on the authority of Abū Ḥanīfah and ath-Thawrī to the effect that a divorce pronounced under the influence of *banj* is binding if the user when he drank it knew what it was he was taking, but it is not binding if he did not know. However, al-Bazzāzī himself and Qāḍīkhān (d. 592/1196), whom he quotes, think that it is not binding under any circumstances.[6] Ibn al-Humām (d. 861/1457),[7] however, finds that no sin exists in the case of *banj* or opium, as they are

---

al-Qazwīnī (d. 665/1266), is meant here. A perusal of these widely preserved works will bring the decision. For al-Māwardī, ar-Rūyānī, and al-Qazwīnī, see *GAL, Suppl.*, I, 668, 673, and 679, respectively. The Yale volumes of al-Māwardī's *Ḥāwī* (see below, p. 124, n. 6) do not include this section.

[1] Ḥājjī Khalīfah, 1023, lists "*ash-Shāfī fī furūʿ ash-Shāfiʿīyah* by Abū l-ʿAbbās Aḥmad b. Muḥammad al-Jurjānī who died in 482/1089-1090." A brief obituary notice of this man which, however, makes no reference to any scholarly activity of his appears in Ibn al-Jawzī, *Muntaẓam*, IX, 50 (Hyderabad 1357-1359).

[2] The reading of the text (below, p. 196) is correct and to be translated as above. Two mss. have something like *thzy' wa-ṭaraban*, seemingly two parallel adverbial accusatives.

[3] These *Fatāwī* appear to be the work listed in *GAL, Suppl.*, I, 649, No. III: *at-Tajnīs wa-l-mazīd fī l-fatāwī*.

[4] For ʿUthmān b. ʿAlī az-Zaylaʿī, cf. *GAL, Suppl.*, II, 265. His statement is cited in the margin of al-Fanārī. The negation seems to have been omitted by mistake, for in his *Tabyīn al-ḥaqā'iq*, VI, 47 (Būlāq 1313-1315), az-Zaylaʿī refers to the ineffectiveness of a divorce declared by a person asleep and by a person whose mind is affected by *banj* and kumiss.

[5] Cf. Ms. Yale A-166 (Catalogue Nemoy, No. 888), fol. 62a.

[6] Qāḍīkhān, *Fatāwī*, II, 33 (Calcutta 1835), makes the same statement as az-Zaylaʿī, cited in n. 4.

[7] For Ibn al-Humām, cf. *GAL, Suppl.*, II, 91. His statement is quoted by al-Fanārī.

principally used for medical purposes; consequently, the divorce is not binding. But the use of narcotics for pleasure and with the intent to cause harm changes the situation. In such a case, the divorce is binding (apparently, because this involves a sin). The author of the *Risālah fī ḥurmat al-banj* decides that a divorce declared under the influence of drugs is binding, as it is in connection with wine, as a deterrent against their use, and the same view is credited to "our (Ḥanafite) scholars" in a discussion apparently by at-Timirtāshī.[1]

The question was presumably one of considerable practical importance. It may not have been the result intended, but the preference expressed in favor of the assumption that a divorce declared under the influence of drugs is binding, while it might have worked hardship on the wife in certain cases, could also have been for her a means to obtain a divorce from a husband who was an addict. This would otherwise have been quite difficult for her. Our hashish stories happen not to talk about divorce, and no reports on actual cases are, as we must expect, available. Thus, once again, the jurists' concern serves us as a reflection of reality. Even if it cannot be corroborated, it appears to be a true reflection.

5. The Feeding of Hashish to Animals

Animals must not be made drunk. Likewise they must not be fed hashish. Az-Zarkashī adds, without indicating his authority, that animals would not eat hashish.[2] Al-Aqfahsī (fol. 20a) adds that if the purpose in feeding hashish to animals is to increase their appetite and fatten them, it can be considered permissible.

6. The Punishment for Drug Use

Since the use of hashish was generally adjudged a crime, the proper form and extent of punishment had to be discussed, even if this discussion had to be held in the rather vague terms customary in Muslim jurisprudence. As usual, it revolves around *ḥadd*, the punishment fixed by the Religious Law, and *taʿzīr*, the punishment left to the discretion of the judicial authorities. Clearly, if it was possible to equate hashish with wine, the *ḥadd* penalty for wine would apply. Otherwise it would have to be *taʿzīr*. However, there

[1] According to the Gotha Ms., quoted in part above, p. 48.
[2] Cf. below, p. 195.

were slight variations. Again it would seem that general considerations concerning the danger inherent in the use of drugs, to a greater degree than strict reasoning according to school tradition, determined the individual scholar's attitude. The strong feelings of the Ṣūfī Shaykh al-Ḥarīrī against hashish naturally led to the conviction that the *ḥadd* punishment was applicable to hashish with even greater force than to wine.[1] Expectedly, Ibn Taymīyah showed himself adamant in his insistence upon the *ḥadd* of either eighty or forty stripes for those who believe that hashish is unlawful, yet take it.[2] However, he was faced with the fact that other jurists did not think the way he did and included hashish in the category of drugs that were non-intoxicating such as *banj*, in which case *taʿzīr* was indicated.[3] We have already seen[4] that the Mālikite al-Qarāfī ranged himself among those. He considers hashish as corruptive but non-intoxicating and draws the conclusion that in such a case, *taʿzīr* is indicated, and only in the case of intoxication (not applicable to hashish) the *ḥadd* punishment. In the course of time, a strong tendency seems to have come to the fore in the direction of moving away from the theory that the *ḥadd* punishment should go with hashish.

In the view of the Shāfiʿite colleagues of an-Nawawī, the use of non-liquid substances and medicines "such as *banj* and this known *ḥashīshah*" were forbidden like wine but entailed *taʿzīr*, and not *ḥadd*, for punishment.[5] The Shāfiʿite az-Zarkashī considered the application of *ḥadd* obligatory on the basis of his assumption of an intoxicating character for hashish. What is really decisive for him is the property of giving pleasure and an emotional uplift. Thus there is no contradiction in the statement of al-Māwardī who required *ḥadd* for the use of plants causing strong emotion,[6] and that of ar-

[1] Cf. also Ibn Taymīyah, below, pp. 161 f.

[2] Cf. Ibn Taymīyah, *Fatāwī*, IV, 312.

[3] Cf. Ibn Taymīyah, *Siyāsah*, and *Fatāwī*, IV, 310, 312.

[4] Cf. above, p. 110.

[5] Cf. an-Nawawī, *Majmūʿ (Sharḥ al-Muhadhdhab)*, III, 9.

[6] The passage from al-Māwardī's *Ḥāwī* appears on fol. 182a of Vol. 23 of the Yale Ms. L-267 (Catalogue Nemoy, No. 1030). Al-Māwardī discusses two other possibilities: Plants like *banj* that cause intoxication but do not cause strong emotion, which are forbidden to eat but do not require the *ḥadd* penalty and, if necessary, may be used for medical purposes, and plants like *dād(h)ī* "Judas tree" which do not cause intoxication by themselves but only in connection with something else. For *dād(h)ī*, cf., for instance, M. Meyerhof and G. P. Sobhy, *The Abridged Version of "The Book of Simple Drugs" of ... al-Ghāfiqī by Gregorius Abu'l-Farağ (Barhebraeus)*, I, 488-490 (Cairo 1938),

Rāfiʿī who rejected *ḥadd* in connection with non-intoxicating plants, because the crucial consideration is the effect of emotion. Thus, according to ar-Rāfiʿī, *banj* does not require *ḥadd* because it does not cause pleasure and emotion and, in addition, is not strictly addictive.[1] In az-Zarkashī's view, since this is different with hashish, the *ḥadd* penalty for hashish is also implied in the position taken by ar-Rāfiʿī.[2] Another Shāfiʿite, ʿIzz-ad-dīn, rejected in his *Qawāʿid* the applicability of *ḥadd* to the use of non-intoxicating drugs such as *banj* whose destructive effect he considered to be of an extremely rare occurrence. He declared it appropriate in connection with alcoholic beverages such as wine and *nabīdh*, for they, he argued, were so very harmful just because of their ability to generate joy and emotion. Az-Zarkashī made no comment as to whether this included hashish.[3] He might have wanted to leave it to the reader's judgment as to how the emotional aspect of the inebriating qualities of alcoholic beverages could be reconciled with the effects of hashish. The Shāfiʿite judge Ḥusayn al-Marwarrūdhī would certainly not have used the word hashish in the eleventh century, but according to al-Qalqashandī's discussion of hashish,[4] he held the view that intentional drug use was a major sin marking the user as "wicked" *(fāsiq)* (as are winedrinkers). Unintentional or medical use did not have this consequence. This then suggested the conclusion that hashish users are to be classified as "wicked"; yet, they are not subject to the *ḥadd* penalty. To conclude our survey of the Shāfiʿite position, we may quote, again from az-Zarkashī, the colleagues, presumably Shāfiʿites, of a certain Ẓahīr-ad-dīn at-Tizmantī[5] who acknowledged that they were confronted with three different views. Hashish, as a plant, may be equated with wine and *nabīdh* because it involves intoxication, as this is the crucial point. It may be equated with wine only if it is in liquid form, so as to have complete

and for the possibility of intoxication caused only in connection with other substances, cf. above, p. 115.

[1] Cf. above, p. 97, n. 1.

[2] Cf. az-Zarkashī, below, p. 189. Ar-Rāfiʿī is better known as the historian of Qazwīn, who died in 623/1226, cf. *GAL*, *Suppl.*, I, 678.

[3] Cf. pp. 190 f.; Ibn ʿAbd-as-Salām, *Qawāʿid*, I, 164 (Cairo, n.y.).

[4] Cf. al-Qalqashandī, *Ṣubḥ*, II, 146, and above, p. 114, n. 3.

[5] This seems to be the correct reading, after Tizmant, a town in Egypt. Ibn Ḥajar, *Durar*, II, 61 (Hyderabad 1348-1350), mentions a certain Jaʿfar at-Tizmantī as a law teacher of al-Ḥusayn b. ʿAlī b. Sayyid-al-kull (646-739/1248(9)-1338). I do not know whether he was this Ẓahīr-ad-dīn. The entire passage concerning him occurs only in one-half of the Zarkashī manuscript tradition.

correspondence. And it may be equated with wine only if it can be shown that it produces the same effects as wine, such as generating energy, bravery, daring, and exhilaration[1] in the head. We may well assume that only in the first case could there be *ḥadd* punishment, since hashish was rarely used in liquid form and was not really believed to have the qualities associated with wine.[2]

For the Ḥanafites whom az-Zarkashī quotes from the *Fatāwī al-Khulāṣah*, medical use, even if it leads to mental derangement, remains exempt from the *ḥadd* punishment. However, if the use of a drug (*banj* was presumably the word originally used) is intended to produce intoxication, ash-Shaybānī favors *ḥadd*, while Abū Ḥanīfah himself and Abū Yūsuf opt for *taʿzīr*.[3] With express reference to *banj*, this view is also reported in the marginal notes of al-Fanārī as having been stated by al-ʿAynī (?).[4] *Ḥadd* punishment is also demanded, for the use of *banj* leading to intoxication, by the *Tanwīr al-abṣār*, az-Zaylaʿī, and the *Tātarkhānīyah*.[5] The authoritative Ḥanafite view with regard to the use of hashish was evidently the one quoted by al-Fanārī from al-Ḥaddād(ī)'s commentary on al-Qudūrī: "(Hashish) is less strictly forbidden than wine. Eating a small amount of it does not require the *ḥadd* penalty, even if intoxication results. It is like drinking urine and eating faeces. It is forbidden but does not require the *ḥadd* penalty but a *taʿzīr* less severe than *ḥadd*."

The user was thus criminally culpable, but he was not condemned as harshly as was the person who "declared the use of hashish lawful and permissible" (who, of course, mostly was, but need not always have been, a user himself). At least for Ibn Taymīyah, an individual who thus distorted the intent of the divine law was an apostate *(murtadd)* and was to be treated as such. He must be asked to repent, and failing to do so, he must be killed. His corpse must not be washed, the funeral prayers must not be performed for him, and he must not

---

[1] This appears to be the meaning of *nashāh*, apparently from the root *n-sh-w*. No doubt the same word occurs in Ibn Taymīyah, *Fatāwī*, IV, 324 (= II, 252) (below, p. 148, n. 4), where the printed text offers *nash'atuhā* or *shiyātuhā*, neither easily explainable in the context by its ordinary meaning. *Nashāh* also appears repeatedly in Ibn Ḥajar al-Haytamī, *Taḥdhīr ath-thiqāt*.

[2] *Nashāṭ* "energy" is mentioned as an effect of hashish in the Ḥaydar story (above, p. 51), but cf., in particular, al-Qarāfī, above, pp. 109 f.

[3] Cf. az-Zarkashī, below, p. 190.

[4] I am not sure whether this is the correct reading and, if so, whether he is the well-known historian who died in 855/1451.

[5] For the *Fatāwī at-Tātarkhānīyah* of Ibn ʿAlāʾ (d. ca. 750/1349), cf. *GAL*, *Suppl.*, II, 643.

be buried among Muslims.[1] We do not have further evidence on this point, but a late jurist, probably at-Timirtāshī (quoting an-Nasafī?),[2] ascribes to "our scholars," meaning the Ḥanafites, the view that those who say that eating hashish is lawful *(man qāl bi-ḥill aklih)* are not only innovators and "wicked" but also heretics *(zindīq)*. This may mean that they considered the severe fate awaiting heretics as reserved also for those people. In the same discussion, users are thought deserving of severe *taʿzīr*.

In this connection, we also find an express statement as to what is to be done legally with those who traffic in hashish. Their punishment is *ta'dīb* "chastisement," which is one, or rather some, of the forms the *taʿzīr* punishment could take.[3] Both the growers of hashish and hashish sellers suffered destruction of their product. This obviously entailed considerable financial loss for them,[4] but it was a practical matter which appears to have found little repercussion in legal theorizing.

What the actual legal practice was as distinct from the theory would be of particular importance for us to know in our quest to understand hashish as a social problem, but if we wish to be honest with ourselves, we must admit that our knowledge in this respect is almost non-existent. Documented information can be expected to come forth from Ottoman archives and literary sources. For earlier times, there is little hope that even the most careful sifting of the preserved material will present us with something like a documented and coherent picture.

The *ḥadd* punishment put a severe stigma upon those convicted to it, and it was generally considered as more stringent than *taʿzīr*. It was in fact held by the majority of schools that the *taʿzīr* should not go beyond the extent of the prescribed *ḥadd*, but this could be measured unambiguously in the case of hashish only when the applicable *ḥadd* consisted of stripes like that for drinking wine (according to the prevailing theory, even though the practice often substituted jail for it). *Taʿzīr* could therefore result in practice in penalties that hit the culprit harder than *ḥadd*.

---

[1] Cf. Ibn Taymīyah, *Fatāwī*, IV, 302, 310, 312.

[2] Cf. above, p. 48.

[3] Cf. above, p. 49, and the anecdote, above, p. 39. Ibn ʿAbd-aẓ-Ẓāhir singled out the grower of hashish as deserving of chastisement whereas the user should be denounced publicly (*sh-h-r* VIII) (which would also qualify as "chastisement"), cf. al-Ghuzūlī, *Maṭāliʿ*, II, 129; Ibn Ḥijjah, *Thamarāt*, I, 364.

[4] Cf. below, pp. 133 ff.

Before either *ḥadd* or *taʿzīr* could be administered, the difficult hurdle of providing evidence had to be cleared. Under many, if not most, circumstances this might not have been possible. The establishment of guilt when a suspected user was brought before the authorities probably depended as a rule upon witnesses or the finding of hashish in the suspect's possession. Some glimpse at the procedures that might at times have been followed is granted us by a passage in al-Badrī (fol. 55a). Signs of hashish intoxication are redness and dullness *(futūr)* of the eyes, a sallow pale ("dirty yellow") complexion of the face, and difficulties in moving about combined with physical and mental apathy *(kasal, khabāl)*. These signs are used by the authorities *(ḥākim)* to prove the case against a defendant. If the accused denies his guilt, he may be given sour milk to drink and be ordered to throw up, as the greenness of hashish would go down (rather, come up?)[1] with it. If the accused refuses, he should be beaten until he complies.

For a judge, regardless of school affiliation, a decision was certainly never easily arrived at. Defenders of the use of hashish could not only claim that there was no law against it. Under ordinary circumstances, they could be also fairly certain that the law would not attempt to reach out for them.[2]

A special situation existed in the case described by al-Badrī (fol. 57a). On 25 Ramaḍān 867/13 June 1463, shortly before the *maghrib* prayer, an individual was apprehended in Damascus with hashish in his hand and ready to eat it. He confessed that he had obtained it from someone who had ground *(ṣ-ḥ-n)* it and that he had meant to eat it at the time of the call to prayer. Both he and his source were beaten and publicly denounced and then banished. In this case, the crime of using hashish was combined with an intended desecration, at least on the part of one of the culprits, of the fast of Ramaḍān. How the punishment would have turned out under less incriminating circumstances is hard to say.

When the government decided to proceed energetically against the use of drugs, severe penalties were demanded and apparently also imposed. This included the death penalty. In the thirteenth century, Baybars prohibited the consumption of wine and hashish and invoked the sword as the punishment (expressed by the word *ḥadd*) for it.[3]

---

[1] *Tanzil*, cf. *nizāl*, below, p. 164, n. 1?
[2] Cf., for instance, above, p. 76, or below, p. 164, verse 16.
[3] Cf. below, pp. 135 f.

In the latter part of the fourteenth century, Sūdūn ash-Shaykhūnī punished people accused of making hashish with the extraction of their molars, and many suffered this fate, as al-Maqrīzī tells us. The seventeenth-century anecdote reported by Ibn al-Wakīl al-Mīlawī has two old men go to a park in Qaṣr al-ʿAynī, then outside Cairo, in order to eat hashish and smoke tobacco undisturbed. They were afraid of being found out by the governor, Ḥusayn Pasha,[1] and decided that one of them should always watch the road. They alternately ate hashish and smoked tobacco, but the effect of hashish caused the watcher to fall asleep. He woke up only upon hearing the clatter of the horses of the men of Ḥusayn Pasha. Quickly he hid the smoking apparatus *(dawāh)* under the garment on the back of the other man. When Ḥusayn Pasha came and asked them what they were doing there, he told him that he was a barber getting ready to shave his companion's head. The companion felt the heat of the smoking utensil and squirmed, and when Ḥusayn Pasha who was aware all the time that they had been smoking, asked him why the man was squirming, the "barber" blamed the heat of the razor. Ḥusayn Pasha called his attention to the fact that he had no razor. So he said that he was squirming because he was afraid of his clumsiness and inexperience in barbering. Ḥusayn Pasha broke out laughing. All the while, however, the man suffering from the burning heat accused his companion in Arabic of having burned his back, only to be told to be quiet and patient since "the burning of fire was milder than decapitation." Both naturally thought that Ḥusayn Pasha did not know Arabic and did not understand them, but he did. Yet he did not have the men arrested but gave them some gold and silver coins as a payment, he said, for the barbering, and then left them alone.[2] The prime offence here was not hashish but smoking, which was hotly debated at the time.[3] The death penalty was at stake, but enforcement was evidently lax.

[1] He was Deli Ḥusayn Pasha, who died in 1069/1659 and was governor of Egypt from 1045/1635 to 1047/1637, cf. I. Parmaksızoğlu, in *EI*², s. v. Ḥusayn Pasha. The date of his governorship in Egypt provides the exact chronological setting for the story.

[2] Cf. Ibn al-Wakīl al-Mīlawī, *Bughyat al-musāmir*, in the Cambridge Ms. ar. 136 (Qq 194), fols. 113b-114a. For the author and the work, cf. F. Rosenthal, in *JAOS*, LXXXIII (1963), 454.

[3] The unsuccessful repressive actions against the use of tobacco in the Ottoman Empire are described, for instance, in Ḥājjī Khalīfah, *The Balance of Truth*, trans. G. L. Lewis, 50 ff. The little treatise (cf. also above, p. 16, n. 2) presents a good picture of the theoretical and legal arguments then in vogue.

It would seem that the occasions when the government was determined to take drastic steps against hashish (for reasons never stated in satisfactory detail but at best in generalities such as counteracting moral laxity) were infrequent, and the action not very successful. One might also suspect that at other times, the number of individual cases that reached the courts was limited and stood certainly in no proportion to the number of addicts. The legal theory left some loopholes, although by and large it was agreed upon the criminal character of drug use. But it was fighting a losing battle with the reality of the societal environment and seems to have given up and failed when a strong stand was sorely needed. At the end, the prevailing attitude in society appears to have been one of complete resignation.[1]

[1] This, at least, is the impression one gains from the just cited work by Ḥājjī Khalīfah for the first half of the seventeenth century.

CHAPTER FIVE

HASHISH AND ITS USERS IN SOCIETY

1. Economic Aspects

With its continued growth, the hashish habit quite naturally came to play a certain role in economic and commercial life. The extent and character of this role can be assumed to have varied a good deal from country to country and from locality to locality, but we do not have the details that would be necessary to make any precise statements about this situation.

One of the outstanding features about hashish was its comparative inexpensiveness. It might have been only under rare conditions that it was beyond the reach of anybody.[1] Hashish was so cheap that it could be said by the historian Ibn ʿAbd-aẓ-Ẓāhir in the thirteenth century that one dirham of hashish readily bought as much intoxication as did one dīnār of wine.[2] This, of course, is not to be taken literally, but it gives a good idea of the economics involved. Wine, in contrast to hashish, was a luxury item that the poorer sections of the population were unable to afford, a fact repeatedly commented upon. The production of hashish also was much less refined and complicated than the cultivation and the processing of grapes, nor should it be forgotten that hashish was a much less bulky and more easily handled merchandise than wine. Moreover, the trade in it did not require the capital and organization that can be assumed to have been required in the merchandising of wine. Thus, even if hashish had not been a subject to be treated gingerly and to be bypassed wherever possible, we could not expect to find for it even a small part of the information that exists on viticulture and the wine trade. Understandably, the jurists, too, paid much less attention to it.

Hemp was grown for purposes that were entirely legitimate such

[1] Cf. above, p. 99.

[2] Gf. al-Ghuzūlī, *Maṭāliʿ*, II, 129; Ibn Ḥijjah, *Thamarāt*, I, 364. For a similar comparison with respect to weight, cf. above, p. 106.

European observers in the past always stressed the cheapness of hashish as compared to other narcotics, cf. Silvestre de Sacy, *Mémoire sur la dynastie des Assassins*, 48, 50.

as the production of rope.[1] For use as a drug, the wild variety could be used and was, in fact, recommended for use.[2] But primarily, it was cultivated in "gardens," as already Ibn al-Bayṭār tells us. Quite apart from the possibility that it often was home-grown in small patches of land, the acreage used for planting it even commercially was no doubt as a rule small. However, we also hear that in certain parts of the Delta of the Nile, the major crop sown was hashish, and the daily consumption of hashish in Cairo amounted to ten thousand *nuqrahs* (= dirhams), presumably referring to the monetary value of the hashish consumed.[3] There may be considerable exaggeration here, especially with respect to the statement of hemp being the principal crop in some of Egypt's most fertile land, but there is little reason to doubt that hemp as the source of hallucinatory cannabis was not negligible as a factor in agriculture. The cultivation of hashish was largely forbidden no less than its use. An additional verse to be found in adh-Dhahabī's *Kabā'ir* stresses this point (although it should be noted that the second line also occurs in connection with wine):[4]

> To eat it and to grow it as something lawful—
> These are two calamities for the unfortunate individual.

According to az-Zarkashī,[5] growing hashish for use as an intoxicant is forbidden, while growing it for medical purposes is permitted. Ibn Taymīyah might not have made an express pronouncement on the subject since all az-Zarkashī quotes in this connection as Ibn Taymīyah's view is a *fatwā* of his that forbade the cultivation of a kind of grapes to be found in certain places in Syria which could not be used as raisins but were good only for wine.

Between the grower and the seller, we find the "maker" or "producer" *(f-ʿ-l, ṣ-n-ʿ)* of hashish, evidently the entrepreneur who turned the plant into the product ready for sale and use. At times,

---

[1] Cf. S. D. Goitein, *A Mediterranean Society*, I, 86, 105 f. (Berkeley and Los Angeles 1967).

[2] Cf. above, pp. 57 f.

[3] Cf. al-Badrī, fol. 4b, where, in spite of the use of "I say," the statement seems to go back to the alleged source, al-Bunduqī's *Ṣaḥīḥ* (see above, p. 28, n. 4). The Damiette region in particular seems to be meant for hashish being the major crop there. Although the phrasing is somewhat strange *(yustaʿmal fīhā kull yawm bi-ʿasharat ālāf nuqrah ḥashīsh)*, the preposition *bi-* suggests that *nuqrah* cannot be understood as referring to "lumps" of hashish.

[4] Cf. the Berlin Ms. (but not the Princeton Ms.) of Ibn Ghānim.

[5] Below, p. 196.

he might of course have been identical with either the grower or, more likely, the seller, if not both. This probably depended upon the volume of local demand and the resulting profitableness of any of these activities. When severe punishment was meted out in connection with the making of hashish,[1] it probably affected those involved in all the stages, from growing to preparation to consumption. And the curse pronounced in *Qamʿ* upon "the maker and consumer of hashish"[2] was no doubt also intended to be all-inclusive. However, the producer of hashish from the harvested hemp crop was a further link in the economic chain of drug use.

That tax farming *(ḍamān)* was undertaken in connection with hashish (see below), in whatever form it might have been, clearly shows that it was a commercial item of some importance. We do not know anything about the profits of the sellers marked for chastisement in Transoxania,[3] but a local addict who maintained himself by importing and selling hashish was certainly not just compelled by his habit to continue in business, but he also found it lucrative and was not greatly bothered by occasional monetary fines imposed upon him.[4] The hashish seller *(bayyāʿ al-ḥashīsh)* of the *Arabian Nights* is described as selling also preparations with, it seems, no hashish in it.[5] However, his appears to have been an established business, and presumably a profitable one. The confection called *ʿuqdah*[6] provided its inventor with a flourishing business, even if it had to be a clandestine operation. A success story paralleling that of *ʿuqdah* is reported by al-Badrī (fols. 29a-30a) as having taken place in his own lifetime, in the years 869-870/1464-1466. A Persian called ash-Sharīf (but not a descendant of the Prophet, *min ghayr shaṭfah khaḍrā')* came to Damascus and set up two tents in which he sold herbs and confections. He had a good business and soon received a missive from Egypt expressing the desire of Egyptians for his product and beginning with the verse: "Anyone going to Damascus underneath its fortress—Please greet the seller of the paste *(maʿjūn)* in the tent(s)." He accepted the invitation and set up a candy shop in Cairo where his employees produced pears, apples, red and green dates, and other (candied fruits). He was so successful that it was rare to find a

[1] Cf. above, pp. 128 f.
[2] Cf. *Qamʿ*, fol. 275b: ...*al-ḥashīshah qātal Allāh fāʿilahā wa-mubtaliʿahā.*
[3] Cf. above, p. 49.
[4] Cf. above, p. 39.
[5] Cf. the story referred to above, p. 32, n. 4.
[6] Cf. above, p. 33.

Cairine, man, woman, or child, without candies from ash-Sharīf in the pocket. But then it happened that the wife of an *amīr al-ʿasharāt* went to the public bath and her companion *(khushdāshah)* gave her one of the dates *(bal[a]ḥah)* from the Sharīf establishment to eat. It was her first experience with them, and she had hardly entered the bath when she lost contact with reality *(ghābat ʿan wujūdihā)*. Applying a shampoo *(nūrah)*[1] to her head, she felt its pleasant itch and started to scratch but then was unable to stop until her tresses fell out. Her husband was shocked when he saw her. He got together with the *muḥtasib*, and they accused ash-Sharīf of putting hashish in his confections. Ash-Sharīf denied it and gave them his recipe. They had it checked out with a druggist, and it was found that the candies did not contain hashish. There was disagreement among people as to what could have been the intoxicating ingredient. Some suggested that it might have been *ḥāfir al-ḥimār*,[2] others thought of *dāt(h)ūrah*, and others still of other plants.[3] Anyway, when the *amīr al-mushidd*[4] heard about the matter, he gave ash-Sharīf a large salary which enabled him to set up a chain of candy stores all over Cairo. If hashish had been involved or, if it was, could have been proven to be involved, he probably would have been put out of business, but the story suggests that a skilful retailer could have done very well with hashish confections, at least for some time.

The need to keep the hashish trade under cover was no doubt the result of the legal attitude toward activities of this sort. Az-Zarkashī declared it permissible for the drug to be sold if it was intended to serve useful pharmacological purposes the same way as was done by scammony and opium, but even in this case only on condition that

[1] Lit., "depilatory," cf. A. Louis, in *EI*², III, 145a, *s. v.* ḥammām, on modern Tunisian *ṭfal* "fuller's clay, dry mud."

[2] There is a plant called *ḥāfir al-muhr* "colchicum" (cf. M. Meyerhof, ed. and trans. of Maimonides, 134 f.), but there also is a *ẓilf al-ḥimār* (*ẓilf* being a synonym of *ḥāfir*), cf. H. P. Renaud and G. S. Colin, *Tuḥfat al-aḥbāb*, 184 (Paris 1934, *Publ. de l'Institut des Hautes Études Marocaines* 24). Dioscurides' reference to *ḥawāfīr al-ḥamīr* and *aẓlāf al-maʿz* (II, 42, 44; ed. Wellmann, I, 134; Dubler and Terés, II, 141) is, however, of no help as no plant names are involved.

[3] With reference to the *zaqqūm* legend, above, p. 46, n. 2.

[4] As in the case of the poet so named (above, p. 91, n. 5), who was a superintendent of government bureaus, this refers to some high rank in the Mamlūk administration. For the various possibilities, cf. W. Popper, *Egypt and Syria under the Circassian Sultans*, 94 f. For the "amīr of ten(s)," cf., for instance, D. Ayalon, *Studies on the Structure of the Mamluk Army*, in *BSOAS*, XVI (1954), 470.

it be traded in small quantities only. Selling hashish to those who were definitely known as addicts was forbidden.[1] On the other hand, if we can take al-Aqfahsī literally, the purchase of hashish was not unlawful, in contrast to that of wine.[2]

In order to curb the use of hashish, it was necessary to hit it at the source, that is, primarily, either the growers or the sellers. Sometimes, urban development eliminated a popular source of hashish. This happened when the Kāfūr Park in Cairo was built up in 651/1253. It put an end to the use of the park for cultivating hashish there.[3] The word employed in connection with the destruction of hashish is "burning." What was burned is somewhat ambiguous, but we may assume, with good reason, that it predominantly referred to burning down the hemp fields (or rather, the cut plants), and only rarely if at all to the burning of the finished product, the stock of hashish in the hands of dealers. We have already heard that the Ḥanafites and Shāfiʿites of Transoxania agreed, presumably at a comparatively early date in the history of hashish, that it was to be burned with considerable loss to the owners.[4] If this loss was due to its great value, it would seem to mean the destruction of the finished product held by merchants, but if it resulted from lack of recompensation, it would also be possible to think of the burning down of the plants in the fields. When the governor of Cairo, Mūsā b. Yaghmūr (599-663/1202(3)-1265), was ordered by al-Malik aṣ-Ṣāliḥ Najm-ad-dīn Ayyūb in 643/1245 to prevent the growing of hashish in the Kāfūr Park, he had a large amount of it collected and burned, quite obviously, the harvested plants,[5] but a slight ambiguity in this respect attaches to the famous report of the attempt, undertaken in Egypt under al-Malik aẓ-Ẓāhir Baybars in 665/1266-67, to proceed against moral laxity in the population. It involved revocation of the

[1] Az-Zarkashī (below, p. 195) continues: "as it is forbidden to sell grapes to winemakers. The statement that hashish is intoxicating leads through analogical reasoning to the conclusion that the sale (of it) is invalid, even if it is clean, like musical instruments." Al-Aqfahsī, fol. 22b, adds to this the view expressed by Shaykh Abū Ḥāmid that selling grapes to winemakers is not forbidden since they might repent. He concludes that this could also be considered applicable to hashish. Abū Ḥāmid would be the famous Shāfiʿite, Aḥmad b. Muḥammad al-Isfarāʾinī (344-406/955(6)-1016), cf. al-Khaṭīb al-Baghdādī, *Taʾrīkh Baghdād*, IV, 368-370 (Cairo 1349/1931); as-Subkī, *Ṭabaqāt ash-Shāfiʿīyah*, III, 24 ff.

[2] Cf. above, p. 105.

[3] Cf. al-Maqrīzī, II, 25, and I, 457.

[4] Cf. above, p. 49.

[5] Cf. al-Maqrīzī, II, 26.

ḍamān for hashish and the destruction of it by fire as well as the destruction by fire of houses where intoxicating beverages were available, breaking the wine vessels found there and pouring out the wine.[1] Since the wine was the finished product stored in taverns ready for consumption, we might think that also the hashish was the finished drug available from dealers; this, however, is quite obviously uncertain, and the burning of hemp plants might rather be meant. Accordingly, the *ḍamān* would refer to tax revenues obtained from the growers, rather than from sales of the finished product purchased by users. When Qudādār (d. 730/1329) became governor of Cairo in 724/1324, he confiscated much hashish in Bāb al-Lūq and had it burned at Bāb Zuwaylah where at the same time also large quantities of confiscated wine were destroyed. Hardly a day went by for an entire month when this was not done.[2] It is difficult to say whether it was processed hashish or the hemp plants that were uprooted and burned. Certainly, when Sūdūn ash-Shaykhūnī (d. 798/1396) went after various places in and around Cairo, such as al-Junaynah,[3] Ḥakr Wāṣil in Būlāq, and Bāb al-Lūq, in order to have those "accursed shrubs" destroyed, there can be little doubt that the growing plants were meant which were burned in the places where they were growing.[4] Whatever it was that was destroyed when action was taken against hashish, it is clear that people were hurt economically to some degree.

Altogether, hashish provided for or contributed to the livelihood of quite a number of individuals and had some importance in the economy, at least in Egypt, practically the only country for which we have some information. This might have contributed to make the fight against hashish use more difficult, but to all appearances, it cannot have been a very weighty factor. We may suspect that the hashish trade made its contribution to the ever present danger of bribery in the judiciary. Our sources, however, contain no examples

---

[1] Cf. al-Kutubī, *Fawāt*, I, 170 (in the life of Baybars), and II, 387 (in the life of Muḥammad b. Dāniyāl); Ibn Dāniyāl, *Ṭayf al-khayāl*, cf. G. Jacob, *Das Schattentheater*, 7 (Berlin 1901); al-Maqrīzī, I, 106, ed. G. Wiet, in *Mém. de l'Institut Français d'Archéol. Or. du Caire*, XXXIII (1913), 90, and II, 302; Ibn Iyās, *Badā'i'*, I, 104-107 (Būlāq 1312), *anno* 665 (not available); 'Alī Ṣ. Ḥusayn, *Ibn Daqīq-al-'īd*, 40 f. (Cairo 1960); S. Y. Labib, *Handelsgeschichte Ägyptens im Spätmittelalter*, 249 (Wiesbaden 1965).

[2] Cf. al-Maqrīzī, II, 149; Ibn Kathīr, XIV, 113, where Qudādār's closeness to Ibn Taymīyah is stressed.

[3] Cf. above, p. 95, n. 7.

[4] Cf. al-Maqrīzī, II, 128.

for the use of money derived from the trade to protect its merchants and customers against legal action.

2. The Asocial Character of Drug Use

As described by al-Maqrīzī, addicts tended to gather in certain sections of town. In Cairo, Arḍ aṭ-Ṭabbālah and Bāb al-Lūq were known as notorious centers of vice, certainly also because they were gathering places for hashish eaters. From a later time, we hear about a bridge then known as Qanṭarat al-Ḥashshāshīn which had acquired this nickname because it was one of the places where addicts met.[1] There were special hideouts and taverns frequented by them.[2] We hear about a scholar in Baghdād leaving a "hashish house."[3] But, it seems, there was nothing really comparable to the winehouses mentioned for the Cairo of Baybars, let alone anything like the famous monasteries and taverns we hear about mainly from ʿAbbāsid times.

Hashish parties of a private character were not unusual.[4] Thus, at a party gathered in some pleasant spot *(muntazah)*, people passed hashish around *(adārū)*, but one of those present, the young poet Ibn al-ʿAfīf at-Tilimsānī, refused to take any. He was goaded by verses of another participant, called Jūbān al-Qawwās:

> When opportunities show themselves for you, seize them,
> For the times for enjoying them are brief.
> Get them from something amber-scented, the color
> Of myrtle, with a touch of green.
> It circulates in the palms, no cup is needed
> For it, and its jars are small pockets.
> Leave aside anything else if you are afraid of being shamed
> As sipping anything else means humiliation and shame.[5]

---

[1] Cf. al-Bakrī, *Kawākib.*

[2] As in Granada, cf. above, p. 55.

[3] See below, p. 145.

[4] Cf. also below, p. 172, n. 4.

[5] Cf. al-Badrī, fol. 56a:

> *idhā furaṣun badat laka fa-ntahizhā*
> *fa-aʿmāru s-surūri bihā qiṣāru*
> *wa-khudhhā min muʿanbaratin bi-lawnin*
> *ka-lawni l-āsi yalḥaquhā khḍirāru*
> *taṭūfu ʿalā l-akuffi bi-ghayri ka'sin*
> *lahā wa-ḥibābuhā l-jiyabu ṣ-ṣighāru*
> *wa-daʿ ʿan ghayrihā in khifta ʿāran*
> *fa-ḥaswatu ghayrihā dhullun wa-ʿāru.*

For Ibn al-ʿAfīf's reply, see above, p. 93. On Jūbān, see al-Kutubī, *Fawāt,* I, 213-219.

Ibn al-ʿAfīf, however, remained steadfast in his refusal. In this case, the hashish eaters were in the company of one, or, presumably, more than one, person who did not mind their activities but also felt free not to participate in them. We also hear about individual hashish eaters in a group of people not using the drug.[1] Sharing the hashish habit seems to be understood as a bond of friendship in verses by a certain Muḥammad b. Makkī b. ʿAlī b. al-Ḥusayn al-Mashhadī. They were the favorite poem of an impoverished addict:

> The use of hashish is censured by all silly persons
> Weak of mind, insensitive.
> Really, do not listen, friend,
> To the censure coming from stupid and envious individuals.
> Share hashish with a goodly young man firm
> In the preservation of friendship and appointments.
> Is it not a relaxation for the mind? Thus enjoy
> It, all you sensible men!
> It is the subtle meaning. Which words could accomplish
> A description of the centerpiece of the necklace of pearls?
> Use it—it is no sin—
> To obtain joy and happiness.
> Its excellence has emotion and pleasure as witnesses.
> Such witnesses are among the best of witnesses.
> That this is the right view of it is indicated
> By the soul's joy freed from worry.[2]
> Reveal what it harbors: a secret concealed,
> And bring about removal from existence in existence![3]

---

[1] Cf. above, p. 67.

[2] *Ṭarīd* could be feminine and refer to *an-nafs*, but in this case it should have the definite article.

[3] Cf. al-Badrī, fols. 22b-23a (in connection with the story of ʿAṭīyah al-Ḥaṣkafī, below, p. 159):

> *yalūmu ʿalā l-ḥashīshati kullu fadmin*
> *sakhīfi r-ra'yi dhī ḥissin balīdi*
> *fa-lā tasmaʿ bi-ḥaqqika yā ḥabībī*
> *malāma min ghabīyin aw ḥasūdi*
> *wa-wāfiq fī l-ḥashīshi fatān muqīman*
> *ʿalā ḥifẓi l-mawaddati wa-l-ʿuhūdi*
> *a-mā hiya rāḥatu l-arwāḥi fa-nʿam*
> *bihā yā ṣāḥiba l-ʿaqli r-rashīdi*
> *hiya l-maʿnā l-laṭīfu wa-ayyu lafẓin*
> *yaqūmu bi-waṣfi wāsiṭati l-ʿuqūdi*
> *ʿalayka bihā fa-mā fīhā junāḥun*
> *li-taẓfara bi-s-surūri wa-bi-s-suʿūdi*
> *shawāhidu faḍlihā ṭarabun wa-lahwun*
> *wa-shāhidu dhāka min khayri sh-shuhūdi*
> *yukhabbiru ʿan ṣawābi r-ra'yi fīhā*
> *surūru n-nafsi ʿan hammin ṭarīdi*
> *wa-aẓhir mā lahā sirrun khafīyun*
> *fa-ghayyib fī l-wujūdi min-a-l-wujūdi.*

While common need and wishful dreaming thus tended to draw users together, the enjoyment of hashish was by and large considered a lonely, asocial activity. Because of legal and social objections, it was the better part of wisdom to keep one's habit concealed as much as possible. The defiant declaration that "hashish must be eaten openly, no matter how much one's friends are against it,"[1] was more easily made in an anonymous poem than in reality. Likewise, the supreme contempt for the opinions of others expressed in the verses:

> Many a hashish user
> Gets to be hated by mankind.
> When they give him an earful of vilification,
> He swallows it and keeps silent,[2]

constituted an expression of hope as to how things should be, rather than the ordinary reaction to the demands of the societal environment. The eater was afraid of being found out, and he would not even mind to seclude himself in a toilet so as to be able to indulge in his habit unobserved.[3]

Primarily, however, it was the very character of hashish intoxication itself that made the addict seek privacy even in public places and in the company of others. He tries to withdraw from the world around him and to be left alone with his dreams. He does not react to what is going on around him. "If he is spoken to, he does not listen."[4] Under the influence of the drug, he is as quiet and somnolent as in a trance.[5] He would not want to have anything to do with that

---

Min in the last line should probably be corrected to *ʿan*.

The poet, al-Mashhadī, is repeatedly quoted by al-Badrī, but I have no further information on him. I doubt that he is identical with the man, whose grandfather was named ʿUthmān, mentioned by Ibn Ḥajar, *Durar*, IV, 264; J. Sublet, in *Bulletin d'Études Or. de l'Inst. Français de Damas*, XX (1967 [1969]), 51, no. 121.

[1] Cf. al-Badrī, fol. 8a:

fa-lā budda min akli l-ḥashīshati jahratan
wa-in asrafū l-ikhwānu minhā wa-aktharū.

Minhā probably should be corrected to *fīhā*. The crucial understanding of the second line is, however, doubtful.

[2] Cf. al-Badrī, fols. 10b and 17b, where the verses are ascribed to al-Hā'im:

wa-rubba ḥashshāshin ghadat — lahū l-barāyā tamqutu
in asmaʿūhu shatmahū — yablaʿuhā wa-yaskutu.

Shatmatan, not *shatmahū*, is the reading indicated in the ms. However this may be, the suffix *-hā* in the following line refers to hashish (and not to a possible *shatmah*).

[3] Cf. the poem by Ibn Ghānim, verse 6, below, p. 169.

[4] Cf. above, p. 87.

[5] Cf. above, p. 110.

quarrelsome lot of winebibbers whose companionableness often ends in violent altercations when they are drunk. This is considered an advantage of sorts for the hashish user,[1] but it points up the lonesome character of his vice. Fuzūlī depicts hashish personified as someone who is convinced of his uniqueness and who claims that he is everything in the world and nothing else counts. His attitude, Fuzūlī states, represents the most pronounced egoism.[2] The clear implication is that hashish, and its user, wants to live in a world of his own, apart from reality and unconcerned with society.

There is no contradiction between the addict's need for privacy and his need for congregating with his fellows. Urban society in Islam tended to segregate those who by their personal habits did not live up to the expected norm, at least outwardly. This included the majority of the economically less favorably placed hashish users. They had to band together in poor and undesirable neighborhoods in order to pursue their essentially lonely activity.

3. The Addict's Social Standing

One thing stands out clearly in the entire discussion of hashish. While its use cut through all layers of the population and, as al-Badrī (fol. 1b) put it, was, like wine, common to Zayd and ʿAmr, meaning everybody, a certain class distinction was made between confirmed addicts and the rest of the people. This distinction was no doubt largely fictitious, yet, it enjoyed the reputation of being true and definite. Hashish eaters were believed to be low-class people either by nature or by being reduced to that state through their habit which impaired all their faculties but in particular those moral and character qualities that determine the individual's standing in society. It also threatened impoverishment and reduction to beggary *(ḥarfashah)*. Briefly put, hashish "generates low social status *(safālah)* and a bad moral character *(radhālah)*" and brings the addict down to a level where almost nothing human remains in him.[3]

[1] Cf. above, p. 110, n. 2, or the poem of al-Isʿirdī, verse 14, below, p. 164. The hashish eater can dispense with the company of the drunk *(ṣuḥbat al-makhmūr)*, according to a poem by a certain Sharaf-ad-dīn Abū l-ʿAbbās Aḥmad b. Yūsuf from the first half of the thirteenth century, cf. al-Maqrīzī, II, 26.

[2] According to Rescher and Lugal in their translation of Fuzūlī, 154.

[3] The concluding portion of this sentence is al-Maqrīzī's comment on the words in quotation marks, reported by him as a statement made by the

As one of the poems against hashish implies, he combines all the qualities that negate the existence of a well-ordered society and is, in short, a criminal.[1]

A reaction against the accusation of social inferiority is to be found in the stress addicts constantly placed on their "elitist" standing. They were distinguished from and elevated above the common herd of people by being privy to the "secrets" resting in the drug. This theme, already developed in the Ḥaydar story, always served them, we may assume, to bolster their morale. They claimed that on the contrary the use of hashish lifted a person above the lowly state in which life had placed him:

> Let me have some green *Kāfūrī*
> Which takes the place of the best of yellow wine.
> The poor person who partakes of a dirham's weight
> Of it feels superior to amīrs.
> You would think him to be the strongest of men, but when he has none,
> We count him among the weak.[2]

This naturally describes merely a subjective state as seen by users and, perhaps, by sympathetic observers. In reality, hashish did not improve anyone's social status, even in the eyes of those friendly disposed toward hashish use.

The contrast between hashish and wine in this respect is noteworthy. Wine had had a long and mostly honorable history everywhere in the pre-Islamic world, including the Arabian peninsula. It seems to have been forbidden by the Prophet mainly because wine consumption was a luxury which the early adherents of the new religion could not afford and therefore should do without. It remained in a sense a luxury and as such was cherished by the highest strata of society and their entourage and followers. Most importantly, this involved the world of belles lettres with its prime representatives, the innumerable poets whose wine poetry expressed the longings for an unrestrained life for themselves and for those who felt that their social position placed them above the great mass and

---

brother of his maternal grandmother, Tāj-ad-dīn Ismāʿīl b. Aḥmad b. ʿAbd-al-Wahhāb, who died, about eighty years old, in 803/1400 (cf. as-Sakhāwī, *Ḍaw'*, II, 290), on the authority of ʿAlā'-ad-dīn Ibn Nafīs. Unless there is an omission in the text and Ibn Nafīs was not the direct authority of Tāj-ad-dīn, he could hardly be the famous physician who died in 687/1288. It is not excluded that some other Ibn Nafīs (whose honorific may or may not have been ʿAlā'-ad-dīn) is meant.

[1] Cf. below, p. 171.

[2] Cf. al-Maqrīzī, II, 25.

entitled them to disregard for the societal restraints supposed to apply to all alike. According to all we know, there seems to be a good measure of truth to the claim advanced by the proponents of wine in al-Isʿirdī's poem that no caliph or sultan ever used hashish while many rulers, probably the vast majority of them, were devoted to wine.[1] When al-Maqrīzī speaks of the rulers of Hurmuz and al-Baḥrayn in connection with the spread of hashish, it is well to note that he does not say that they themselves were users but it was their entourage *(aṣḥāb)* that was reponsible for propagating the evil habit,[2] a point which, however, was not stressed in al-Badrī's version. Whatever the actual situation, hashish was believed to be incompatible with the responsibility for ruling others, at least on the highest levels of power.[3] Poets and singers also did not proclaim the glories of hashish as they did those of wine. Though the frequent quotations of poems here would seem to suggest that hashish poetry was well cultivated, it is little as compared with the overabundance of verses on wine that continued to be composed all the time. Repetitiveness is rampant, and much of the poetry, in addition to being perfunctory, also was apologetic one way or other.[4] There was none of the joy and exuberance in it that continued to suffuse wine poetry even through its centuries of decay.

Hashish was believed to be anathema to all members of society of the highest social standing. We do not hear anything about the attitudes and practices of the extremely important military component of society. Nor do we have any information about drug use among the rural population. This, however, does not mean much since little attention is paid in the literature to peasants, notwithstanding their large numbers and their importance. Urban craftsmen and merchants of good standing are not too often described as users but our stories contain at least some precise statements as well as quite numerous indications by implication that they were indeed open to the blandishments of drug use and willingly exposed themselves to its dangers.[5] However, hashish was clearly assumed to have its true home among Ṣūfīs and scholars. Together they represented

[1] See below, p. 166, verse 37.
[2] Cf. above, pp. 52 f.
[3] For a highly placed emir, Jānibak at-Tājī (d. 868/1464), being suspected of the use of hashish, cf. Ibn Taghrībirdī, trans. W. Popper, VII, 103 (Berkeley and Los Angeles 1960, *University of California Publications in Semitic Philology* 23).
[4] Cf. also above, pp. 5 and 72.
[5] Cf. also below, p. 160.

a kind of third estate, having connection with the rulers and the military establishment above and the mass of subjects below. During the time under consideration here, Ṣūfism and religious scholarship in its various manifestations were so closely intertwined in the same persons that a clear distinction can rarely be made. And even where there was open hostility, there was constant interaction.

Scholars were often quite poor, and Ṣūfīs even more so as a result of their pretense to economic self-sufficiency. Hashish was cheap and easily accessible. Its acquisition could be done clandestinely. Its use was more easily concealed than that of wine and less affected by the inescapable religious odium attaching to wine, quite apart from the fact that even very small quantities of hashish were more powerful than wine.[1] There was nothing to give away its being used: "The palm of my hand serves as cup for it, and my pocket is its cask; I never gave away its secret by a jug."[2] Hashish can claim to be the friend of dervishes and to be available in the corner of every mosque and among all kinds of scholars.[3] If anyone were to enter the largest class in al-Azhar and produce some hashish or opium or *barsh*, so the author of *Qamʿ* informs us,[4] nobody would want to let him do it because righteous scholars are convinced that it would be unlawful. This may be so but the very idea that somebody could be imagined to be doing such a thing raises the suspicion that it was not inconceivable in reality. Indeed, in an earlier age, hashish could be praised for being suitable for use in every monastery *(ribāṭ)* and mosque, in contrast to wine, as al-Isʿirdī maintains.[5] And when Ibn ʿAbd-aẓ-Ẓāhir inveighed against hashish, he singled out *masājid* and *jawāmiʿ* as the places that should be cleansed of it.[6] More than ordinary people, Ṣūfīs and scholars might have been concerned as they had particularly close ties with life in religious establishments.

Hashish can claim to be the shaykh of scholars, just as wine boasts

---

[1] Cf. above, p. 106.

[2] Cf. also, for instance, above, pp. 63 f., and below, pp. 172 f. The verses referred to above are from a poem, already mentioned above, p. 45, n. 5, and p. 57, n. 2, in al-Badrī, fol. 5b:

kaffī lahā qadaḥun wa-jaybī dannuhā
lam ulqi ʿanhā sirrahā bi-inā'i.

[3] Cf. Fuzūlī, 167.

[4] Cf. *Qamʿ*, fol. 276a. The passage was quoted by al-Fanārī.

[5] Verse 3, below, p. 163.

[6] Cf. al-Ghuzūlī, *Maṭāliʿ*, II, 129; Ibn Ḥijjah, *Thamarāt*, I, 364. Cf. above, pp. 66 f. and 80.

of being the boon companion of rulers.[1] Sometimes we are told that the action of hashish had no influence upon a scholar's ability to discharge his teaching duties in an acceptable manner. Thus a shaykh credited with much wit, a certain Muslim al-Ḥanafī, who was a lecturer in the Barqūqīyah, was able to give lectures on traditional and intellectual subjects in a state of hashish intoxication. One day, however, a mishap occurred. His turban fell off, and out came a few pills (?) of *zīh.*[2] On the lower rungs of scholarship, we hear about a copyist of Burhān-ad-dīn al-Miʿmār whose poetry he copied and who introduced him to hashish *(muḥammaṣ* and *kibāsh)*. He spent all his money on the drug and on the food, much of it sweets, that he consumed alternately with hashish while doing his chores as a copyist. Yet, in spite of his drug consumption, he was able to write a complete quire of paper of a certain size *(qaṭʿ kāmil al-baladī)* with thirty-one lines per page without making a mistake.[3]

---

[1] Cf. Fuzūlī, 171.

[2] Cf. al-Badrī, fol. 28a-b, and above, p. 62, n. 6. The story is quite similar to that of a preacher who had the same happening to him with *banj*. It was included in the eighteenth-century work of J. F. de la Croix, *Anecdotes arabes et musulmanes* (Paris 1772), under the year 950, and was quoted by Robert P. Walter, *Marihuana*, 11 (Philadelphia 1938). The source of de la Croix was, expectedly, B. d'Herbelot, *Bibliothèque Orientale*, 200b, *s. v.* Benk (Paris 1697). The anticlerical sally at the end and, since it is not in d'Herbelot, the date are additions by de la Croix. D'Herbelot states that his source was the Turkish *Laṭāʾif* of Lāmiʿī (d. 939/1532-33, or in the preceding or the following year, cf. Ibn al-ʿImād, *Shadharāt*, VIII, 235; T. Menzel, in *EI*, *s. v.* Lāmiʿī).

The same Muslim al-Ḥanafī, al-Badrī tells us, once bought a chicken at the Zuwaylah Gate and ordered it sent home to his house *(bayt Muslim)* at the Barqūqīyah. The vendor wondered whether not everybody in the Barqūqīyah was a Muslim, which gave our witty and somewhat malicious scholar the opening for the reply that he was the only "Muslim" there.

[3] Cf. al-Badrī, fol. 23a, and above, p. 29, n. 7, and pp. 78 f. Al-Badrī adds the following verses by al-Miʿmār on this copyist of his:

A copyist whose heart is attached to
The green one with seeds and leaves,
I noticed patches on his garment.
I knew he was really torn up.

wa-nāsikhin qalbuhū muʿallaq
bi-l-akhḍari l-mubazzari l-muwarraq
raʾaytu fī thawbihī riqāʿan
ʿalimtu tamzīqahū muḥaqqaq.

Mubazzar is a likely correction of *al-m-b-dh-r* "scattered (?)" found in the ms. The allusions of the second verse escape me. It seems to refer to the copyist's neglect of his appearance and poverty caused by his habit, but this is quite uncertain.

For another copyist who praised hashish, cf. below, p. 154.

Mostly, however, scholars are depicted as having suffered the same fate as others who fell under the spell of hashish, that is, they lost a good deal of the dignity that was expected of them. The story of Ibrāhīm Ibn al-Aʿmā al-Baghdādī (who may have been more of a littérateur than a scholar) contains many of the popular elements. He spent the evening in the "hashish house," reciting bawdy poetry such as the following verses:

This hashish has made my time pleasant.—Its softness (?) is my share of this world.[1]
Would you could see me running around inebriated
In the street, swaying like a drunk,
Being myself in his condition, man!

Up seems down to me.—This hashish has made my time pleasant.—Its softness is my share of this world.
I am, as you know, a beggar and vagabond.
I do not stop being fed hashish,[2]
Some small tablet without capital provided (??).

On beggary an expert, a *muftī*.—This hashish has made my time pleasant.—Its softness is my share of the world.[3]

This no doubt was shockingly unbecoming, but at least it was not out in the open. But then, Ibn al-Aʿmā remembered his college, the Mustanṣirīyah, and he left the hashish house to return to it. On the road, he thought that the light of the moon was water from the Tigris which he believed had overflowed its banks. He took his sandals in

[1] *Lynw'* (requiring two long syllables) may be *līnū*, for *līnuhū*, to be translated as indicated. The meaning would seem to be that the user finds the world as soft and easygoing as hashish. Like that of other passages of this poem, the translation is, however, by no means certain.

[2] *Kaff* may have here the double meaning of "hand" and "hashish," with a probable double meaning also in *maḥshūsh*.

[3] Cf. al-Badrī, fol. 14a:

hādhā l-ḥashīsh ṭayyab waqtī — līnū mina-d-dunyā bakhtī
law raytanī asʿā nashwān
fī s-sūqi mā'il ka-s-sakrān
wa-('a)nā bi-ḥālih yā insān
fawqī takhayyal lī taḥtī — hādhā l-ḥashīsh ṭayyab waqtī — līnū min-a-d-dunyā bakhtī
wa-('a)nā kamā tadrī ḥarfūsh
bi-l-kaffi mā nabraḥ maḥshūsh
luwayḥ bi-lā ra'sin manbūsh (?)
fī l-ḥarfashah ʿālim muftī — hādhā l-ḥashīsh ṭayyab waqtī — līnū min-a-d-dunyā bakhtī

The doubtful reading *luwayḥ* ("tablet" in the sense of "pill") is a correction of *lwʿ* in the ms. Reading *ra's* as two syllables is another dubious feature, perhaps *leg. ra's māl*.

his hand, girded up his clothes, and grabbed his *jarīd*[1] with his hand. The people he encountered shouted at him and made him feel ashamed.

A similar story, from the *Ṭārid al-humūm* of al-ʿUkbarī, tells of the author walking one night in Mosul *(balad al-Mawṣil)* when he met with a well-dressed individual reciting these verses:

I have combined hashish with wine
And become so drunk that I cannot find my way.
You there whoever you are who will show me the way to my College
Will indeed be rewarded for it most generously.

The narrator, ready to help, inquired which College it was he wanted to go to, and told that it was the Badrīyah, he took him there. It turned out that he was the imām of the College and a very learned man.[2] Strangely enough, the verses quoted are also ascribed to ʿAlam-ad-dīn Ibn Shukr, who was a contemporary of al-ʿUkbarī but lived in Egypt.[3] If the story does in fact go back to al-ʿUkbarī, one would have to assume, I believe, that the ascription to ʿAlam-ad-dīn is not correct and that, perhaps, ʿAlam-ad-dīn recited the verses when he found himself, in reality or in fiction, in a similar situation. He was, as we have seen,[4] also a successful teacher for some time, in spite of his indulgence in hashish.

We also hear about a certain Abū Jurthūm al-Ḥimṣī who taught grammar to a certain al-Muʿizz Amīn-ad-dīn al-Ḥimṣī, a high official *(kātib al-inshā' ash-sharīf)*. One day, his student found Abū Jurthūm in a state of great emotional upset under the influence of hashish, dancing around completely uninhibited, urinating, holding his penis, shouting aloud, and reciting verses on flowers.[5]

---

[1] Even if *jarīd* were to mean "staff," this would hardly yield a suitable meaning in the context, since a staff is naturally carried in the hand. Perhaps, *jarīd* is some part of the dress or, as seems most likely, it is a slang variant of *jurdān* "penis."

[2] Cf. al-Badrī, fol. 14a-b.

[3] Cf. Ibn Kathīr, XIII, 315, with very slight variations.

[4] Cf. above, p. 84.

[5] Cf. al-Badrī, fols. 10a-b, 12a-b, and above, pp. 26, n. 5, 82, n. 5, and 91, n. 1. That the personalities and the historical setting are not quite traceable is due to lack of information, but it may also be noted that in one version, al-Badrī's often quoted colleague al-Hā'im (d. 887/1482) plays a role in the anecdote, and in the other Ibn Ḥijjah al-Ḥamawī, the author of the *Thamarāt* (d. 837/1434). (It may, however, be noted that *GAL, Suppl.* II, 12, refers to Ibn al-Hā'im as Aḥmad b. Muḥammad [b. ʿAlī], whereas al-Badrī calls him Aḥmad b. ʿAlī, but I believe that the identification is correct. Amīn-ad-dīn al-Ḥimṣī can, however, not be identified with Muḥammad b. Muḥammad b. ʿAlī who died in 800/1397, cf. Ibn al-ʿImād, *Shadharāt*, VI, 367.) Some of the

Naturally, it was also assumed that scholars, like anybody else, could be ruined by their uncontrollable addiction mentally, physically, and socially.[1] No matter how much fiction all these stories contain, and they probably are entirely fictitious or, at best, grossly exaggerated, they also would seem to be a reflection of an actual situation and an illustration of what was possible and did occur on occasion. There is one strange and noteworthy fact, though. Prominent scholars, and, for that matter, other successful members of society, are only rarely accused of hashish use, although this would have been an easy and effective kind of slander. Ibn Khallikān, the famous biographer, sounded out a friend about his reputation among Damascenes, and he was told that his competence as a scholar was generally accepted, but his claim to descent from the Barmecides was doubted, and it was whispered that he loved boys and ate hashish. Ibn Khallikān's reply with respect to the last item is supposed to have been that if it was inevitable for him to do something forbidden by the law, he would rather drink wine than eat hashish because it was much more pleasurable.[2] Ibn Khallikān was also a prominent judge and as such traditionally subject to slanderous rumors. Why, as far as is known, there is no more of the sort reported in our sources is puzzling. Perhaps the lack of a long established tradition for hashish as a moral and religious sin is responsible for it.[3]

---

flower verses are by Ṣafī-ad-dīn al-Ḥillī, cf. his *Dīwān*, 381, ll. 8-10, 12-13, quoted again by al-Badrī, fol. 79a. There may be certain allusions here. The story of Aḥmad al-Khaffāf (al-Badrī, fols. 12b-13b, above, p. 29, n. 1, and p. 80, n. 5) centers around flower symbolism, the rose representing wine, and basil *(rayḥān)* hashish.

[1] Cf., for instance, above, pp. 47 f.

[2] Cf. al-Kutubī, *Fawāt*, I, 102; Ibn Ḥijjah, *Thamarāt*, I, 29.

[3] Just in passing, and in the only express reference to hashish in his section on wine, al-Badrī, fol. 138b, says of ʿImād-ad-dīn al-Wāsiṭī *al-wāʿiẓ*, who was the second person to hold the appointment as preacher at the Tawbah Mosque in Damascus in the early years after its founding in 632/1234-1235 (cf. Ibn Kathīr, XIII, 143), that he was "fond of the use of wine and hashish." Al-Wāsiṭī's name was Aḥmad, according to an-Nuʿaymī, *Dāris*, II, 426 f. (Damascus 1367-1370/1948-1951), who, incidentally, refers to the same story and the same verses as al-Badrī. I do not know whether he is to be identified with the Wāsiṭī who is cited by al-Badrī, fol. 18b, as the author of verses asking for a gift of hashish:

> Show your noble generosity to me by giving me a green morsel,
> Most generous one of those who walk the earth...
>
> *jud lī karaman bi-farmatin (?) khaḍrā'i*
> *yā akrama man mashā ʿalā l-ghabrā'i...*

For *farmah* in the meaning of "small piece," cf. Dozy and Hava. However,

What mainly distinguished the Ṣūfīs from the scholars in their attitude toward hashish was their quasi-religious devotion to it, the cult and ritual they made of its use.[1] It was this that made some among them fervent missionaries of the drug while others like ʿAlī al-Ḥarīrī at times bitterly opposed it. But there can be little doubt that hashish was rather widely employed by them as a supposed aid for achieving enlargement of the individual's powers of sense and, especially, spiritual perceptions. By tasting the "secret" and the "meanings" of hashish, Ṣūfīs more than others hoped to gain additional mystic experience. Those who were sympathizers with Ṣūfism rather than avowed mystics generally saw in hashish a way toward religious uplift. They made, as attested also by their adversary Ibn Taymīyah,[2] the use of the drug "an act of worship" *(ʿibādah)*, corresponding to the drinking of wine and the gazing at handsome boys, and they deserved for it the condemnation reserved for those other practices that were so greatly abhorred by the orthodoxy. Ibn Taymīyah went into some valuable detail in formulating the query concerning *ghubayrā'*, which precedes his *fatwā* concerning it:[3] "A query as to young and old men who are pilgrims, who painstakingly observe the religious obligations incumbent upon them concerning fasting, prayer, and worship, some of whom are highly regarded and known for their trustworthiness and integrity (in word and action), who show no outward signs of evil and wickedness. Their minds *(ʿuqūl, adhhān)* and view are now determined to insist upon eating *ghubayrā'*. Their stated belief with respect to *ghubayrā'* now is that it is (a sin and) evil. Yet, they adduce with regard to their belief the evidence of the Qur'ān where it is said that 'good (deeds) make evil ones disappear' (11 : 114/116). They say that it is forbidden, but (they think that) they perform special prayers *(wird)* at night and acts of worship. They think that when the exhilarating effect[4] of *ghubayrā'* goes to their heads, it commands them to do such acts of worship, and does not command them to do anything evil or

---

the Paris Ms. indicates two dots for the first letter, which, though written together, could also indicate one dot each for the first and second letters, but no suitable meaning suggests itself for *q-r-m-h*. A correction to *q-r-n-h* (above, p. 62) would not seem entirely impossible.

[1] Cf. also above, pp. 69 ff.

[2] Cf. *Fatāwī*, I, 59, II, 268. For Ibn Taymīyah's understanding of "religious worship" (*ʿibādah*), cf. *Fatāwī*, II, 361 ff.

[3] Cf. *Fatāwī*, II, 252, IV, 324, with variants translated in brackets.

[4] See above, p. 126, n. 1.

sinful. They assert[1] (that it causes no harm to any human being in contrast to fornication, winedrinking, and theft, and) that it(s eater) does not require any punishment *(ḥadd)*. It is, however, connected with opposition to a divine command, yet, God shows forgiveness for whatever takes place between the servant (and His Master). A truthful person, having been in touch with them, now reports this view of theirs. He is now in agreement with them regarding the eating of *ghubayrā'* through their positive assessment of it and the expression of their views and has adopted all that for himself."

Needless to say, everything here is terribly erroneous in the view of Ibn Taymīyah. He considers it worse than certain Christian practices which Christians believe to be acts of divine worship but which no Muslim in his right mind would acknowledge as such. What incenses him most is that those men were ordinary, decent citizens who thought of themselves as good Muslims and outwardly were. They were no extremists in their mystic attitudes and beliefs, even if they were allied to Ṣūfism and were infected by Ṣūfī ideas.

Others, it seems, went considerably farther in their quasi-religious devotion to hashish. The claims they made for it are described for us by the sixteenth-century Fuzūlī. His statements are filtered through his poetical imagination, but this was no doubt also the way in which the intellectual elite among Ṣūfīs looked at things in actuality. They claimed for hashish to be the master of Ṣūfī teaching, whereas wine can claim to be only an eager disciple setting the world afire. The shaykh of love is the very refuge of hashish, whereas wine merely shows the way to it. Both wine and hashish are considered almost equals as far as love is concerned, but it is not worldly love, at least not primarily, that is meant here but the mystic love that is the highest goal of the religious world with which hashish is thus connected.[2] A mystic disciple in al-Baṣrah became addicted to hashish *(esrār)*. His understanding shaykh recognized that this meant that he had reached the ultimate degree of perfection. It was because of this insight that he ceased giving him further instruction. This proves that hashish is the perfect being, sought after by mankind with great eagerness. It may not be the perfect being for everybody, but it most certainly is for the seeker of mystic experience.[3]

No matter how eloquently vocal exponents of scholarship and

---

[1] For *wa-nasabū* or *wa-yuthbitūhā* (!), read, possibly, *wa-athbatū*.

[2] Cf. Fuzūlī, 171.

[3] Cf. Fuzūlī, 168 f.

mysticism defended the possibilities for individual improvement inherent in cannabis, they were not able to make a convincing case for this being of benefit to society. The adversaries of the drug also concentrated on the degradation of the individual but it was very clearly implied and understood by them that individual degradation was upsetting to the established social structure. Hashish was generally branded as something inherently dirty and bestial. The mental deterioration it is assumed to cause turns men into dumb, irrational beasts.[1] The fact that it comes from a plant is constantly stressed to make it clear that only animals, and people as irrational and inferior as animals, would care to consume it. Even worse, it was food for the devil, as wine was the devil's drink. When Baybars decided to curb the use of wine and hashish, Judge Nāṣir-ad-dīn Ibn al-Munayyir (620-683/1223-1284)[2] rhymed:

> Iblīs has no desire to stay with us.
> He prefers to make his home elsewhere, and not in the Amīr's country.
> You have prevented him from obtaining both wine and hashish.
> You have thus deprived him of his water and his fodder.

Someone else phrased the same idea in similar words:

> Aẓ-Ẓāhir has outlawed hashish as well as wine.
> In consequence, Iblīs turned his back and left Egypt in a hurry.
> He says: Why should I stay in a country
> Where I do not have the enjoyment of water and fodder?[3]

It seems that ʿIzz-ad-dīn ʿAbd-as-Salām (Ibn Ghānim) also branded hashish as fit only for animals when he replied to those who claimed that it was wrongly declared unlawful:

> It destroys mind and temper alike
> With various kinds of craziness and disease.
> Those who say that it is permitted speak the truth.
> It is indeed permitted but for cattle.[4]

---

[1] Cf., for instance, above, pp. 110, 140, and below, p. 168, etc.

[2] Mālikite of Alexandria, Aḥmad b. Muḥammad b. Manṣūr, cf. al-Yūnīnī, *Dhayl Mir'āt az-zamān*, IV, 206-210 (Hyderabad 1374-1380/1954-1961); adh-Dhahabī, *ʿIbar*, V, 342; Ibn Farḥūn, *Dībāj*, 71-74 (Cairo 1351/1932).

[3] Cf. al-Kutubī, *Fawāt*, I, 170, and above, pp. 135 f.

[4] The text as it appears on the title-page of the Istanbul Ms. Murad Molla 1408 of Abū Sulaymān as-Sijistānī (cf. above, p. 101, n. 4) reads:

> *tudhhibu (?) l-ʿaqla wa-l-mizāja jamīʿan*
> *bi-funūni l-junūni wa-l-asqāmi*
> *ṣadaqa l-qā'ilūna bi-l-ḥilli fīhā*
> *hī ḥalālun lākin ʿalā l-anʿāmi.*

The crucial last word is unclear and seems rather to be *al-anām*, but it can hardly be doubted that the correct reading is as indicated. For the stated

Since there were animals such as the gazelle that were standard poetical metaphors for female grace and beauty, the idea could also be turned around, as was done by Ibn al-Wardī, who meant to be facetious and did not seriously intend to come out in favor of hashish:

> A pretty girl high on hashish,
> When I blame her for what is going on,
> Says: Every gazelle
> Feeds on green grass.[1]

There were many other different interpretations of the green color of hashish. It might suggest the unnatural paleness of the addict's complexion as against the rosy hue that appears on the cheeks of winedrinkers.[2] It also lent itself to positive evaluation inasmuch as

---

author of the verse, see above, pp. 6 f., and for the verses that provoked this rejoinder, above, p. 101. The first verse appears also in the Gotha Ms. (above, p. 18) with the variant reading *tufsidu*, which, however, could hardly be the word intended in the Ms. Murad Molla. The Gotha Ms. indicates as the name of the author a certain imām Maḥmūd b. Abī l-Qāsim b. Nadmān al-Ḥanbalī, whose name remains uncertain pending identification. The Gotha Ms. has altogether three verses:

> The worst intoxication is hashish intoxication, and
> Intoxication is forbidden by express statement of the best of men.
> It corrupts mind...
> Which (read *ayyu* for *fī*) view would permit what affects the
> Mind and by (the power of) its intoxicating effect shows contempt for wine?

The fact that the first verse here ends in *al-anām* could be a further argument for eliminating the possibility of reading this word in the Murad Molla Ms.

For hashish "grass" being the proper feed only for cattle, cf. also Ibn Ghānim, below, p. 168. Al-Badrī, fol. 55b, has another couplet to the same effect, blaming the Ṣūfīs for eating hashish, by Ibn al-Mushidd (apparently, Sayf-ad-dīn al-Mushidd, above, p. 91, n. 5).

[1] Cf. Ibn al-Wardī, *al-Kawākib as-sāriyah ʿalā mi'at jāriyah*, in the Istanbul Ms. Topkapusaray, Ahmet III 2373, fol. 181a:

> *malīḥatun masṭūlatun — in lumtuhā fī-mā jarā*
> *taqūlu kullu ẓabyatin — tarʿā l-ḥashīsha l-akhḍara.*

Ibn al-Wardī's verses are quoted in al-Badrī, fol. 33a. Ibn al-Wardī, furnishing a good example for the impossibility to rely upon a poet's statements as indicative of his personal views, also expresses himself seemingly against the use of hashish. His many terrible sins, he says, at least do not include homosexuality, *nabīdh*, and hashish (*Dīwān*, 256). Again, he lists hashish among the five sins with which Iblīs tries in vain to tempt him during his sleep in the night. However, here the devil has the last word: "Go on sleeping, you are just a wooden oaf *(ḥaṭabah)*" (*Dīwān*, 232). The theme of the nocturnal Satanic temptation goes back to Abū Nuwās, *Dīwān*, 554 f. There are other imitations, such as the one by Ṣafī-ad-dīn al-Ḥillī, *Dīwān*, 450, where Satan starts out by suggesting a *shaqfah kabshīyah* (above, p. 30) to drive off sleeplessness, or the one by al-Badrī, fols. 33b-34a. For pederastic verses using the image of the grazing gazelle, cf. al-Badrī, fol. 30b.

[2] Cf. al-Isʿirdī, verse 34, below, p. 166.

its green color enabled hashish to claim the famous al-Khiḍr "the green one" as its patron saint.[1] Its "green dress" and general decorativeness as a plant bespeak the wholesomeness of hashish, as indicated in the verses of, as usual, disputed ascription but probably, as stated by al-Maqrīzī, by ʿAlī b. Makkī, a gifted lute and tambourine player in early thirteenth-century Baghdād:[2]

Now drive sadness away from me as well as harm
With the help of a virgin(al being), wedded in its green dress.
It reveals itself to us adorned with brocade.[3]
No metaphor in verse or prose is strong enough for it.
It appears, filling the eyes with light through its beauty,
A beauty that puts to shame the light[4] of meadow and flowers with a bright sheen(?).
It is a bride whose hidden secret gladdens the soul.
Coming in the evening, it is found in all the senses in the morning.
In its clarity it gives to taste the taste of honey.
Through its odor it gives to smell the choicest scent of musk.
It makes touch dispense with bashful maidens.
Mention of it makes music superfluous for the ear.[5]
Its color presents sight with the most beautiful diversion.
Sight turns to looking at this color rather than that of any other flower.
It is composed of bright red color[6] and white, and it bends

---

[1] Cf. Fuzūlī, 153, 167.

[2] The identity of ʿAlī b. Makkī appears to be clarified by an anecdote told by al-Badrī, fols. 7b-8a, which, in spite of the confused source situation (see above, p. 74, n. 5), may be credited with historicity as far as the persons mentioned in it are concerned. Makkī was a poet in the days of an-Nāṣir (1180-1225). His son, ʿAlī b. Makkī, visited the epileptic Ẓahīr-ad-dīn Muḥammad b. Ismāʿīl b. al-Wakīl whose father had been *ḥājib dīwān al-majlis* "Chamberlain of the Caliphal Council" in Baghdād, and on this occasion introduced the reluctant Ẓahīr-ad-dīn to hashish for medication. It cured him completely, but he became an addict who could not for a moment be without the drug. As appears from G. Gabrieli's index of the biographies in aṣ-Ṣafadī's *Wāfī*, a certain Abū l-Muẓaffar ʿAlī b. Makkī b. Muḥammad b. Hubayrah ad-Dūrī has an entry in the *Wāfī*, but I am unable to check whether he might be identical with our ʿAlī b. Makkī.

Al-Badrī, fol. 5a, mentions a certain Nūr-ad-dīn al-Iṣfahānī as the author of the verses, and he seems to suggest that his source was the *History* of al-Manbijī (see above, p. 45).

[3] This refers to the silvery and golden glow on the plant when it is covered with dew in the morning sunlight.

[4] "Light" seems more likely to be meant than "blossoms."

[5] The verse is missing from al-Maqrīzī and found in al-Badrī:
wa-fīhā ghinan bi-l-massi ʿan khurradi sitrin
wa-fī dhikrihā li-s-samʿi mughnin ʿan-i-z-zamri.
It clearly belongs to the original poem.

[6] For the old Arabian color spectrum, cf. W. Fischer, *Farb- und Formbezeichnungen in der Sprache der altarabischen Dichtung*, 237 and *passim* (Wiesbaden 1965). For the red-colored wood of the plant, cf. above, p. 47.

Proudly over the flowers, high of stature.
The light of the sun is eclipsed by its red color.
The face of the moon is put to shame by its whiteness.
It ranks high in beauty. It is as if it were
The emerald of a meadow drenched by copious rain.
It appears—and makes hidden feelings appear.
It comes—and turns away the army of my worry and pensiveness.
Beautiful of shape, mighty in rank,
It grows high, and high does my verse grow in praise of it.
Thus, rise and banish the army of worry[1] and stay the hand of distress
With an Indian (maiden) more effective than white (swords) and brown (spears),
With an Indian as to origin, showing people
How to eat it, not an Indian in color like the brown ones.[2]
Eating it removes the burning worry from us
And gives us enjoyment secretly and openly.

The green color, and possibly also the fact that hashish was cultivated in "gardens" *(basātīn)*, permitted its association with gardens, and the word "garden" naturally evoked the idea of *the* garden, Paradise. Although hashish appears fiery and hot like the fire of Hell, it still is Paradise, as expressed in verses by al-Isʿirdī,[3] or in the following lines of the Syro-Egyptian Muḥammad b. Sharīf Ibn al-Waḥīd (647-711/1249(50)-1312):

Something green whose action red wine is unable to duplicate,
It rocks the guts and stays put.
It kindles a fire in the guts, although it is a garden.
It brings forth the bitter taste (of wine), although it is a plant.[4]

---

[1] Al-Badrī: "and protect the army of fun." The "army" of worry is a very common metaphor in hashish poetry.

[2] Al-Badrī: "and greenness (?)" *(wa-l-khuḍri)*.

[3] Verse 6, cf. below, p. 163.

[4] Cf. aṣ-Ṣafadī, *Wāfī*, III, 151; al-Kutubī, *Fawāt*, II, 438; Ibn al-Qāḍī, *Durrat al-ḥijāl*, as quoted by al-ʿAbbādī (above, p. 55, n. 3); Ibn Taghrībirdī, *Nujūm*, VII, 360, *anno* 688, who does not know the name of the poet; al-Badrī, fol. 10a, who also omits the poet's name. For the aspersions on Ibn al-Waḥīd's orthodoxy, cf., in addition to the *Wāfī*, Ibn Ḥajar, *Durar*, III, 452-456. The translation "bitter taste" follows the reading of aṣ-Ṣafadī, al-Kutubī, and Ibn Taghrībirdī, as against "pleasant life" in Ibn al-Qāḍī. The second verse reads in al-Badrī: "It kindles a fire, although in the heart it is a garden. It shows you the taste of wine..." *(ta'ajjaju* [read *tu'ajjiju*] *nāran wa-hya fī l-qalbi jannatun — wa-tūrīka ṭaʿma l-khamri...)*. Usually, it is wine that is said to kindle a fire in the drinker, and the opposition of "fire" and "gardens" is a topic of wine poetry, cf. al-Ghuzūlī, *Maṭāliʿ*, I, 166, 168. "Fire" even functions as a nickname for wine, cf. al-Badrī, fol. 64a, quoting a verse by Ibn Ḥabīb al-Ḥalabī (710-779/1310-1377) beginning: "Kindle for us the fire which is a garden" *(awqid lanā n-nāra llatī hiya jannatun)*. The play is, of course, on the double meaning of fire = Hell and garden = Paradise.

According to verses cited by al-Maqrīzī (cf. above, p. 140, n. 1), hashish was like a bride dressed in green silk:

No wonder that in spite of Ibn al-Waḥīd's talent as a scholar and calligrapher, there were rumors casting doubt on his religious sentiments and suspecting him of grave sins, such as putting wine or *nabīdh* in the ink which he used for copying the Qur'ān.

The defenders of hashish also found it easy to score a point in favor of hashish as against wine with respect to natural dirtiness. The preparation of hashish was a cleaner process than that of wine. Also, as we have seen, wine was proved legally unclean much more easily than hashish, and hashish was never used for cultic purposes among non-Muslims as was wine. All these aspects are brought together in verses variously ascribed to the Spaniard Ibn Khamīs (650-708/1252-1308)[1] and the Syro-Egyptian Ibn al-Aʿmā (d. 692/1292):[2]

Give up wine and drink from the wine of Ḥaydar,
Amber-scented,[3] green the color of emerald.
It is presented to you by a Turkish gazelle, slender,
Swaying like a willow bough, delicate.
In his hand, you would think, as he turns it,
It is like the traces of down on a rosy cheek.
The slightest breeze makes it reel,
And it flutters toward the coolness of the continuing breeze.[4]
The greyish pigeons coo upon its branches in the morning,
And the cadences of the warbling of doves cause it emotion.
It has many meanings the like of which are unknown to wine.
Therefore do not listen with respect to it to the words of the old censor.[5]

They brought into our (read *lanā*) bridal chamber a fire, and we thought
A garden had come to us coupled with light.

[1] Cf. M. Hadj-Sadok, in *EI*², *s. v.* Ibn Khamīs.

[2] His name is usually given as ʿAlī b. Muḥammad, and not as Muḥammad b. ʿAlī as we find in al-Maqrīzī and *GAL*, *Suppl.*, I, 444 f. The Berlin fragment of al-Badrī has Muḥammad b. al-Mubārak but indicates in the margin that "ʿAlī b." is to be inserted before Muḥammad. ʿAlī b. Muḥammad appears in al-Badrī, fol. 3b. Cf. above, p. 53, n. 1.

The text translated here is that of al-Maqrīzī. Ibn Khamīs, as quoted by al-ʿAbbādī from Ibn al-Qāḍī, adds the last verse and omits the verse before last as well as verses two to five. The order of the rest is different, to wit: 1, 2, 5, 4, 6-11. The Berlin fragment of al-Badrī breaks off after verse 5.

[3] Ibn Khamīs: "A fine draft."

[4] Silvestre de Sacy translates: comme chancelle un homme étourdi par la vapeur du vin.

[5] The statement recurs in al-Isʿirdī, verses 24 and 45 (below, pp. 165 f.), and the editor of al-Kutubī notes that *mufannid* means "declaring a liar." The root is common in poetry, and the meaning "to blame" is more likely applicable here. *Mufannid* is meant to refer to those who censure the use of hashish without having any traditional (or rational) arguments to fall back on. In this poem, as in al-Isʿirdī and generally according to the rules of prosody,

It is virginal, not deflowered by rain,
Nor has it ever been squeezed by feet or hands.
No Christian priest has ever played around with the cup containing it,
Nor have they ever given communion from its cask to any heretic's soul.[1]
Nothing has been said expressly by Mālik to declare it unlawful,
Nor is the *ḥadd* penalty for its use found prescribed in ash-Shāfiʿī and Aḥmad (Ibn Ḥanbal).
An-Nuʿmān (Abū Ḥanīfah) has not established that it must be considered unclean *per se*.
Thus take it with the sharp edge of steel.[2]
Stay the hands of worry with *kaff* and achieve joyful repose.[3]
Do not lightly postpone the day of joy till tomorrow.
"The days will show you what you were ignorant of,
And someone for whom you did not provide (to serve as your messenger) will bring you the news."[4]

The poet of these lines, whoever he was, was influenced by al-Isʿirdī, unless more likely both used common material. Wine is dirty, *banj* and hashish are clean, and not only in the ritual sense.[5]

Hashish may have been not as dirty as wine by nature, but the general opinion was that it made the addict physically dirty, and he was not only socially déclassé but also contemptible in character and mores. He is a "vile" *(khasīs)* individual. The word *ḥashīshah* easily combines with the adjective *khasīsah* "vile"[6] and should rather be written *khasīsah*. Adh-Dhahabī (?) repeats this graphic pun in an

the short vowel preceding the rhyme letter can be *a*, *i*, or *u*. Al-Isʿirdī uses *mufannid* to rhyme with *muqallid* in the first verse. Thus, a reading *mufannad* "a mentally and/or physically weak old man" is unlikely and, anyhow, excluded by the meaning required. But it suggested to me the addition of the adjective "old."

[1] The classical love poetry, for instance, Abū Nuwās, *Dīwān*, 64, made *qarrab qurbān* familiar to every Muslim poet as a Christian cultic term. However, it is not entirely excluded that the intended sense here was rather: "have brought near to its cask." Anyway, the "heretic's soul" would still seem to be that of a non-Muslim who indulged in wine for cultic purposes. If, however, Muslims whose winebibbing made them heretics are meant, the line could be a slur directed against Ismāʿīlīs, accusing them of drinking wine. I have no explanation for al-Maqrīzī's reading *muqʿad* "cripple," for "heretic." Al-Badrī has "cask" for "cup," and "tavern" for "cask."

[2] If this is the correct translation, it seems to refer to the harvesting of hemp with a sharp knife, a process more easily accomplished than winemaking.

[3] Cf. above, p. 26. For "achieve joyful repose," al-Badrī has *wa-ṣṭabiḥ* "have a morning drink," and goes on with *wa-lā tadʿu* (?) *ayyāma*, which seems quite doubtful.

[4] Al-Maqrīzī does not have this famous quotation from Ṭarafah's *Muʿallaqah*. In the context, its meaning appears to be that hashish should be tried and the experience will be found rewarding and pleasurable.

[5] Cf. Fuzūlī, 171.

[6] Cf. below, p. 170, and Ibn Kathīr, XIII, 314.

addition in his text to what is found in Ibn Taymīyah's *Siyāsah*: "By God, Iblīs has never had any joy like the one he has from hashish, because he made it appear nice to vile souls so that they considered it lawful and permissible."[1] He further adds the verses:

> Say to those who eat hashish in ignorance:
> You live the worst life imaginable when you eat it.
> The worth of a man is a jewel. Why then,
> You fools, do you sell it for a bit of grass *(ḥashīshah)*?[2]

The idea that hashish or *ghubayrā'* is a bad bargain and offers little that is valuable in exchange for the devastating harm it does to the user's physical condition and social position was also expressed by Ibn Taymīyah, if in a slightly different form.[3] An anonymous rhymester cited by az-Zarkashī and al-Aqfahsī repeats the verses just quoted with some minor variations (although Ms. A of az-Zarkashī has the same text as adh-Dhahabī for the first half-verse of the second verse):

> Say to those who eat hashish in ignorance:
> You vile fellows, you live the most contemptible life imaginable.
> The blood money for the mind is a purse full of money. Why then,
> You ignoramuses, do you sell it for a bit of grass?

When hashish is mentioned as something helpful in love affairs, it means hitting at the low social standing of addicts due to their moral corruption. The evil nature of the drug makes it a willing accessory to licentiousness.[4] It has the effect of facilitating seduction. In this respect, as al-Isʿirdī implies, wine and hashish are equals. Both break down the resistance of the beloved and increase the chances for success in amorous affairs. Already in the early thirteenth century, al-Jawbarī cited some verses to this effect which are also to be found in the much later al-Maqrīzī and al-Badrī. They ascribe them to a littérateur named Aḥmad b. Muḥammad al-Ḥalabī and

---

[1] The same phrase occurs also in Ibn Ghānim. His text continues: "They (Ms. Princeton: he?) took it as a *qurbah*, something to bring them near to God."

[2] The quotation in Ibn Ḥajar al-Haytamī, *Zawājir*, does not include these verses. The Berlin Ms. (but not the Princeton Ms.) of Ibn Ghānim adds the verses at the very end, written in a different hand. The second verse begins: "The ornament of man is his mind *(ʿaql)*...". Al-Badrī, fol. 55a, has the verses with the variant reading in the first verse: "...intentionally: You live, miserable friend, the worst life imaginable *(ʿamdan — ʿishta yā ṣāḥi wayka aqbaḥa ʿīshah)*." In the second verse, it is "pearl," for "jewel."

[3] Cf. Ibn Taymīyah, *Fatāwī*, IV, 325 (= II, 253).

[4] Cf., for instance, al-Badrī (above, p. 66), or an-Nuwayrī, *Nihāyah*, XI, 29.

known as Ibn ar-Rassām, who according to al-Badrī had the honorific Shihāb-ad-dīn. His identity has not yet been established, nor is the form of his name quite certain. Al-Jawbarī,[1] on the other hand, claims rather dramatically that the poet was a member of a caste of advanced standing within the hierarchy of professional swindlers and crooks. This group pretended to be composed of learned shaykhs. In fact, it agreed upon the legality of eating hashish and considered as permissible the commission of acts of immorality involving married women and boys from good families:

Many a slender one, seemingly standoffish, have I observed
Whom I was never able to meet[2] except him frowning.
One night I encountered him laughing,
Good tempered, docile, at a party,
His eyes seeking out a chaste lover.
Drunkenness is kind to lovers, not unkind.
I accomplished what I wanted from him and thanked[3] him
As he had become, after mutual avoidance, my good friend.
He gave me this reply: Do not thank my natural disposition.
Rather, thank your intercessor, the wine of the bankrupt.
For the herb of good cheer[4] intercedes with us
In behalf of lovers by gladdening the soul.
When the capture of a standoffish gazelle is on your mind,
See to it that he grazes on cannabis hashish,
And thank Ḥaydar's band for having shown
To those of lewd inclinations the method of the fivefold one.[5]
Leave the killjoys and let me be
Among those who hide from the good opinion of the people.[6]

Al-Jawbarī also lengthily describes criminals who induce children of

[1] *Kashf al-asrār*, 14 (Cairo 1316). Al-Maqrīzī and al-Badrī lack verse 3 and add the two concluding verses.

[2] The meter requires a long last syllable in *altaqīhī*.

[3] Al-Jawbarī: "left."

[4] Al-Jawbarī: "the spirits" (*al-arwāḥ*, for *al-afrāḥ*).

[5] This could be the meaning of *al-mutakhammis*, as in the edition of al-Maqrīzī and, it seems, in the ms. of al-Badrī, and refer to the shape of hemp leaves (cf. above, p. 27). *Al-mutaḥammis* seems less likely. It could mean "strictly pious" (cf. Lane) and indicate the wish of the user to appear to the world as one of those pious Ṣūfīs who introduced hashish.

[6] According to Silvestre de Sacy, we should understand this verse to mean that the poet desires to have a hiding place (*mutanammas*, not *mutanammis*) and be protected by the good opinion in which the Ṣūfīs who introduced hashish were generally held, see also the preceding note. The last two verses would thus express the longing of hashish eaters for respectability in the eyes of the world. This, however, hardly fits in with the contents of the earlier verses. Therefore, the last two verses (provided they belong together with what precedes) are better explained as showing callous indifference to the world and public opinion.

wealthy parents to leave their homes,[1] but in this connection, the role of hashish, if it was indeed hashish which seems unlikely, was probably merely that of a narcotic to make the victims unconscious for the purpose of abduction. However, he also purports to know of swindlers who shave their beards, wear irons, and, in some cases, pierce the penis and put a ring through it in order to gain the confidence of their intended victims. These people, he says, "are unable to remain for one day without eating hashish. When they eat it, their minds become confused, and they do everything evil. For hashish is one of the strongest intoxicants. Everything intoxicating is forbidden, and those who eat what is forbidden do everything evil. Iblīs gains control over their brains."[2]

The condemnation of hashish eaters as low-class rabble might conceivably have already led to giving the sect of the Assassins their name.[3] It was not only moral degradation which contributed to the social downfall of addicts. Hashish prevented them from earning a decent living, and the expenses connected with the habit directly or indirectly brought about serious financial difficulties. An addict would try to raise money by borrowing to sustain his habit, but failing to do that, he had to sell all he owned.[4] During a long drawn-out bout of debauchery with wine and hashish lasting for ten days, the money might naturally run out. The only thing left to sell was a carpet. A prospective buyer claimed that it had been stolen from a murdered cousin, and this had dire results for the unfortunate reveler.[5] Despite of its cheapness, hashish was at times too much of an expense for those poor people who craved it.[6] Those who were in the beginning quite well-off financially might find their undoing in a craving for food and expensive luxuries such as large amounts of sweetmeats and fruits, coming on top of the expenses caused by general dissipation. This could cause a large inheritance to dwindle and disappear, reducing the addict to beggary and vagabondage *(ḥarfūsh, ḥarfashah)*. The story goes that this happened to a certain

[1] Cf. al-Jawbarī, 15 f.

[2] Cf. al-Jawbarī, 14 f. Aziz Ahmad, *An Intellectual History of Islam in India*, 45 (Edinburgh 1969), states: "Another *malāmī* order was that of the Ḥaydarīs, whose bizarre practices included adorning themselves with iron necklaces and bracelets and wearing a ring attached to a lead bar piercing their sexual organs in order to eliminate any chance of sexual intercourse."

[3] See above, pp. 42 f.

[4] Cf. al-Badrī, fol. 22b. Cf. also above, p. 62, n. 3.

[5] Cf. al-Badrī, fol. 45a.

[6] Cf. above, p. 99.

Aḥmad, the son of Burhān-ad-dīn Ibrāhīm aṣ-Ṣūfī ad-Dimashqī,[1] and also to a certain ʿAṭīyah al-Ḥaṣkafī. The depth of degradation into which the latter fell is illustrated by the story that he lost everything and had to leave town. He was encountered by someone who knew him. He was naked, and when he was asked about it, he lied that he was having his garment *(qumāsh)* washed and had nothing else to wear. The acquaintance took off his woolen coat (?)[2] and made him wear it. When the craving for hashish *(muʿāṭāt* [?] *al-khaḍrā')* came again over him and he did not find anything else to spend or sell, he tore off the sleeve of the garment and sold it to buy hashish for himself from the proceeds.[3] Because of the abject poverty that was their lot, some addicts depended on charity, and in fifteenth-century Egypt, it was one of the good deeds of a pious Ṣūfī to distribute food he himself had received as a gift from the nobility, to hashish eaters who were passing by his door.[4]

Men of the Middle Ages did not clearly pose for themselves the problem whether man's innate baseness led him at times to excessive use of drugs with the consequence that his status in society slipped, or whether poverty and a depressed social status created a fertile soil for turning to drugs in the first place. The first alternative obviously held greater appeal for them in keeping with their religious and political preconceptions. In any event, the association of drug use with the status of social outcast appears to have had a firm grip on majority opinion.

4. Hashish, the Individual, and Society

In conclusion we must state again that our knowledge is very limited. The gaps are tremendous. The nature of the information we do have is not easily assessed. Its applicability to the realities

---

[1] Cf. al-Badrī, fols. 56b-57a.

[2] The word is twice clearly written in the ms. as *jndh,* whose precise meaning and derivation are not known to me. For another occurrence, cf. as-Sakhāwī, *Ḍaw',* IV, 254, l. 12. ʿAlī b. Dāwūd al-Jawharī, *Inbā',* ed. Ḥ. Ḥabashī, 264 (Cairo 1970), shows *kh.*

[3] Cf. al-Badrī, fol. 22a-b, and, for other details of the story, above, p. 29, n. 2, and p. 138.

[4] Cf. ash-Shaʿrānī, *aṭ-Ṭabaqāt al-kubrā,* II, 76 f. (Cairo, n. y.), in the biography of ʿUmar al-Kurdī, cited by A. Schimmel, in *Festschrift Werner Caskel,* 281 (Leiden 1968).

Among further examples for impoverishment as the result of addiction are, for instance, the stories mentioned above, pp. 80 and 94.

prevailing over the immense extension in time and space of medieval Islam is often suspect. Partisanship pro or con, coupled with a seemingly widespread ignorance of hard facts, obscures everything. Statistics naturally are non-existent.

Our sources give the impression of a westward march of hashish that had its serious beginnings in the twelfth century and gathered speed during the thirteenth century. A certain confirmation of these dates may be found in the further impression that voices seemingly in favor of hashish would appear to belong largely to the earlier stages of literary attestation. This would indicate that at first a restricted use of the drug presumably by Ṣūfīs made it possible to view it as something affecting individuals rather than society and therefore limited in the harm that it was considered to be able to cause. Soon, however, the alert went out. Hashish was branded as a danger to society. The voices raised against it were at first strong and insistent. When Ibn ʿAbd-aẓ-Ẓāhir wrote a sort of official paper against it, he implied that first it was wine that had to be fought against, but now, he stated, hashish had become a fashion and thereby a social danger.[1] Human resistance began to assert itself, and the broad assumptions that governed the edifice of Islam as a religious and legal structure were put to the test. It cannot be said that they were found wanting, but they did not provide the aggressive and irresistible strength that would have been necessary. Jurists clung to the lifeline thrown to them by the prohibition of wine. In theory it seemed very strong but had itself worn thin in stretches by custom and abuse. Thus they were unable to provide much support for the strict prohibition of hashish which most of them seem to have thought necessary.

The addicts, on their part, felt that they could be at peace with their Muslim conscience. Where pure hedonism was not a sufficient excuse for indulgence, the drug could also be claimed to open up new spiritual and intellectual vistas and thus to contribute to an otherwise unobtainable sharpening of the religious experience, thereby bringing mankind closer to what was imagined to be its essential goal. The spread of hashish was facilitated by its easy accessibility. This recommended it to the urban masses. The by and large asocial character of hashish use was a welcome help in fighting the frustrations of daily life, again something particularly desirable in an urban

---

[1] Cf. al-Ghuzūlī, *Maṭāliʿ*, II, 129; Ibn Ḥijjah, *Thamarāt*, I, 364.

environment. The social stigma and loss of respectability associated with hashish were, it seems, no real deterrents, all the less so since the use of it was easily concealed.

Society did not have to fear the potential harm that hashish was able by prolonged use to inflict upon individual users. Its most important problem, which called for action, was the cumulative effect produced by large numbers of addicts. The periods when secular authorities tried openly and energetically to fight drug use were sporadic. They were certainly not the result of a revival of religious fervor where doctrinal considerations as such determined the government's attitude. They reflected an acute fear that a potential social evil threatening the welfare of the state might eventually get out of hand. In general, the use of hashish and other cannabis confections remained an underground affair, and this was so most of the time and not only in periods of governmental campaigns of repression. There was, however, an attempt made to set restrictions aside and to find out what the result would be. At least this, al-Maqrīzī tells us, was what happened in the year 815/1412-13. Hashish was at that time used in public without any inhibition, and it was discussed openly without embarrassment. Al-Maqrīzī for one took a dim view of the resulting effect upon society: "Character and morals became overwhelmingly vile, the veil of bashfulness and shame was lifted, people used foul language, boasted of faults, lost all nobility and virtue, and adopted every possible ugly character quality and vice. Were it not for their (human) shape, nobody would think them human. Were it not for their sense perception, nobody would adjudge them living beings." Such transformation *(maskh)* of the human quality of life is "a warning sign," foreboding great danger for individuals and society. It is, as the author of *Qamʿ* stresses in the beginning of his work, a great potential danger to Islam. Islam here is a synonym of our term "society."

Whatever one may think of the uncompromising and harsh attitude of Ibn Taymīyah, he must be given credit for having recognized the societal aspect of hashish addiction and to have stated it clearly and succinctly in so many words, and not only by indirection. Given their outlook as determined by Islam and their limited factual knowledge, thoughtful Muslims will have understood and shared his view. "Hashish," Ibn Taymīyah says,[1] "requires the *ḥadd* penalty

---

[1] *Fatāwī*, IV, 226, omitted in the parallel passage, II, 254.

more than wine. The harm a hashish eater causes to his own person is greater than that caused by wine. On the other hand, the harm a winedrinker causes to the people is greater (in view of the quarrels and the like provoked by alcohol). However, in these times, because the consumption of hashish is spreading, the harm coming from it to the people is greater than that of wine." "The people" here is another word for our "society." Hashish had become a threat to it, and the fight was on. Effective countermeasures were not readily available, once mere repression proved futile, until, perhaps, as among the later Wahhābites, it was accompanied by an entirely changed orientation. The conflict between what was felt to be right and morally and socially good and what human nature craved in its search for play and diversion went on.

APPENDIX A

SOME HASHISH POEMS TRANSLATED

1. Al-Isʿirdī's *Rangstreit* of Hashish and Wine

"Verses by al-Isʿirdī[1] expressing preference for the wine of the poor:

1) May all be well with you! Do not listen to the word of the old censor[2]
And do not let not following tradition shape your legal decisions.[3]
2) You have asked about the relationship between the green one and wine. Thus listen to
What a person of correct and straightforward views[4] has to say.
3) Surely wine does not possess some of the qualities of (hashish).
Can it be drunk openly in a (Ṣūfī) monastery or a mosque?
4) You ought to obtain it, a green one, not to be acquired at an excessive price
For the white of silver or the red of gold.
5) Rather, in contrast to wine, it comes as a gift
Removed from purchase without (the need for) abstemiousness.
6) It is something belonging to meadows[5] whose greenness resembles the gardens (of Paradise),
Whereas their wine is like a burning firebrand.
7) Their wine makes (you) forget all the meanings there are, while this one
Recalls the secrets of Beauty declared unique.
8) It is the secret. In it, the spirit ascends to the highest
Spots on a heavenly ascent *(miʿrāj)* of disembodied understanding.
9) Rather it is, indeed, the spirit (itself). On its plain, worries do not

---

[1] From al-Kutubī, *Fawāt*, II, 331-334, see above, p. 6.

[2] See above, p. 154, n. 5.

[3] If I understand the verse correctly, it refers to the view that there is no traditional basis for the prohibition of hashish. As indicated in verse 25, the situation is different with respect to wine, and it is stated that the traditional view prohibiting wine should not be accepted.

[4] Hardly, "an informed, correct, straightforward person."

[5] *Riyāḍīyah* here is an adjective formed from the plural of *rawḍah*.

Alight, nor is anyone not enjoying right guidance able to take hold of it.

10) The squeezers of grapes have not trampled on it on purpose, nor have they dirtied
The casks with a seal of black pitch.

11) The bodies are not tired when it is evacuated[1]
And by vomiting as they have the appearance of an inflated wine-skin.

12) People do not disparage your intellect among themselves,
I swear, and you are not called by them a corrupter.

13) In the handkerchief's edge may be the place to keep it,
Instead of having to carry a glass in the hand.

14) You escape from sin and punishment. You are not considered
Lowly, and you get away from quarrelsome boon companions.

15) You may drink it constantly, in good and bad circumstances.
The nights of pious devotions are not to be feared in connection with it.[2]

16) You are safe from sudden and deceitful assaults by the militia,
And you escape from the injustice of the government, and you have to pay no penalty.

17) You find yourself[3] clean, virtuous, bright,
Witty, and unencumbered by excessive dullness.

18) You discover yourself not hated by the people,
And you are favored with (?)[4] the best friendship all around.

19) When the beloved tastes it, he will sneak away from
The invidious backbiter and come to you without an appointment.

20) Among its excellent medical qualities is that it is good for digestion.[5]

---

[1] Presumably, through vomiting, as this seems to be the meaning of *nizāl*. The usual sexual meaning of the word is not applicable here. The variant reading *zawālihā*, rejected by the editor of al-Kutubī, could hardly mean: "when it stops exercising its effect." Cf. above, p. 128, n. 1.

[2] Hashish, in contrast to wine, permits Ṣūfīs and other devout people to spend the night in prayer. Cf. also above, p. 148.

[3] The literal meaning, "to be, become in the morning," suggests the idea that in contrast to wine which leaves the drinker with a hangover after a night of quarrels, the effects of hashish taken in the evening are gone by next morning.

[4] *Tumnaḥu* could hardly be followed by the preposition *bi-*. Read *tumdaḥu* ?

[5] According to the medical authorities cited by al-Maqrīzī, hashish is good for digestion *(jayyidah li-l-haḍm)* but also difficult to digest *('asir al-inhiḍām)*, cf. above, p. 114, n. 7. Al-Is'irdī's *jūdatu haḍmihā* is, however, hardly intended to mean "easy digestibility."

How impossible it is to enumerate all its manifold virtues!
21) Especially, if my boon companion in (eating hashish) is
A gazelle, like the bent branch of a willow,
22) Who keeps (me) company with a pretty poem, and at times
Sings, thereby putting to shame the cooing pigeon.
23) He flirts with me in secret with the eyes of a female gazelle,
And when he smiles, he shows teeth arranged like pearls.
24) Do not listen to what critics may say with respect to it.
They want to keep you away from it. Disobey any old censor!

Other verses by al-Isʿirdī, expressing preference for wine over hashish:

25) I am devoted to you. The light of truth has shone forth. Thus be guided aright,
My boon companion! And be you not one to follow tradition with respect to amusement!
26) Do you like to be similar to a dumb beast
By eating dry grass, not juicy?
27) Do not pay any attention to the opinion of people who are like animals. Do not pass around anything
Except a pearl comparable to a blazing star,
28) Wine! Whenever its light shines for a caravan that
Went astray some night, it is guided back to the right path by the light.
29) Their hashish covers the respectable person with ignominy
So that you meet him like a killer acting with premeditation.[1]
30) It produces[2] upon his cheeks something like its own greenish color
So that he appears with a face darkish, dust-colored.
31) It ruins his appearance as the boon companion's mind imagines it
So that the white of the morning appears like black (darkness).[3]
32) Our own wine covers the lowly person with respectability
And dignity so that you find every master beneath him.[4]
33) It shows up—and clears up every boon companion's worries.
When he drinks it, his thirsty heart is sated.

---

[1] The hashish eater is furtive and afraid to be seen like a murderer?
[2] Read *wa-tubdī*, or *wa-yabdū* "there appears."
[3] His nightly apparition *(khayāl)* is so disturbing to his friend that the coming of morning brings no relief.
[4] Hardly, "it subjects every master to him."

34) It appears—and his secret appears and gladdens him.
He resembles its color with a rosy cheek.
35) Contrary to hashish, it contains beneficial qualities.
Thus speak about all the meanings it has and describe and enumerate them!
36) The other substance contains all sorts of harm for mankind.
Thus tell all the evil about its bad qualities!
37) Surely, no caliph ever tasted hashish,
Neither did a king who possessed mastery over people.
38) Nor did a poet ever make a serious effort to praise it
With artistic words like the tunes of Maʿbad.[1]
39) Nor have the strings been plucked in a gathering in its behalf.
This happens only with the roseate drink.
40) Is a palm ever tinged by anything other than wine?
When it appears in the cup, it shows up on the hand.
41) Under its influence, the beloved bends down, drunk, swaying
In a shape like a bent willow branch,
42) Giving you wine like it in his saliva
And his mouth like well-arranged bubbles (?).[2]
43) One reluctant to join his lover grants him the favor.
Then he forgets all that took place on the following day.
44) Friend, would any intelligent person refrain from something of this nature?
I was not well advised when I left it alone.
45) Were it not for those meddlers, I would not spend the night sober,
Nor would I listen concerning (wine) to what the old censor says.
46) Thus take it and do not listen to what censorious people say,
Even if it is some time forbidden according to the religion of Aḥmad.[3]

Consider (al-Kutubī comments) these two poems and the contrast and interconnection established by the poet between them. It shows his great skill. He praises a thing and blames its opposite, then reverses the order, thereby causing sympathy for what he has praised, and aversion for what he has blamed, without changing the reality of the one or the other."[4]

[1] The famous Medinese singer who died in 743.

[2] "Well-arranged teeth" would hardly fit in. Moreover, *ḥabāb* does not seem to have the meaning of *ḥabab*.

[3] *ʿAlā dīni Aḥmadi*, referring to the Prophet Muḥammad.

[4] One more poem making similar points may be cited. It is quoted in al-

2. Poems against Hashish by Ibn Ghānim and an Anonymous Poet

Ibn Ghānim's authorship is assured not only by the fact that the verses appear in his work[1] but also by the reference, at the end, to

Badrī, fol. 45a-b, and ascribed to a certain Ibn Abī Saʿd al-Warrāq al-Bannā':

People said about *maʿlūm*
As it was being compared to wine:
The daughter of cannabis cannot
Be compared to the daughter of the vine.
No comparison between them
Is possible for an intelligent man.
How could it be! Wine is pressed in
Shops with the foot.
It has a cask and a jug
And a strainer and a bowl.
The cask of the daughter of cannabis is
A purse, and the hand is the cup.
It has no hangover
Causing harm to the head.
Those (things) become dispensable for
One whose garment is poverty.[a]
Thus eat *maʿlūm* openly—
There is nothing wrong with *maʿlūm*—
In blooming gardens
Adorned by roses and myrtle,
From the hands of a Turkish
Gazelle that shows no refractoriness,
His glances wide awake but
His eyes full of sleep.

qāla fī l-maʿlūmi nāsu
idh bihī li-l-khamri qāsū
ibnatu l-qunbusi laysat
bi-bnati l-karmi tuqāsu
laysa fī-mā bayna hātay-
ni li-dhī lubbin qiyāsu
kayfa wa-l-khamratu fī l-ḥā-
nāti bi-r-rijli tudāsu
wa-lahā dannun wa-ibrī-
qun wa-rāwūqun wa-ṭāsu
wa-bnatu l-qunbusi kīsun
dannuhā wa-l-kaffu kāsu
wa-hya mā fīhā khumārun
yata'adhdhā minhu rāsu
wa-bihā ʿan tilka yaghnā
man lahū l-faqru libāsu[a]

[a] This verse, it seems, has its proper position before the preceding two verses.

[1] Cf. above, pp. 6 f.

"Maqdisī wine," an apparent allusion to Ibn Ghānim's gentilic. The second half of the poem beginning with verse 7 can be understood only as an invitation to accept the mystical teachings of the author, to drink the lawful wine he, and he alone, has to offer, instead of continuing the hashish habit.[1]

1) O you who are similar to dumb beasts, having become[2]
Like an ox grazing on cannabis hashish!
2) Indeed, you are more similar to a dumb beast. Only[3]

---

fa-kul-i-l-ma'lūma jahran
laysa bi-l-ma'lūmi bāsu
fī riyāḍin yāni'ātin
zānahā wardun wa-āsu
min yaday ẓabyin min-a-l-at-
rāki mā fīhi shimāsu
yaqiẓa ('a)lḥāẓuhu lākin
mil'a 'aynayhi nu'āsu.[b]

[b] The meaning of the last verse is clear, but the text as read shows too many metrical and grammatical irregularities (in an otherwise very regular poem) and probably requires correction.

---

[1] Al-Badrī, fol. 55b, quotes the first six verses with the omission of verse 4. The text of Ibn Ghānim's poem is as follows (the variant readings of the Princeton and Berlin Mss. are listed in the footnotes to the translation):
yā man tashabbaha bi-l-bahīmi wa-qad ghadā
ka-th-thawri yar'ā fī ḥashīshi l-qunbusi
wa-la-anta ashbahu bi-l-bahīmati innamā
khālaftahā fa-labista mā lam talbasi
abadat bika l-bankā fa-ruḥta bi-sukrihā
tamshī ka-mashyi l-akmahi l-mutaḥassisi
wa-l-wajhu yaḥkī fī ṣafāqati nasjihī
athwāba khazzin ma'dinīyin aṭlasi
a-raḍīta wayḥaka an turā bayna l-warā
a'mā aṣamma tushīru mithlu l-akhrasi
wa-la-ṭāla-mā ukilat bi-bayti siqāyatin
khawfa r-raqībi wa-khissatan fī l-anfusi
fa-idhā aradta ḥalāla khamrin muskirin
fa-dkhul ilā ḥānī wa-dūnaka majlisī
tajid-i-z-zajājata bi-l-mudāmati ashraqat
wa-ṣafat li-shāribihā bi-ṣafwi l-ak'usi
wa-tarannamat alḥānuhā fī ḥānihā
bi-laṭā'ifi l-ma'nā l-'alīyi l-anfasi
khudhhā bi-lā thamanin fa-inna sharābahā
lā yustabāḥu li-ghayri 'abdin muflisi
fa-shrab wa-ṭib wa-ṭrab bi-ghayri taḥashshumin
wa-shṭaḥ wa-qul hādhā sh(?)-sharābu l-Maqdisī.

[2] Ms. Princeton omits *wa-qad ghadā* and vocalizes *qanbas* (above, p. 22, n. 5).

[3] The seemingly correct *innamā* has been corrected by the scribe of the Berlin Ms. at the bottom of the page to read *ma'kalan* "with respect to food."

You have distanced yourself from it by wearing cloth it does not wear.
3) The drug has settled down in you,[1] and through its intoxication you have turned to
Walking as does someone born blind, feeling his way.[2]
4) The face[3] resembles in its compact weave
Garments of smooth, *maʿdinī* silk.[4]
5) Does it please you, hapless man, to be seen among mankind
Blind and deaf, using sign language like a deaf person?
6) Quite often has it been eaten in a privy
Out of fear of an observer and vileness in the souls.[5]
7) If you wish something lawful in the way of intoxicating wine,[6]
Enter my tavern and help yourself to my salon,[7]
8) And you will find the glass sparkling with wine[8]
And pure for the drinker in the purity of cups,
9) Its tunes resounding in its tavern
With the finesses of noble, most precious meaning.[9]
10) Take it gratis, for this wine
Is permitted only for a bankrupt[10] human being.
11) Drink and be of good cheer and be uplifted emotionally, without inhibition!

---

[1] This is the reading suggested by al-Badrī, who, however, continues with a metrically impossible *wjb*. *Ankā bika l-balwā* "the calamity has befallen you(?)" seems to be the reading in the Berlin and Princeton Mss., *balwā* constituting a correction in the Berlin Ms. whereas the Princeton Ms. has a clearly written السلى. Perhaps, some other nickname for hashish is concealed here.

[2] Al-Badrī clearly shows *mutajassis* with *j*. Ms. Princeton has something like *bi-t-tajassusi* which does not fit the meter, but Ms. Berlin takes pains to indicate *ḥ*. Ms. Berlin has *aʿmā aṣamma* (cf. verse 5) here at the beginning of this line. Since this makes the verse too long, the scribe reconstructed it to read: *Aʿmā aṣamma ka-akmahin mutaḥassisi*.

[3] Ms. Princeton: *fa-l-wajhu*.

[4] The face is so bland and devoid of expression. Both *maʿdinī* and *aṭlas* must be understood as adjectives belonging to "silk"; they cannot be interpreted as "*maʿdinī* satin." For *maʿdinī*, cf. Dozy, *Supplément*, II, 104b, to which R. B. Serjeant, in *Ars Islamica*, IX (1952), 71, has little to add.

[5] Ms. Berlin corrects the last two words to *wa-khashyata l-mutajassisi* "out of fear of a spy." This is suspect if only because of its simplicity.

[6] Ms. Princeton has *khamra ḥalālin ladhdhatan*. The first two words are metrically not possible in this order, but *ladhdhatan* "for pleasure" may be correct.

[7] Ms. Princeton: *majlisi*.

[8] Ms. Princeton: *al-mudāmata bi-z-zajājati* "the wine sparkling in the glass."

[9] Ms. Berlin has *al-mʿly* for *al-maʿnā*. *Al-anfusi* "high of souls, high-minded" seems less likely.

[10] In the sense of poor, Ṣūfī.

Get ecstatic and say: This is the Maqdisī wine.[1]

The author of the other poem, from the Gotha Ms.,[2] is unknown. There is nothing to indicate that he might have been the same man who is mentioned in connection with verses immediately preceding in the ms. (see above, p. 150, n. 4). The poem paints quite a complete picture of the alleged general corruption of addicts, their unpleasantness as members of society, and their criminal character. It plays with the idea that *ḥashīsh* is a misspelling for *khasīs* "vile"[3] because its outstanding trait is vileness, the vile moral character it generates in its users.[4]

1) They say: The secret of poverty (Ṣūfism) is eating a herb.
This secret has been brought to us by some Persian(s).
2) Grief and worry and modesty are gone from us.
This is indeed the life of dumb beasts.[5]
3) I said to them: You have misspelled the secret of your poverty.
Your operation has resulted in disgrace by having your turbans seized (?).[6]

---

[1] The article may have to be omitted. Ms. Princeton has *s(h)rb al-mqds*.
[2] See above, p. 18.
[3] Cf. also above, p. 155.
[4] The text reads:
yaqūlūna sirru l-faqri aklu ḥashīshatin
atānā bi-hādhā s-sirri baʿḍu l-aʿājimi
tabāʿada ʿannā l-ghammu wa-l-hammu wa-l-ḥayā(')
wa-hādhā ʿalā t-taḥqīqi ʿayshu l-bahā'imi
fa-qultu lahum ṣaḥḥaftumū sirra faqrikum
wa-li-sh-shayni ʿāmaltum bi-khaṭfi l-ʿamā'imi
wa-law ṣaḥḥafa l-qawmu l-ḥashīshata wuffiqū
li-taḥqīqi waṣfin li-l-ḥashīshati lāzimi
ta'ammal raʿāka llāhu aḥwāla ahlihā
fa-fī l-ḥāli minhum ʿibratun li-l-masālimi
waqāḥatu wajhin wa-ṭṭirāḥu murūwatin
wa-tarku ktirāthin bi-qtiḥāmi l-maḥārimi
wa-daʿwā wa-lā burhāna fīhi li-muddaʿin
wa-shaṭḥun ʿarīyun ʿan shurūṭi l-makārimi
riyāḍatuhum shatmu l-anāmi wa-luṭfuhum
zukāmun (?) wa-mā fī l-qawmi ghayru mulā'imi
wa-ʿīshatuhum(?) fī-mā jarā yajʿalūnahā
wasīlata ḥazzin li-jtilābi l-maṭāʿimi
fa-mā sakhkhara z-zaqqūma illā ḥashīshatun
yakhuṣṣu bihā fī n-nāsi ahlu l-ma'āthimi.
[5] In the first line, the reading could possibly be *tubāʿidu ... l-ghamma*, etc., "it removes ... grief...". The second line is the gnomic comment of the poet. It is interesting that he considers a life free from worries as something less than human.
[6] *Shayn*, the opposite of *zayn* "ornament," is the vocalization indicated in

4) If people were to misspell hashish, they would succeed
In realizing a correct and necessary description for it.
5) Consider—may God watch you—the conditions of its people.
At once, they will provide a lesson for the Muslims.
6) Ugliness of face, discarding manly virtue,
Indifference to affronts to the womenfolk (?).[1]
7) A claim where the claimant has no proof.
An ecstasy free from the requirements of noble qualities.[2]
8) Their (mystic) exercise is vilifying people. Their grace is
A catarrh (?) and whatever is inappropriate among people.[3]
9) Whatever happens, they make their way of living[4]
A lucky means for obtaining food.
10) Nothing has ever subdued the *zaqqūm* tree[5] except an herb
Which among mankind is the special property of criminals.

3. Poems on Hashish from the *Dīwān* of Ṣafī-ad-dīn al-Ḥillī[6]

(a)

1) Present it to me[7] mixed with a plant
From the purse's opening, not from cups,
2) A wine whose casks are ivory boxes
And whose cups are the palms of my hands.
3) It has not been dirtied by the admixture of water, but

the ms., but there may be here an allusion to the letter *shīn* which distinguishes *ḥashīsh* from *khasīs*. The removal of turbans may be a punishment for hashish use. Or "seizing turbans" may imply false claims to scholarship.

[1] The translation reflects the idea that addicts lose their sense of honor with respect to their women (cf. above, p. 85 f.). However, *iqtiḥām al-maḥārim* more immediately suggests the translation: "to rush into doing forbidden things."

[2] *Shaṭḥ*, and not as one might think *sharṭ* "requirement, condition," is the correct reading. For *'arīyun*, instead of *'ārin*, cf., for instance, as-Sakhāwī, *Ḍaw'*, VI, 58, l. 16.

[3] Some metaphoric meaning unknown to me may go with *zukām* "catarrh." If not, a correction would seem necessary, perhaps, *ziḥām* "crowding others." The ms. has *mulākim* for *mulā'im*.

[4] The ms. has something like *wa-'ayshuhumū*. The verse appears to refer to the alleged inordinate desire of hashish users for food.

[5] See above, pp. 46 f. I doubt whether *zaqqūm* is meant to be the subject, and hashish the object, in which case hashish would be subservient to *zaqqūm* which pressed it into service as its most valuable servant.

[6] Cf. his *Dīwān*, 450-452 (Damascus 1297-1300), reprinted Beirut 1382/1962, 628-631. The superscription reads: "On *al-mufarriḥ al-Ḥaydarī*" (see above, p. 25).

[7] Read *'āṭinīhā* as required by the meter *(khafīf)*.

Often it has been followed by sweet water.[1]
4) It has no hangover, except subtle thinking
That cheers the soul to the last breath.
5) An intoxication such as that of wine is unable to
Offer. How could an old woman have the grace of a young girl?[2]
6) The law stipulates no penalty for it, nor
Has the *ḥadīth* of reliable transmitters said anything about its being forbidden.
7) Ascetics have become acquainted with it. Then they used it
In pastes and electuaries.
8) They nicknamed it at times "rouser of thought,"
And at times "digester of food."
9) I said when the scent of musk spread from it
And the bashful maidens revealed themselves in their garments:
10) It is the right of him who has spent the night wooing you
To give the daughter of the vines a document of privilege.[3]

(b)

1) In the purse, not in the cup, I have a wine
Whose taste or smell makes me drunk.
2) The text of the Holy Writ has not forbidden it, neither
Has there been consensus in the law on its censure.[4]
3) Obviously useful, it possesses a (power of) intoxication
That saves the souls from their worries.
4) The gratitude owed to it is greater than the drunkenness caused by it,
And its usefulness is greater than the sin of using it.

(c)[5]

1) For me the purse has a substitute for what the cup contains,

---

[1] Meaning that some water is drunk after eating hashish?
[2] Wine is "aged," hashish is "new."
[3] Read:

ḥaqqu man bāta khāṭiban laki an yuʿ-
ṭiya binta l-kurūmi khaṭṭa barāti.

The "document of privilege" would seem to be a divorce or a passport to leave.
[4] Cf. also the invitation to a hashish party in *Dīwān*, 375:

In our house there is a wine which neither the text
Has forbidden nor general consensus.
If wine is forbidden to us,
In our house we have hashish and beer *(fuqāʿ)*.

[5] The poem is quoted in al-Badrī, fol. 45b, omitting verses 3 and 4.

And pieces of paper for what the bowl holds.
2) My desire goes for the new one, not for something aged
That the devil inspires people to use,
3) A wine which has neither devilish whisperings in the head
That cover[1] the souls, nor Satanic inspiration in the breast.
4) It does not charge a soul with anything beyond its capabilities,
Neither is there fear of harm and bankruptcy from it.
5) How great is the difference between a wine whose drinker has to fear punishment,
And a wine where there is nothing wrong with drinking it
6) And where when we want to drink it, we do not have to spend the night
With guardians and watchers waiting at the door!
7) The inkwell serves as its shop.[2] Its bag (takes the place of)
A cask. Its cups are fingernail and paper.

(d)

1) Hashish makes you dispense[3] with wine,
The new leaves with the old one,
2) And the green one with pure red wine.
How great is the difference between emerald and carnelian!
3) A wine that is honorably (?) preserved in pockets
And drunk in the open streets.
4) In crushed form held in the hand, it scoffs at
The good scent of crushed musk.
5) Thus drink it and divorce anything beside it,
And you will live among people with a cheerful face.

(e)

1) Take its story from those who know it,
And preserve[4] those who revel in it from shame with respect to it!
2) A wine whose drinker does not have to fear punishment,
And it does not make the intelligent person stupid.
3) We have found in it lasting bliss.

---

[1] The "covering" belongs to the intoxicating effect, cf. above, p. 107.

[2] Read *ḥānun*. The editions have *j'n* and *jānin*, respectively.

[3] *Taghānā* = *tataghānā*, hardly *taghānī*, for *taghānīya* (infinitive with suffix) "makes me dispense." The *taghāna* of the Beirut edition does not fit the meter *(wāfir)*.

[4] Read, apparently, *wa-('a)'fi*.

It has become a paradise for those who choose it.
4) Eating it is permanent[1] and a shady shelter.
You can see those deserving of it[2] taking up residence in it.

(f) On combining hashish and wine

1) Intoxication with both the red one and the green one
Provides safety from the black and the yellow (biles).
2) The one boils without fire, and the other has had
Its curving parts swagger without (motion of the) air.
3) Break with the help of the lassitude of the one the vehemence[3] of the other
And wonder at the harmony of the parts.
4) For the intoxication between them combines
The laziness of hashish and the energy of wine.

[1] As is Paradise?
[2] Or, simply, "its people."
[3] The translation is *not* meant to suggest a correction of *shirrah* to *shiddah*.

APPENDIX B

THE ARABIC TEXT OF AZ-ZARKASHĪ'S *ZAHR AL-'ARĪSH*

For a brief description of the mss., see above, p. 10:

A Berlin Ms. Wetzstein II, 1809
B Berlin Ms. Wetzstein II, 1801
C Gotha Ms. 2096
D Berlin Ms. Petermann II, 407

Mss. A and B are related as are C and D. Mss. B and D are much more carelessly written than A and C. Beyond this, it is hardly possible to make any precise statements regarding the affiliation of the mss. The text given here is therefore highly eclectic. Additional material found in AB and not found in CD belongs to the author's text, but additional material found only in either A or B is of rather uncertain origin, as far as our present knowledge goes.

All variant readings have been listed, including even almost all of the numerous foolish oversights of the scribes of B and D. Differences in the use of diacritical dots have only rarely been noted. The indirect tradition has been checked, but its variant readings have as a rule not been listed in the apparatus. Certain modern spelling conventions have been adopted in the text with no further reference to what is actually found in the mss. However, seeming solecisms have not been corrected; in fact, they have been preferred occasionally in cases of differences between the mss. Some further corrections have been discussed in the footnotes to passages translated above.

(It may be added here that Ibn al-Marāghī studied the *Zahr* with its author, apparently in 788/1386, cf. as-Sakhāwī, *Ḍaw'*, VII, 161.)

بسم الله الرحمن الرحيم

[١]الحمد لله على نعمائه والصلاة والسلام على سيّدنا محمد صفوة أصفيائه وعلى آله وصحبه خير أوليائه[١] أمّا بعد فهذه فصول فى الكلام على الحشيشة اقتضى الحال شرحها [٢]لعموم [٣]بلوى كثير[٣] من السفلة بها وتوقّف كثير من الناس فى حكمها لمّا لم يجدوا [٤]للسلف فيها[٤] كلاما[٢] —

الفصل الأول

فى[٥] تسميتها[٦] ووقت ظهورها والأطبّاء[٧] يسمّونها القنّب الهندى ومنهم من يسمّيها ورق الشهدانج[٨] وتسمّى بالغبيراء وبالحيدريّة[٩] والقاندريّة[١٠] ويقال كلّ ورقة منها[١١] بقدر[١٢] أصابع اليد

ثمّ قيل [١٣]كان ظهورها[١٣] على يد حيدر[١٤] فى سنة [١٥]خمسين[١٦] وخمسمائة[١٥] تقريبا ولهذا سمّيت حيدريّة وذلك أنّه خرج هائما لتنفّره[١٧] من أصحابه فمرّ

---

١ - ١ قال الشيخ الاستاذ بدر الدين الزركشى رحمه الله تعالى C ; قال الشيخ الامام ابو عبد الله بدر الدين محمد بن عبد الله الزركشى الشافعى المصرى رحمه الله والغفران D ٢ - ٢ D deest ; C in marg. ٣ - ٣ البلوى كثيرا B ٤ - ٤ فيها للسلف B ٥ عن D ٦ اسمها AD ٧ فالاطباء A ٨ الشهرانج D ٩ او بالحيدرية B ١٠ وبالقلندرية AC ١١ A deest ١٢ بمقدار اربع A ١٣ - ١٣ ظهورها كان CD ١٤ حيدرى B ١٥ - ١٥ خمسمائة وخمسين A ١٦ خمس B ١٧ ليفر CD

على هذه الحشيشة فرأى أغصانها تتحرّك من غير هواء فقال فى نفسه هذا لسرّ فيها فاقتطف [١]ثمّ أكل منها[١] فلمّا رجع إليهم أعلمهم [٢]أنّه رأى[٢] فيها سرّا وأمرهم بأكلها وقيل[٣] ظهرت على يد أحمد الساوجى[٤] القلندرى[٥] ولذلك[٦] سمّيت قلندريّة وقال أبو العبّاس[٧] بن تيميّة إنّما لم يتكلّم فيها الأئمّة الأربعة وغيرهم[٨] من علماء السلف[٩] لأنّها لم تكن فى زمنهم وإنّما[١٠] ظهرت فى أواخر[١١] المائة[١٢] السادسة وأوّل المائة السابعة حين ظهرت دولة التتر[١٣] وكذا[١٤] قال غيره إنّها كانت [١٥]شرّا داخلا[١٥] على[١٦] بلاد[١٧] العجم حتّى[١٨] استولى على [١٩]من فيها[١٩] التتر[٢٠] ثمّ انتقلت إلى بغداد وقد علم ما جرى على أهلها من [٢١]قبيح الأثر[٢١]

الفصل الثانى

فى مضارّها فى [٢٢]العقل والبدن[٢٢] وذكر[٢٣] بعضهم أنّه جمع فيها مائة وعشرون[٢٤] مضرّة [٢٥]دينيّة ودنيويّة[٢٥] وقد[٢٦] أجمع الأطبّاء على[٢٧] أنّها[٢٨] تورث الفكرة[٢٩] والفكرة[٣٠] تثير[٣١] الحرارة الغريزيّة[٣٢] وربّما قويت على الحرارة الغريزيّة[٢٦] فعزلتها[٣٣] عن الجسد واستولت على البدن فجفّفت الرطوبات

١-١ منها وأكل B ; وأكل منها CD ٢-٢ ان B ٣ وقد D ٤ السارجى A ; المسارجى C ; المسارحى D ٥ القلندرية C ٦ ولهذا D ٧ القاسم C ٨ وغيره B ٩ والخلف +B ١٠ وانها C ١١ CD deest ١٢ الائمة D ١٣ التتار BCD ١٤ وكذلك (D ?) B ١٥-١٥ شر داخل BC ; داخل D ١٦ D deest ١٧ من +B ١٨ حين D ١٩-١٩ فيها من B ٢٠ التتار B ٢١-٢١ فتح التتر A ٢٢-٢٢ البدن والعقل CD ٢٣ ذكر A ٢٤ وعشرين AC ٢٥-٢٥ دنيوية ودينية D ٢٦-٢٦ وقد . . . على الحرارة الغريزية C in marg. ٢٧ CD deest ٢٨ انه D ٢٩ الفكر C ٣٠ D deest ٣١ تورث B ; تشير D ٣٢ D deest ٣٣ فغربتها B

واستعد[١] للأمراض الحارّة واليابسة[٢] والحمّيات[٣] قال محمّد بن زكريّاء الرازى أكل ورق الشهدانق[٤] البستانى يصدع[٥] الرأس ويقطع المنىّ ويجفّفه ويورث[٦] الفكرة[٧] والعلّة فى ذلك أنّ رطوبات[٨] الأبدان[٩] الكائنة[١٠] على[١١] حدّ الاعتدال هى تقع تبعا لبقاء[١٢] الحيوان فما[١٣] يجفّف الرطوبة منها[١٤] فإنّه[١٥] مضرّ معين على إتلافه[١٦] وهى تورث موت الفجأة واختلال العقل والدقّ والسلّ والاستسقاء والأبنة[١٧] وقال بعض الأئمّة كلّ ما فى الخمر من المذمومات موجود فى الحشيشة وزيادة [١٨]فإنّ أكثر[١٩] ضرر[١٨] الخمر فى الدين لا فى البدن وضررها فيهما وهى تشارك الخمر فى السكر وفساد الفكر[٢٠] ونسيان الذكر وإفشاء السرّ وإنشاء الشرّ وذهاب الحياء وكثرة المراء وعدم المروّة [٢١]وكشف العورة[٢١] وقمع[٢٢] الغيرة وإتلاف الكيس[٢٣] ومجالسة إبليس وترك الصلاة[٢٤] والوقوع فى المحرّمات هذا بعض ضررها فى الدين أمّا[٢٥] البدن فتفسد العقل وتقطع النسل وتولد[٢٦] الجذام [٢٧]وتورث البرص[٢٧] وتجلب الأسقام وتكسب[٢٨] الرعشة وتنتن[٢٩] الفم وتجفّف المنىّ وتسقط شعر[٣٠] الأجفان وتحرق الدم [٣١]وتحفر الأسنان[٣١] وتظهر الداء الخفىّ وتضرّ الأحشاء وتبطل الأعضاء وتضيق النفس

---

١ واستبعد B ٢ والسيسه B ; والمدسيه C ; D deest ٣ والحمايات BC ; D deest ٤ الشهدانج AD
٥ يصعد D ٦ وتولد CD ٧ الكفرة D ٨ رطوبة B ٩ البدن D ١٠ منه D ١١ عن A
١٢ لباقى D ١٣ فيما D ١٤ فيها A ; منه CD ١٥ D deest ١٦ اكلها D ١٧ الابنة ؟ D
١٨-١٨ فمضرة D ١٩ C deest ٢٠ العقل D ٢١-٢١ والعورة D ٢٢ وذهاب D
٢٣ الكنيس ؟ (B ?) A ٢٤ الصلوات C ٢٥ فى + BD ٢٦ وتورث AB
٢٧-٢٧ والبرص B ٢٨ وتنسب B ٢٩ ونتن D ٣٠ D deest ٣١-٣١ وتضر الانسان D

وتقوّى الهوس وتنقص القوى وتقلّل[١] الحياء[٢] وتصفّر الألوان وتسوّد الأسنان وتنقب[٣] الكبد وتوهج المعدة وتولد[٤] فى الفم البخر وفى العين الغشاوة وقلّة النظر وفى المخيّلة[٥] كثرة الفكر[٦] ومن أوصافها المذمومة أنّها تكسب أهلها[٧] الكسل وتورثه[٨] الفشل وتجعل الأسد كالجعل[٩] تعيد[١٠] العزيز ذليلا والصحيح [١١]عليلا إن[١١] أكل لا يشبع وإن أعطى[١٢] لا يقنع وإن كلّم لا يسمع تجعل الفصيح أبكما والصحيح أبلها تسقط[١٣] المروّة وتزيل الفتوّة [١٤]ثمّ إنّها[١٤] تفسد الفكرة وتبلّد الفطرة[١٥] وتجمّد[١٦] الفطنة وتولد[١٧] البطنة جعل[١٨] الأكل فنّه والنوم له مظنّه فهو[١٩] بعيد عن السنة طريد عن الجنّة موعود من الله باللعنة الّا[٢٠] أن يقرع من الندم سنّه ويحسن بالله ظنّه [٢١]ولله درّ[٢٢] القائل

قل لمن يأكل الحشيشة جهلا   يا خسيسا قد[٢٣] عشت أزرى[٢٤] معيشه
قيمة[٢٥] العقل جوهر[٢٦] فلما ذا   يا سفيها [٢٧]قد بعته[٢٧] بحشيشه[٢١]

[٢٨]قلت[٢٩] ومن أعظم دائها أنّ متعاطيها[٣٠] لا يكاد يتوب لتأثيرها[٣١] فى مزاجه وأنت ترى أهلها أبعد الخلق ضلالا[٣٢] وتجافيا[٣٣] عن الاستقامة وأقرب[٣٤] إلى الدنيئة وأسفه[٣٤]

---

١ وثقل D   ٢ قوله الحياء هذا اللفظ تقدم وينبغى مكان الحياء الحيلة تأمل C + marg. note
٣ وتنقب A ; وتفتت D   ٤ وتورث B   ٥ الحيلة D   ٦ الفكرة A   ٧ اكالها B ; كالها D   ٨ وتورث AD   ٩ C + marg. note   ١٠ تصير D   ١١-١١ عيلان D
١٢ يعطى D   ١٣ وتسقط AC   ١٤-١٤ D deest   ١٥ D deest   ١٦ وتخمد C ; D deest
١٧ ? D   ١٨ يجعل (تجعل ؟) AD   ١٩ وهو D   ٢٠ الى B   ٢١-٢١ CD deest ; B after the following verse   ٢٢ B deest   ٢٣ B deest   ٢٤ ? A   ٢٥ دية B
٢٦ بدرة B   ٢٧-٢٧ تبيعه B   ٢٨-٢٨ A after the following verse (next page)
٢٩ قيل A ; B deest ; اى الزركشى C + in marg.   ٣٠ معانيها CD   ٣١ لتاثرها C
٣٢ ؟ ; ظلالا AB ; صلاحا D   ٣٣ ونجاة D   ٣٤-٣٤ حمقا وافسد D

أحلاما [1]وأفسد تصرّفا[1] ٢٨، [2,3]وقد قال آخر[3]

وأصغر دائها والداء جمّ   بغاء أو جنون أو نشاف

وكان الشيخ علىّ الحريرى بدمشق يغلّظ على من يتعاطاها وأرسل إليه رجل من أصحابه يعاتبه فى ذلك فقال[4] الشيخ للرسول هذا المذكور إن كان من أصحابى ولى عليه سمع وطاعة فليترك الحشيش أربعين يوما حتّى يفرغ[+4] منها[5] جسده وأربعين يوما حتّى يستريح منها بعد الفراغ ثمّ يجىء إلى[6] عندى حتّى أخبره عنها[7]

الفصل الثالث

فى أنّها مسكرة ومفسدة[7] للعقل والذى أجمع عليه الأطبّاء والعلماء بأحوال[8] النبات أنّها مسكرة منهم[+8] أبو محمّد عبد الله [9]بن أحمد[9] المالقى العشّاب ابن[10] البيطار فى كتابه الجامع لقوى[11] [12]الأدوية والأغذية[12] قال ومن القنّب الهندى نوع ثالث يقال له القنّب ولم[13] أره بغير مصر ويزرع فى البساتين ويسمّى الحشيشة أيضا وهو ينكر[14] جدّا إذا تناول منه الإنسان يسيرا[15] قدر درهم أو درهمين حتّى أنّ من[16] أكثر منه أخرجه إلى حدّ الرعونة وقد استعمله[17] قوم فاختلّت[18] عقولهم وربّما قتلت[19] وقال فى علاجها القىء بسمن

١-١ BD deest; لله + C ٢-٢ CD deest ٣-٣ ولله القائل B ٤ وقال A +٤ ينفرغ A
٥ منه A ٦ A deest ٧ او مفترة A ٨ باقوال B +٨ فمنهم D ٩-٩ D deest
١٠ وابن A ١١ القوى فى D ١٢-١٢ الاغذية والادوية A ١٣ وقال لم A ١٤ مسكر A
١٥ يسير B ١٦ B deest ١٧ استعمل B ١٨ فاخلت A; خلت D ١٩ قلت B

وماء سخن حتّى تنقى المعدة [١]وشراب الحماض[١] لهم فى غاية النفع

وأمّا الفقهاء فقد صرّحوا بأنّها مسكرة فمنهم[٢] الشيخ أبو إسحق الشيرازى فى كتاب التذكرة فى الخلاف والنووى فى شرح المهذّب ولا يعرف فيه خلاف[٣] عندنا وقد[٤] يدخل فى حدّهم السكران بأنّه[٥] الذى اختلط كلامه[٦] المنظوم وباح بسرّه المكتوم أو الذى لا يعرف السماء من الأرض ولا الطول من العرض ويحكى عن بعض من يتناولها[+٦] أنّه[٧] إذا[٨] رأى القمر [٩]يظنّه لجّة ماء فلا[٩] يقدم عليه

وبلغنى عن أبي العبّاس ابن تيميّة أنّه قال الصحيح أنّها مسكرة كالشراب فإنّ آكليها ينشون عنها[١٠] [١١]ولذلك يتناولونها[١١] بخلاف[١٢] البنج وغيره فإنّه لا ينشى[١٣] ولا يشتهى[١٤] ولم أر من خالف[١٥] فى[١٦] ذلك إلّا أبا[١٧] العبّاس القرافى فى قواعده فقال نصّ العلماء[١٨] بالنبات فى كتبهم على[١٩] أنّها مسكرة والذى يظهر لى أنّها مفسدة[٢٠] قال وتحرير الفرق بين المفسد [٢١]والمرقد والمسكر[٢١] أنّ[٢٢] المتناول من هذه إمّا أن تغيب معه الحواسّ أو لا فإن غابت معه[٢٣] الحواسّ كالسمع والبصر واللمس والشمّ والذوق فهو المرقد وإن[٢٤] لم تغب معه[٢٥] الحواسّ فإمّا أن يحدث معه[٢٦] نشوة وسرور وقوّة نفس عند التناول غالبا أم

١-١ وشرب الحامض A ٢ منهم AD ٣ (نعرف . . .) خلافا C ٤ وهو AB ٥ D deest
٦ كلام D ٦+ تناولها CD ٧ وانه D ٨ A deest ٩-٩ فظنه بحرا فلم A ١٠ منها D
١١-١١ وكذلك يتناولها D ١٢ خلاف B ١٣ ينشر D ١٤ يسهى D ١٥ يخالف B
١٦ ممن فى B ; CD deest ١٧ D deest ١٨ العما B ١٩ A deest ٢٠ مفترة A ;
مسكرة C (لعل هذه اللفظة مفسدة بدليل الاقسام الآتية .C in marg) ٢١-٢١ والمسكر والمرقد CD
٢٢ D deest ٢٣ عنه AB ٢٤ فان D ٢٥ عنه AB ٢٦ عنه A

لا فإن حدث فهو المسكر وإلّا فهو المفسد فالمسكر هو المغيّب للعقل مع نشوة[١] وسرور كالخمر والمفسد هو المشوّش للعقل[٢] مع [٣]عدم السرور[٣] الغالب كالبنج [٤]ويدلّك على ضابط المسكر[٥] قول الشاعر

ونشربها فتتركنا ملوكا   وأسدا ما ينهنها[٦] اللقاء[٤]

فالمسكر[٧] يزيد فى الشجاعة والمسرّة[٨] وقوّة النفس والميل إلى البطش [٩]فى الأعداء[٩] والمنافسة فى العطاء [١٠]ومنه قول القاضى عبد الوهّاب

زعم المدامة شاربوها أنّها   تنفى الهموم وتصرف[١١] الغمّا
صدقوا سرت بعقولهم[١٢] فتوهّموا   أنّ السرور لهم[١٣] بها تمّا
سلبتهم أديانهم وعقولهم   أرأيت عادم دين[١٤] مغتمّا[١٠]

قال وظهر[١٥] بهذا أنّ الحشيشة مفسدة وليست مسكرة[١٦] لوجهين أحدهما[١٧] أنّها تثير[١٨] الخلط الكائن فى الجسد كيف ما كان فصاحب الصفراء تحدث[١٩] له حدّة[٢٠] [٢١]وصاحب البلغم تحدث له سباتا[٢١] وصمتا وصاحب السوداء[٢٢] تحدث له [٢٣]بكاء وجزعا[٢٤] وصاحب الدم تحدث له[٢٣] سرورا بقدر حالهم[٢٥] فتجد فيهم[٢٦] من يشتدّ بكاؤه ومنهم من يشتدّ صمته وأمّا الخمر والمسكرات فلا تكاد[٢٧] تجد أحدا ممّن

---

١ نشاة C   ٢ deest D   ٣-٣ عن سرور D   ٤-٤ deest CD   ٥ السكر B
٦ يسهنها B   ٧ والسكر A; فالسكر BD   ٨ والمروة B   ٩-٩ والاعداء D; والانتقام من الاعداء al-Qarāfī   ١٠-١٠ deest CD   ١١ وتصدى B   ١٢ بهمومهم A   ١٣ deest B
١٤ دينه B   ١٥ ويظهر C   ١٦ بمسكرة A   ١٧ احداهما B   ١٨ تبين CD   ١٩ الحديث D
٢٠ مرة A   ٢١-٢١ سبا D   ٢٢ السواد D   ٢٣-٢٣ deest D   ٢٤ وخشوع B; وجوعا C   ٢٥ حاله AB   ٢٦ منهم A   ٢٧ deest A

يشربها إلّا وهو نشوان مسرور بعيد عن تضوّر البكاء والصمت وثانيهما[١] أنّا[٢] نجد شرّاب الخمر تكثر عرابيدهم ووثوب بعضهم على[٣] بعض بالسلاح [٤]وهو معنى البيت المتقدّم فى قوله «وأسدا ما ينهنها[٥] اللقاء»[٤] وأكلة+[٥] الحشيش بخلاف ذلك [٦]بل هم همدة[٧] سكوت[٨] وهم[٦] أشبه شىء بالبهائم وذلك[٩] أنّ القتلى[١٠] توجد كثيرا[١١] مع شرّاب[١٢] الخمر دون أكلة الحشيش وهذا[١٣] الذى قاله[١٤] القرافى ممنوع ولا يساعده عليه دليل وقوله إنّ المغيّب للحواسّ هو المرقد يردّ[١٥] عليه [١٦]الإغماء والنوم[١٦] فإنّهما[١٧] [١٨]يغيّبان الحواسّ[١٨] وليسا[١٩] بمرقد[٢٠] [٢١]والبيت الذى أنشده ليس[٢٢] دليلا على ضابط المسكر لكن على تأثير الخمر فى هذا القائل وأضرابه ولا تساوى الخمر وغيرها فى هذه الخصال وإن تحقّقنا فيه الإسكار كالمزر[٢٣]، [٢١] وما ذكره فى الوجه الأوّل من الفرق ليس باستقراء صحيح فقد[٢٤] بلغنى عن بعض الناس[٢٥] أنّه كان إذا سكر[٢٦] بكى[٢٧] بكاء شديدا وأمّا أهل الحشيش[٢٨] فقد رأيناهم فى أوّل[٢٩] التناول[٣٠] ذوى نشاة[٣١] وطرب[٣٢] ثمّ يعتريهم الخمود[٣٣] والغيبة وكذلك فى أهل الخمر من[٣٤] يفضى به الحال إلى شبه الميت إمّا بحسب الأمزجة وإمّا بحسب قلّة التناول [٣٥]أو كثرته[٣٥] فيهما وما ذكره فى

---

١ وثانيها ABD   ٢ ان (تجد) A   ٣ عن D   ٤-٤ deest CD   ٥ يسهنها B   +٥ وآكل AB
٦-٦ بجدهم بعد هذهم سكون هم D   ٧ يعده ؟ C   ٨ وسكوت A   ٩ ولذلك CD
١٠ كثيرا + A ; القتل D   ١١ deest A ; كثير B   ١٢ شرابة B   ١٣ وهو B
١٤ قال D   ١٥ ويرد B   ١٦-١٦ النوم والاغماء D   ١٧ كانها B   ١٨-١٨ مغيبان للحواس A
١٩ وليس D   ٢٠ بمرقدين C   ٢١-٢١ deest CD   ٢٢ deest B   ٢٣ كالمزروط A
٢٤ وقد D   ٢٥ السفلة A   ٢٦ مسكر D   ٢٧ يبكى A   ٢٨ الحشيشة BD
٢٩ اوائل BC   ٣٠ التنا B   ٣١ نشوة D   ٣٢ وضرب B   ٣٣ الخمر B   ٣٤ deest D
٣٥-٣٥ وكثرته AB

الوجه الثانى باطل[١] أيضا فإنّ الخمر كما قلنا هى مراد الشاعر وهو صاحب هذه الخاصّيّة[٢] وقد ثبت الإسكار لغيره[٣] من أنواع الأشربة وهو دونه[٤] فى ذلك وعلى التنزّل فإنّه من ثوران الأخلاط الرديئة كما سلف فى الحشيش فإنّ المجرم الذاعر[٥] يحدث عنده زيادة عربدة كما فى الشارب[١] وظهر[٦] بهذا أنّ فى الحشيش الإسكار والإفساد فتساوى[٧] الخمر[٨] فى أحكامه[٩] وتزيد بمزيد الإفساد والصواب[١٠] أنّها مسكرة كما أجمع عليه العارفون بالنبات ويجب الرجوع إليهم كما رجع[١١] إليهم فى غيرها من الخواصّ[١٢] وقد كره[١٣] الإمام[١٤] الشافعى الماء المشمّس من جهة الطبّ

ويدلّ على أنّ الحشيش[١٥] مسكرة أنّ[١٦] معنى الإسكار تغطية العقل[١٧] قال الله[١٨] تعالى « إنّما سكّرت أبصارنا »[١٩] أى غطّيت[٢٠] وقد دلّ العقل على أنّه[٢١] يحدث عند تناولها[٢٢] حالة[٢٣] لم تكن قبل تناولها فتلك[٢٤] الحالة هى[٢٥] مبادئ[٢٦] تغيير[٢٧] العقل فإن كان المعنىّ بالإسكار هذا[٢٨] فذاك وإن كان المراد من الإسكار [٢٩]التغيّر الحادث[٢٩] فى[٣٠] المزاج[٣١] المضرّ[٣٢] بالأفعال الاختياريّة[٣٣] المخرج عن حدّ الاعتدال إلى الإفراط والتفريط فهو موجود فيه [٣٤]وقول من قال إنّها[٣٤]

١-١ CD deest ٢ الخاخة B ٣ كغيره B ٤ دنه B ٥ الذاعن B ٦ فظهر A
٧ فساوى AB ٨ D deest ٩ احتكامه B ١٠ فالصواب CD ١١ يرجع A
١٢ الحواس D ١٣ ذكر B ; ذكره D ١٤ BC deest ١٥ الحشيشة D ١٦ فى + A ;
D deest ١٧ D deest ١٨ B deest ١٩ Qur'ān 15 : 15 ٢٠ غطته B
٢١ ان BD ٢٢ فانه + C ; فان + D ٢٣ حا B ; CD deest ٢٤ لتلك A ;
بتلك CD ٢٥ فهى C ٢٦ تودى C ; تنادى D ٢٧ تغير A ; بتغيير C ; بغير D
٢٨ ذلك A ٢٩-٢٩ التغيير الحال D ٣٠ من C ٣١ المعين + B ٣٢ والمضر A
٣٣ D deest ٣٤-٣٤ وقوله انها C ; وقولانها D

مفسدة للعقل[١] باطل لأنّه[+١] لو فسد العقل لجنّ صاحبه إذ فساد العقل ذهابه

الفصل الرابع

فى أنّها حرام وقد تظاهرت الأدلّة[٢] الشرعيّة والعقليّة على ذلك أمّا الكتاب والسنّة[٣] فالنصوص الدالّة على تحريم المسكر[٤] بتناولها وفى صحيح مسلم «كلّ مسكر [٥]خمر وكلّ مسكر[٥] حرام» وأيضا [٦]فإنّها تصدّ[٦] عن ذكر الله وعن الصلاة وما كان هذا وصفه كان حراما كالخمر وقد قال الله تعالى[٧] «ويحرّم[٨] عليهم الخبائث»[٩] وأىّ خبيث أعظم ممّا يفسد [١٠]العقول التى[١٠] اتّفقت الملل والشرائع على إيجاب[١١] حفظها وقد حرّم الله[١٢] إذهاب العقول[١٣] باستعمال ما يزيلها أو يفسدها ويخرجها[١٤] عن مخرجها المعتاد ولا شكّ أنّ تناول الحشيشة يظهر به[١٥] أثر التعدّى[١٦] فى انتظام الفعل[١٧] والقول[١٨] المستمدّ[١٩] كماله من [٢٠]نور العقل[٢٠] شرعا وعرفا

وقد روى أبو داود فى سننه بإسناد حسن [٢١]عن ديلم الحميرى[٢١] قال سألت [٢٢]رسول الله[٢٢] صلّى الله عليه وسلّم فقلت يا رسول الله إنّا بأرض باردة [٢٣]نعالج فيها[٢٤] عملا[٢٣] شديدا وإنّا نتّخذ شرابا من هذا القمح نتقوّى[٢٥] به

---

١ العقل B ; D deest   ١+ لانها C   ٢ الاولة D   ٣ او السنة D   ٤ السكر D
٥-٥ D deest   ٦-٦ ? D   ٧ سبحانه وتعالى B   ٨ وحرم D   ٩ Qur'ān 7 : 157
١٠-١٠ العقل الذى AD ; العقول الذى B   ١١ اقامة C ; ايات D   ١٢ تعالى + CD
١٣ العقل D   ١٤ او يخرجها AB   ١٥ B deest   ١٦ التغيير AB   ١٧ العقل B ; D deest
١٨ القول D   ١٩ المسمة B   ٢٠-٢٠ تصرف العقل C ; التصرف العقلى D   ٢١-٢١ من ويلم الحميدى D   ٢٢-٢٢ النبي B   ٢٣-٢٣ ? D   ٢٤ C deest   ٢٥ فنقوى C ; فنتقوى D

على أعمالنا [١]وعلى برد بلادنا[١] قال هل يسكر قلت نعم قال فاجتنبوه قال قلت[٢] فإنّ[٣] الناس غير تاركيها قال فإن لم يتركوه فقاتلوهم وهذا منه صلّى الله عليه وسلّم تنبيه على العلّة التى[٤] لأجلها حرّم المزر فوجب أنّ كلّ الشيء عمل عمله[٥] يجب+[٥] تحريمه ولا إشكال أنّ الحشيش يعمل ذلك وفوقه

وروى أحمد[٦] فى مسنده وأبو داود فى سننه عن أمّ سلمة [٧]رضى الله عنها[٧] قالت نهى رسول الله صلّى الله عليه وسلّم عن كلّ[٨] مسكر ومفتّر قال[٩] العلماء المفتّر[١٠] كلّ ما يورث الفتور والخدر[١١] فى الأطراف وهذا الحديث أدلّ[١٢] دليل على تحريم الحشيشة[١٣] بخصوصها[١٤] فإنّها إن لم تكن مسكرة كانت مفتّرة مخدرة ولذلك يكثر النوم [١٥]من تعاطيها[١٥] ويثقل الرأس[١٦] بواسطة تبخيرها[١٧] الدماغ

[١٨]وأمّا الإجماع[١٨] على تحريمها فقد [١٩]نقله غير واحد منهم[١٩] القرافى فى قواعده وكذلك ابن تيميّة[٢٠] وهو حافظ[٢١] قال فإن[٢٢] استحلّها فقد كفر وفى هذا نظر لأنّ تحريمها ليس معلوما من الدين بالضرورة سلّمنا[٢٣] ذلك لكن لا بدّ أن يكون دليل الإجماع قطعيّا[٢٤] على أحد الوجهين وقد ذكر[٢٥]

١-١ D twice ٢ فقلت B ٣ وان A ; ان B ٤ D deest ٥ D deest ٥+ بحسب A ٦ بن حنبل + B ; الإمام احمد C ٧-٧ AD deest ٨ D deest ٩ قالت A ١٠ D deest
١١ والتخدر C ; التخد D ١٢ ايضا B ; اول C ١٣ الحشيش B ١٤ وغيرها من المخدرات A ; يحصر وصفها B ١٥-١٥ بمن يتعاطاها A ; من متعاطيها B ١٦ روؤسهم AB
١٧ فى + A ; تبخرها D ١٨-١٨ وبالاجماع B ١٩-١٩ نقل B ٢٠ شيخ الاسلام + B
٢١ الاسلام ومصر والشام نفعنا الله ببركاته وبركات علومه على الدوام + B ٢٢ وان A
٢٣ وسلمنا B ٢٤ قطعا D ٢٥ BD deest

[١]أصحابنا المسكر من غير عصير العنب[٢] كعصير العنب فى وجوب الحدّ لكن لا يكفّر مستحلّه لاختلاف العلماء فيه وقد[١] أجمع الفقهاء من أصحابنا وغيرهم على أنّه يحرم تناول المسكر وعمّموا النبات[٣] وغيره وقال الرافعى[٤] فى باب[٥] [٦]الأطعمة فى[٧] بحر[٦] المذهب إنّ النبات [٨]الذى[٩] يسكر وليست[٨] فيه شدّة مطربة يحرم أكله [١٠]وقال الإمام علاء الدين ابن العطّار صاحب النووى وتلميذه وهو الذى جمع فتاويه وكان فقيها[١١] وأىّ فقيه أمّا الحشيشة المسمّاة بالغبيراء المفسدة للعقول والأبدان المذهبة للأموال والأديان المخبّبة لنوع الإنسان المخنّثة لفحول الذكران فهى أشدّ إثما وتحريمها من الخمر ولم أعلم لتحريمها اختلافا[١٢] بين علماء الإسلام الذين أدركتهم لاكنّهم لم يصرّحوا بوجوب الحدّ فيها مع اتّفاقهم على وجوب التعزير فيها بالضرب وغيره انتهى[١٠] وفى فتاوى المرغينانى[١٣] للحنفيّة[١٤] المسكر من البنج [١٥]ولبن الرماك[١٥] حرام ولا يحدّ[١٦] قاله الفقيه[١٧] أبو جعفر ونصّ عليه شمس الأئمّة السرخسى انتهى [١٨]وفيه فائدة انّ هذا الذى يستعملونه الترك ويسمّونه القمز حرام[١٨]

الفصل الخامس

فى أنّها طاهرة أو نجسة وهذا ينبنى[١٩] على ما سبق من[٢٠] أنّها مسكرة

١-١ BD deest ٢ القنب A ٣ الباب D ٤ الرابعى D ٥ CD deest
٦-٦ اطعمة وفى نحو D ٧ وفى C ٨-٨ المسكر وليس B ٩ لا + D ١٠-١٠ ACD deest
١١ فقيه B ١٢ اختلاف B ١٣ B المرغيانى D ١٤ للسادة الحنفية ان A ; من الحنفية CD
١٥-١٥ CD deest ١٦ شاربه + A ; (ولا حد .corr. in marg) الحد B ; يتحد D
١٧ فقيه D ١٨-١٨ CD deest ١٩ يبنى B ; مبنى D ٢٠ AD deest ; فى B

فإنّ قياس[١] من يقول [٢]بإسكارها أن[٢] يقول بنجاستها ووفى بذلك الطوسى فى المصباح فقال الحشيشة نجسة[٣] إن ثبت أنّها مسكرة[٤] لكنّ الشيخ [٥]محيي الدين قال إنّها مسكرة وليست نجسة[٦] ولم يحك[٧] فيه خلافا ويؤيّده أنّ الشيخ تقىّ[٥] الدين ابن دقيق العيد فيما كتبه على فروع ابن الحاجب قطع بأنّها طاهرة وحكى الإجماع عليه[٨] قال والأفيون وهو لبن الخشخاش أقوى فعلا من الحشيش[٩] لأنّ[١٠] القليل منه يسكر جدّا وكذلك[١١] السيكران[١٢] وجوز[١٣] الطيب مع أنّها[١٤] طاهرة[١٥] بالإجماع وهذا الذى ادّعاه من الإجماع فيه نظر لما[١٦] سيأتى عن القرافى فى مسئلة الصلاة وفى[١٧] شرح قديم[١٨] للوجيز[١٩] قال مؤلّفه إنّه سمع من الأفواه[٢٠] فى نجاسة الحشيش قولين [٢١]وقال ابن العطّار توقّفوا فى تنجيسها إذا علمت (؟) فيه وهى إذا خلطت بالماء وشربت أولى بالتنجيس عند من يقول بنجاسة الخمر[٢١] وذكر ابن الصلاح فى [٢٢]فوائد رحلته[٢٢] [٢٣]عن رواية[٢٣] صاحب التقريب وجها أنّ النبات إذا كان [٢٤]سمّا قاتلا[٢٤] يكون[٢٥] نجسا وأنّه ردّ عليه بنصّ الإمام[٢٦] الشافعى لكنّ القياس فى الحشيش الطهارة وليس لنا نبات[٢٧] نجس العين[٢٨] قطّ إلّا النبات الذى يسقى[٢٩] بالنجاسة فإنّه نجس العين عند

---

١ قاس D ٢-٢ انها مسكرة A ٣ CD deest ٤ فهى نجسة + C ٥-٥ تقى C ; معين D ٦ بنجسة A ٧ ويحل B ٨ B deest ٩ الحشيشة B (e corr.) A ١٠ وان C ١١ وكذاك B ; وكذا D ١٢ D deest ١٣ وكذا جوزة C ; جوزة B ١٤ انه CD ١٥ طاهر CD ١٦ بما D ١٧ عن A ١٨ القديم D ١٩ الوجيز A ٢٠ الافراد D ٢١-٢١ ACD deest ٢٢-٢٢ فوائده وعلقه A ; فوائد وجلبه D ٢٣-٢٣ رواية عن B ٢٤-٢٤ ساقافلا CD ; له ساقا al-Badrī ٢٥ كان A ٢٦ AB deest ٢٧ فبات D ٢٨ D deest ٢٩ ينق ؟ D

الصيدلانى حتّى[١] قالوا[+١] فى [٢]السمّ الذى[٢] هو نبات إنّه طاهر مع أنّه أشدّ ضررا من الحشيش [٣]ولا يتّجه القول بالتنجيس[٤] ولو كانت مسكرة[٣] لأنّ الدليل إنّما انتهض[٥] فى الخمر وغيرها[٦] ليس فى معناها[٧] من كلّ الوجوه والاتّفاق على جواز تناول اليسير منها[٨] ولو كانت نجسة لما جاز ذلك

الفصل السادس

فى أنّه[٩] هل يجب فيها[١٠] الحدّ [١١]والصواب[١٢] الوجوب للإسكار [١٣]فتناولتها أدلّة[١٣] الحدّ[١١] فى المسكر[١٤] ولأنّ[١٥] صاحبها يهذى وإذا هذى[١٦] افترى فيجلد[١٧] جلد الفرية[١٨] وقد صرّح الماوردى بأنّ النبات الذى فيه شدّة[١٩] مطربة [٢٠]يجب فيه[٢٠] الحدّ ولا ينافى هذا[٢١] ما حكاه الإمام[٢٢] الرافعى عن البحر أنّ النبات المسكر لا حدّ على آكله لأنّ مراده ما ليس فيه[٢٣] شدّة مطربة كما صرّح به وقال الرافعى فى باب[٢٤] الشرب ما[٢٥] يزيل العقل من غير[٢٦] الأشربة كالبنج لا حدّ فى تناوله لأنّه لا[٢٧] يلذّ ولا يطرب ولا يدعو قليله إلى كثيره انتهى وهو يفهم إيجاب الحدّ فى الحشيشة لأنّها[٢٨] على العكس من البنج

---

١ حين A +١ قال B ٢-٢ المسلم لذى D ٣-٣ D deest ٤ بالنجاسة B (A ?)
٥ نهض A ; ينهض D ٦ A in marg. ; وغيره CD ٧ معناه CD ٨ B deest ٩ انها D
١٠ منها B ١١-١١ وهو ينبنى ايضا على ما سبق فان قلنا انها مسكرة وجب الحد لتناولها ادلة الحديث A
١٢ الصواب B ١٣-١٣ فتناولها للادلة D ١٤ السكر CD ١٥ وان B ١٦ اهدى B
١٧ فيحل D ١٨ الضرب D ١٩ مثلا D ٢٠-٢٠ توجب B ٢١ B deest
٢٢ AB deest ٢٣ به A ٢٤ حد + A ٢٥ لم B ٢٦ عين D ٢٧ B deest
٢٨ فانها A

[١]ووجدت بخطّ بعض الفضلاء من أصحاب الظهير التزمنتى[٢] أنّ هذه المسئلة وقعت فى عصره واختلف[٣] الفقهاء فى جوابها فقال بعضهم إنّها[٤] تلحق بالخمر والنبيذ إذ العلّة إنّما هى الإسكار وهى شاملة للنبات[٥] والخمر وفصّل بعضهم فقال النبات المسكر إذا أذيب وصار مائعا فهو[٦] ملحق بالخمر لتقع المشابهة الكاملة بين[٧] المشروب المسكر والنبات وفصّل بعضهم تفصيلا آخر فقال إن كان يفيد نشاطا وشجاعة وتجاسرا ونشاة[٨] فى الرأس التحق بالخمر فى سائر الأحكام لأنّ الخمر يفيد هذه الصفات انتهى وكان الشيخ علىّ الحريرى[٩] بدمشق يقول تعاطى الحشيش عندى أعظم خطرا[١٠] من تعاطى الخمر ويحسن عندى[١١] أن يحدّ آكلها أكثر ممّا يحدّ شارب الخمر[١]

وقال القرافى اتّفق فقهاء[١٢] العصر على المنع منها واختلفوا هل[١٣] الواجب فيها الحدّ [١٤]أو التعزير بناء على أنّها مسكرة أو مفسدة للعقل وعن كتاب الذخيرة له[١٥] أنّه يجب فيها الحدّ[١٤] والتعزير[١٦] وفى فتاوى الخلاصة للحنفيّة[١٧] وشرب البنج للتداوى لا بأس به فإن ذهب به[١٨] عقله لا يحدّ يعنى [١٩]بالاتّفاق فإن[١٩] سكر يحدّ عند محمّد وعند أبى حنيفة وأبى يوسف يعزّر ولا يحدّ

وقال[٢٠] الشيخ عزّ الدين فى القواعد فإن قيل هلاّ[٢١] وجب[٢٢] الحدّ

١-١ CD deest   ٢ التبزمنتى B   ٣ واختلاف B   ٤ B deest   ٥ النبات B   ٦ B deest
٧ ومن A   ٨ لو نشاة B   ٩ الحرير B   ١٠ جرما B   ١١ B deest   ١٢ فيها D
١٣ لا هل D   ١٤-١٤ D deest   ١٥ C deest   ١٦ او التعزير A   ١٧ للسادة الحنفية A
١٨ B deest   ١٩-١٩ بالارتفاق فانه D   ٢٠ قال CD   ٢١ هل BD   ٢٢ اوجب D

[1]إذا زال العقل[1] بغير مسكر كالبنج وغيره فالجواب أنّ إفساد العقل بذلك فى غاية الندور إذ[2] ليس فيه تفريح ولا[3] إطراب[4] يحثّان[5] على تعاطيه بخلاف الخمر والنبيذ فإنّ فيهما[6] من التفريح[6] والإطراب حاثّ[7] على شربهما[8] فغلبت[9] لذلك مفسدتهما فوجب الحدّ لغلبة[10] المفسدة[11] ولم يجب فى البنج ونحوه لندرة[12] الإفساد به[13]

الفصل السابع

فى فروع[14] متفرّقة[15] ومولّدات منها هل تبطل الصلاة بحملها[16] وذلك ينبنى[17] على [18]نجاستها وطهارتها[18] وقد سبق وقال القرافى سئل بعض فقهاء العصر عمّن صلّى والحشيشة معه هل تبطل صلاته فأجاب[19] إن صلّى بها+[19] [20]قبل أن[20] [21]تحمّص أو تصلق[21] صحّت صلاته أو [22]بعد ذلك[22] بطلت لأنّها إنّما تغيّب[23] العقل [24]بعد التحميص+[24] [25]أو الصلق[25] أمّا قبله وهى[26] ورق أخضر فلا بل هى[27] كالعصير للعنب[24] وتحميصها كغليانه قال[28] وسألت[29] عن هذا الفرق جماعة ممّن يعانيها فاختلفوا على قولين منهم من سلّمه[30] ومنهم من قال

١-١ ان ازال عقله D ٢ انه D ٣ D deest ٤ طرب C ٥ يجتاز AD ٦-٦ الفريح B ; من التفرح D ٧ C e corr. ; حادث D ٨ شربها C ٩ فغلب ; نقلبت C ; فقلت D ١٠ بقابه C ; بعلة D ١١ للفسدة C ١٢ لندورة B ; لندور C ١٣ D deest ١٤ مشروع B ١٥ مفرقة A ١٦ محلها D ١٧ ينشى ؟ D ١٨-١٨ طارتها ونجاستها C ١٩ اجاب C ; فمنها D +١٩ فيها CD ٢٠-٢٠ قيله D ٢١-٢١ تحمص C ; التحميص D ٢٢-٢٢ بعده D ٢٣ تصيب D ٢٤-٢٤ D deest + ٢٤ التمحيض A ٢٥-٢٥ والصلق B ٢٦ فهو A ٢٧ هو A ٢٨ C deest ٢٩ وسئلت C ; وسلت D ٣٠ سلم هذا الفرق وقال لا تؤثر الا بعد مباشرة النار al-Badrī, 54a

تؤثـر[١] مطلقا وإنّما تحمّـص[٢] لإصلاح[٣] طعمها وتعديل[٤] كيفيّتها[٥] خاصّة [٦]فعلى القول[٦] بعدم الفرق تبطل الصلاة وعلى القول به يكون الحقّ ما قاله المفتى إن صحّ أنّها مسكرة وإلا صحّت بها[٧] الصلاة مطلقا [٨]قال والذى[٩] اعتقده أنّها لا تبطل الصلاة مطلقا[٨]، [١٠]كالبنج وهذا[١١] قاله بناء [١٢]على اعتقاده[١٣] أنّها مفسدة وليست بمسكرة[١٤]

ومنها[١٥] هل يحرم يسيرها الذى لا يسكر صرّح[١٦] النووى فى شرح المهذّب أنّه[١٧] لا يحرم أكل القليل+[١٧] الذى لا يسكر من الحشيش بخلاف الخمر حيث حرم قليلها الذى لا يسكر والفرق أنّ الحشيش طاهر والخمر نجس فلا[١٨] يجوز شرب[١٩] قليله للنجاسة[٢٠] وكلام التنبيه يفهم جواز [٢١]أكل قليل[٢١] الحشيش فإنّه قال وكلّ طاهر لا ضرر فى أكله يحلّ أكله وقليلها طاهر لا ضرر فى أكله[٢٢] وكذلك صرّح به[٢٣] القرافى فقال إنّه يجوز تناول اليسير منها لكنّ ذلك بناء منه[٢٤] على[٢٥] اعتقاده أنّها[٢٦] ليست مسكرة[٢٧] أمّا[٢٨] الشيخ محيي الدين[٢٩] وغيره ممّن يعتقد أنّها مسكرة فلا يحسن منه[٣٠] إطلاق تجويز القليل وقد صحّ فى الحديث «ما أسكر كثيره فقليله حرام» والمتّجه أنّه لا يجوز تناول شىء من

---

١ موثر D ٢ الحمض A ; يخص D ٣ الاصلاح D ٤ او تعديل A ٥ صفتها CD
٦-٦ مصلى قولين D ٧ معها A ٨-٨ B deest ٩ والترمذى D ١٠ CD deest
١١ ما + D ١٢ A deest ١٣ اعتقاد AB ١٤ مسكرة D ١٥ انه + CD
١٦ ذكر A ١٧ بانه C ; بان D +١٧ من + CD ١٨ ولا CD ١٩ شربه D
٢٠ النجاسة B ٢١-٢١ قليل اكل B ٢٢ اكلها CD ٢٣ CD deest ٢٤ به ؟ D
٢٥ ان + B ٢٦ B deest ٢٧ بمسكرة CD ٢٨ واما D ٢٩ النووى + C ; النواوى + D ٣٠ D deest

الحشيش لا قليل ولا كثير وهى أشدّ ضرارة[١] من الخمر

ومنها هل[٢] يجب على آكلها التقيّؤ[٣] [٤]منها [٥]إن قلنا[٥] إنّها مسكرة ولنا خلاف فى وجوب التقيّؤ[٦، ٤] من الخمر ومحلّه إذا شرب قدرا لا[٧] يسكر [٨]أو أكل نجاسة فإن[٩] شرب منها قدرا يسكره[١٠، ٨] لو[١١] تركه فى باطنه[١٢] وجب تقيّؤه[١٣] بلا خلاف لأنّ إزالة العقل محرّمة[١٤] قطعا وحينئذ[١٥] فنقول إنّ من[١٦] أكل من الحشيش قدرا يسكره[١٧] وجب كالخمر قطعا وإلاّ لم[١٨] يجب للطهارة[١٩]

ومنها يجوز أكلها للمضطرّ إذا جاع ولا[٢٠] يتحرّج على الخلاف فى الخمر للعطش لأنّ الخمر إنّما[٢١] امتنعت لكون شربها يزيد فى العطش وأكل الحشيش لا يزيد فى الجوع وغاية ما فيها أنّها[٢٢] تغطّى العقل وتغطية العقل للدواء ونحوه جائز[٢٣] عند قطع[٢٤] اليد[٢٥] المتأكلة[٢٦] فيجب أكلها [٢٧]حفظا للروح[٢٧]

ومنها لو تصوّر[٢٨] شخص[٢٩] يأكل الحشيش ولا[٣٠] يسكر بها[٣١] فالظاهر أنّها لا تحرم عليه[٣٢] للطهارة[٣٣] وعدم الضرر[٣٤] وقد صرّح الإمام بذلك فى[٣٥]

---

١ ضررا A ; ضراوة (C?) B ; ضرورة D   ٢ انه A   ٣ التقى ABC ; اليقيق D
٤-٤ D deest   ٥-٥ اذا قلت A   ٦ التقى ABC   ٧ D deest   ٨-٨ D deest
٩ وان A   ١٠ يسيرا C   ١١ ولو B   ١٢ لا يسكره + B ; لأسكره + D   ١٣ تقييه AC ; تقييد B ; نقيه D   ١٤ تحرم CD   ١٥ وح .AC abb   ١٦ A deest   ١٧ يسكر B ; يسيرا CD   ١٨ ما D   ١٩ الطهارة B   ٢٠ والا A   ٢١ إذا A   ٢٢ D deest
٢٣ جائزة B   ٢٤ القطع D   ٢٥ B deest   ٢٦ D deest   ٢٧-٢٧ عند حفظها الروح D
٢٨ تضرر (.. باكل) CD   ٢٩ شخصا D   ٣٠ ولم B   ٣١ منها C   ٣٢ D deest
٣٣ للطارة B ; لطهارة D   ٣٤ الضرورة BCD   ٣٥ B deest

[١]الشخص الذى لا يضرّه أكل السموم الطاهرة[١] فقال لا يحرم عليه تعاطيها وهذا بخلاف الخمر يحرم شربها على من لا يسكر بها+[١] [٢]وان لم يتضرّر[٢] للنجاسة

ومنها جواز التداوى بها إن ثبت أنّها تنفع[٣] فى[٤] بعض الأدواء[٥] وقد قيل إنّها تحلّل النفخ وتنقى الإبرية[٦] من الرأس عند غسله بها والإبرية[٧] مرض يحدث بسطح الرأس [٨]وهى بثور بيض[٨,٩] والعلّة فى فعلها لذلك[١٠] ما[١١] اشتملت عليه من الحرارة واليبس [١٢]وينبغى الجزم بالجواز[١٢] [١٣]اذا كان يسيرا فينبغى أن تكون على الخلاف فى التداوى بالخمر وأولى بالجواز للخلاف[١٤] على طهارتها وإسكارها بخلاف الخمر بل قد سبق من النووى عدم تحريم اليسير منها عند عدم الحاجة فعند الحاجة أولى[١٣] فإنّ[١٥] الزعفران والمحمودة وغيرهما[١٦] ممّا يقتل كثيره قد أجمع الناس[١٧] على تناول القليل منه للحاجة [١٨]أمّا إذا كان كثيرا فالرويانى صحّح جواز التداوى بالخمر واتّفق الأصحاب فى مثله فى الخمر على منع التداوى به وخصّوا الخلاف باليسير منها أن يكون هاهنا كذلك ويحتمل كلامه لما سبق أنّها أوسع من الخمر ولهذا أنّ الرويانى صحّح جواز التداوى باليسير من الخمر الذى لا يسكر وجوّزه بالنبات مطلقا فقال فى البحر[١٨] ويجوز[١٩] التداوى

١-١ B deest +١ B deest ٢-٢ ان تصور AB ; ان يضرر D ٣ D deest ٤ من CD
٥ الادوية AB ; الادوار D ٦ الابذية D ٧ والابذيه من D ٨-٨ وهو قشور البيض D
٩ وفى بعض كتب الطب الهبرية (الهبرية .leg) فى الراس شىء كالنخالة فيه والابرية الحزاز + A
١٠ ذلك A ; كذلك D ١١ لما A ١٢-١٢ A deest ١٣-١٣ BCD deest
١٤ الخلاف A ١٥ لان A ١٦ وغيرها A ١٧ A deest ١٨-١٨ ثم رايت الرويانى (الرديانى C) فى البحر صرح بذلك فقال BCD ١٩ يجوز A ; ويجو B

به وإن أفضى إلى السكر إذا لم يكن منه بدّ[١] قال وما يسكر مع غيره [٢]ولا يسكر[٢] بنفسه إن[٣] لم[٤] [٥]ينتفع به[٥] فى دواء[٦] غيره[٧] فيحرم أكله وإن كان ينتفع[٨] به حلّ التداوى به[٩] ونصّ الإمام[١٠] الشافعى[١١] على أنّه [١٢]لا يجوز أكل[١٢] الترياق المعمول من لحوم الحيّات إلّا فى حالة[١٣] الضرورة بحيث يجوز له أكل الميتة

[١٤]فائدة تحصّل[١٥] ممّا سبق أنّه يجوز تناولها فى خمسة مواضع[١٦] أكل يسيرها على ما قاله النووى وأكلها لمن لا يسكر بها وأكلها لمن يتداوى بها وأكلها عند قطع اليد المتأكّلة وأكلها عند المخمصة وتجب إن لم نجوّز[١٧] الاستسلام[١٨، ١٤]

ومنها أنّه يحرم إطعامها الحيوان كما[١٩] يحرم إسكاره وقد قيل إنّها لا يأكلها

ومنها[٢٠] أنّه يجوز بيعها[٢١] لأنّه[٢٢] ينتفع[٢٣] بها[٢٤] فى الأدوية كالسقمونيا والأفيون بشرط أن يكون يسيرا نعم بيعها لمن يتحقّق منه[٢٥] تعاطيها حرام كما فى بيع العنب لعاصر الخمر وقياس قولهم[٢٦] أنّها مسكرة بطلان[٢٧] البيع وإن كانت طاهرة[٢٨] كآلات الملاهى

---

١ سبد D ٢-٢ D deest ٣ اذا D ٤ كان لا A ٥-٥ ينتضع ؟ D ٦ دوار D
٧ وغيره C ٨ ينتضع D ٩ AB deest ١٠ AB deest. ١١ رضوان الله تع عليه + C
١٢-١٢ يحرم D ١٣ حال C; D deest ١٤-١٤ D deest ١٥ يحتل B
١٦ الاول + C ١٧ يجز B ١٨ الاستدام C ١٩ مما D ٢٠ C from here to end
written in another hand ٢١ سها D ٢٢ لأنها BCD ٢٣ تنفع CD ٢٤ CD deest
٢٥ منها A ٢٦ AB deest ٢٧ بطلاق B ٢٨ B deest

ومنها أنّ زراعتها لغرض الاستعمال والإسكار حرام ويجوز لغرض التداوى [١]إن جوّزناه[١] وقد أفتى [٢]بعض أئمّة الشأم[٢] بتحريم[٣] زراعة العنب الذى لا يتزبّب ولا يمكن أن يجىء [٤]إلّا خمرا[٤] ببعض[٥] نواحيها[٦]

ومنها أنّه[٧] هل يقع[٨] طلاق آكلها ولا يخفى حكمه ممّا تقدّم وقال الرويانى فى البحر لو شرب دواء أو بنجا لا للتداوى بل [٩]للهو والمجون[٩] فلا نصّ [١٠]للامام الشافعى[١٠] فيه ولكنّ قياس قوله[١١] أنّه يقضى الصلاة أنّه[١٢] كالسكران

[١٣]وقال فى الحاوى فيه وجهان أحدهما[١٤] أنّه كالسكران والثانى[١٣] وبه قال[١٥] أبو حنيفة[١٦] لا يقع طلاقه وإن كان عاصيا وقال الجرجانى فى الشافى[١٧] لو شرب مختارا[١٨] [١٩]أو شرب[١٩] البنج [٢٠]وهو ناو به طربا (؟)[٢٠] فزال عقله وقع طلاقه لأنّ فعله معصية فلزمه[٢١] ما تولّد منه كسراية[٢٢] القطع فى القصاص والسرقة

وفى فتاوى المرغينانى[٢٣] للحنفيّة لو سكر من البنج لا تنفذ تصرّفاته لأنّ[٢٤] نفاذ التصرّف شرع زجرا[٢٥] ولا[٢٦] حاجة إليه فصار[٢٧] كمن ضرب[٢٨]

١-١ BCD deest   ٢-٢ تقى الدين ابن تيمية CD   ٣ تحرم D   ٤-٤ احمر B   ٥ كبعض A
٦ نواحى الشام C ; نواحى D   ٧ B deest   ٨ عليه + A   ٩-٩ للهيق الجنون D
١٠-١٠ للشافعى AB ; رضى الله عنه + C   ١١ قولهم (؟) فى B ; فى + C   ١٢ ان اغمى D
١٣-١٣ الثانى D   ١٤ A deest   ١٥ لامام الأعظم + A   ١٦ رضى الله عنه + A
١٧ الشافعى B   ١٨ D deest   ١٩-١٩ AD deest   ٢٠-٢٠ تهزيا وطربا AB ; وهو ناوى طوبا D   ٢١ فلزم AB   ٢٢ كثر نابه D   ٢٣ المرغينا D   ٢٤ لأنه D   ٢٥ ؟ ; زاجرا BC ; آخر D   ٢٦ اذ لا C   ٢٧ وصار CD   ٢٨ بها + D

رأس نفسه [١]حتّى ذهب[١] عقله

ومنها قال[٢] القاضى حسين[٣] فى باب صلاة المسافر من تعليقه إذا شرب البنج [٤]وغيره ممّا[٤] يزيل العقل فعليه قضاء الصلاة والصيام [٥]بعد الإفاقة[٥] كالسكران لأنّه[٦] [٧]جلب إزالة[٧] العقل بنفسه فيؤاخذ به [٨]والله أعلم[٨]

١-١ فذهب A ٢ deest D ٣ الحسين B ; حسن ؟ D ٤-٤ او غيره ومما D ٥-٥ الآ (del.) بعد فاقة C ٦ لأن B ٧-٧ جيرازال D ٨-٨ وصلى الله على سيدنا محمد وآله وصحبه وسلم + A ; تم كتاب زهر العريش فى تحريم الحشيش والحمد لله رب العالمين وصلى الله على سيدنا محمد وآله وصحبه اجمعين B· ; بالصواب آخر ما علقه مؤلفه منه والحمد لله اولا وآخرا باطنا وظاهرا سرا وعلانية. وحسبنا الله ونعم الوكيل وصلى الله على سيدنا محمد وآله وصحبه وسلم (تم كتاب زهر العريش فى احكام الحشيش للعلامة الزركشى رحمه الله آمين) + C ; والله تعالى اعلم بالصواب D

ADDITIONS

W. Leslau has called my attention to a book by R. Gelpke, *Vom Rausch im Orient und Okzident* (Stuttgart 1966). Although it appears to have little in common with the present work, it does contain some additional references. Informative notes on "Le kif et le hachich" in the modern Maghrib are to be found in R. Brunel, *Le monachisme errant dans l'Islam*, 281-323 (Paris 1955, *Publications de l'Institut des Hautes Études Marocaines* 48).

Sa^{c}d bula^{c} (p. 37, n. 8) refers no doubt to the star of this name, cf. P. Kunitzsch, *Arabische Sternnamen in Europa*, 56, 106 f. (Wiesbaden 1959). It was, perhaps, understood to mean "bliss to eat".

Jamāl-ad-dīn as-Sāwajī (p. 50, n. 3) was named Muḥammad, cf. aṣ-Ṣafadi, *Wāfī*, V, 292 f. The recently published volumes of the *Wāfī* also contain the Ibn Khallikān story (p. 147, cf. *Wāfī*, VII, 313) and offer the reading *al-qinnabīyah*, for *al-mughayyibah*, in the title of Ibn Taymīyah's monograph (p. 9, cf. *Wāfī*, VII, 28).

For *Kitāb al-Khadar* (p. 81, n. 5), see Ms. Aya Sofya 3724, fols. 222b-236b.

The verses ascribed to Abū Nuwās (p. 83, n. 3) may not have spoken of *ḥashīsh* but of something else, perhaps, *jashīsh* "gruel" (?).

"The often repeated standard formula" (p. 88): Qur'ān 5:91/93.

Another ^{c}Alī b. Makkī, mentioned by P. A. MacKay, *Certificates of Transmission* (of al-Ḥarīrī), index, no. 79 (Philadelphia 1971, *Transactions of the American Philosophical Society* 61, 4), comes, it seems, from a different social stratum and, at any rate, is too early to be identical with the one referred to on p. 152.

INDEXES

1. Selected Arabic, Persian, and Turkish Words

2. Proper Names and Selected Topics